The complete
HOME
DESIGN
book

The complete
HOME DESIGN
book

JOHNNY GREY • SUZANNE ARDLEY • DINAH HALL
SYLVIA KATZ • SARAH GAVENTA • BARBARA WEISS

DORLING KINDERSLEY
LONDON • NEW YORK • SYDNEY • MOSCOW

A DORLING KINDERSLEY BOOK

Senior Editor CHARLOTTE DAVIES
Project Art Editor SHARON MOORE
Project Editor ANNA CHEIFETZ
DTP Designer MARK BRACEY
Production Controller MANDY INNES
Managing Editor MARY-CLARE JERRAM
Managing Art Editor AMANDA LUNN

First published in Great Britain in 1998 by
Dorling Kindersley Limited
9 Henrietta Street, London WC2E 8PS

Visit us on the World Wide Web at
http://www.dk.com

A CIP catalogue record for this book
is available from the British Library

ISBN 0 7513 11243

Text film output in Great Britain by R & B Creative Services Ltd
Reproduced in Singapore by Pica
Printed in Italy by Euro Litho, Milan

YOU AND YOUR HOME   6

KITCHEN   14

Fresh food storage   24
Chilled food storage   26
Non-perishable food storage   28
Food preparation   30
Food rinsing and waste disposal   32
Hobs and extractors   34
Oven cooking   36
Eating   38
Washing-up   40
Hardware storage   42
Small kitchen   44
Unfitted kitchen   48
Fitted kitchen   52
Island kitchen   56
Improvised kitchen   60
Family kitchen   64

LIVING AREA   68

Seating   74
Occasional Tables   76
Entertainment   78
Displaying collections   80
Family room   82
Living and dining room   84

BEDROOM 88

Beds 94
Bedside storage 96
Clothes storage 98
Accessories 100
Children's storage 102
Adult bedroom 104
Children's bedroom 110

BATHROOM 114

Bath shapes 128
Specialist baths 130
Shower systems 132
Shower and bath fittings 134
Basin types 136
Basin fittings and materials 138
WCs and bidets 140
Bathroom storage 142
Heating and ventilation 144
Fitted bathroom 146
Unfitted bathroom 150
Improvised bathroom 154
Dual-purpose bathroom 158
Children's bathroom 162
Shared bathroom 166
Unusual shape bathroom 170

HOME OFFICE 174

Long-term seating 188
Occasional seating 190
Workstations 192
Computer desks 194
Office units 196
Meeting areas 198
Workstation storage 200
Remote office storage 202
Dedicated office 204
Dual-purpose office 208
Integrated office 212
Conversion 216
Unusual space 220
Executive office 224

ANCILLARY SPACE 228

Halls, stairs, and landings 234
Lofts and cellars 236
Utility area 238

STUDIO LIVING 242

Space-saving beds 254
Flexible furniture 256
Cooking area 258
Dining area 260
Washing area 262
Space dividers 264
Compact room 266
Open-plan room 270
Large room 274
Galleried room 278
Loft 282

PLANNING DETAILS 286

Natural light 288
Artificial light 290
Soft flooring 292
Hard flooring 294
Wallcoverings 296
Shelving 298
Worksurfaces 300
Concealment 302

INDEX 304

ACKNOWLEDGMENTS 309

CONTENTS

YOU AND YOUR

WHETHER YOU LIVE in a rambling country house or a small studio flat, your home is the one space where you can take full control of your surroundings. Once your door is closed to the outside world it is important for you to be able to completely relax in a comfortable environment that reflects your character and lifestyle. Identifying your needs is the key to achieving a practical layout that works well for you. This book focuses on the function and contents of individual rooms in order to help you plan your home, and to ensure that it is fully integrated.

BACK TO BASICS

Moving into a new house, or re-modeling your current one, involves the challenge of balancing your plans with available budget. Limited finance has one advantage, in that it allows you time to experience the space and develop your ideas before starting expensive improvements. An ideal home does not materialize overnight – the essential elements for even a modest lifestyle take time and effort to assemble. First, invest in the basics of the house, such as structural alterations, heating, re-wiring, and plumbing. Break the work down into logical stages to avoid lengthy spells of disruption whilst the jobs are being carried out. You need to decide how much you can accomplish yourself, and where you need to ask for professional advice

and help from architects and builders. Once finished, the shell of each room will be ready for the plans and ideas you have in store.

INDIVIDUAL STYLE

What is style? It conjures up a different image to everyone, so your taste in furniture and decoration will be individual to you. If you are unsure what will work, leaf through magazines and books for ideas. Although you will want to personalize the decor, these style references can help you decide on a cohesive look. This is usually more satisfying and cheaper in the long run than buying isolated items only to find that they do not work together in a room. The age of the house or shape of the rooms may also dictate or influence your choices. Clarify your ideas and imagine the effect you want to create by planning the layout on paper and making sketches to show the position of main items.

Look at how space is allocated, and if it can be adapted to suit your needs. Two small rooms with limited use could be opened out to make a comfortable family living area, with space for seating, studying, and eating. Consider if a small box room would be better converted into a shower room or study. Ancillary spaces, such as the loft or hallway, can also offer potential room for improvement. They may be able to house a home office, audio-visual equipment, or cleaning materials that would otherwise

HOME

▽ **CHOOSE YOUR OWN LOOK**
The calm, tranquil look of this bathroom draws
on the art of Japanese simplicity for its form and
function. Minimal decoration allows the delicate
light, scent of orchids, and the texture of cedar
wood to create a feast for the senses.

ADAPTING YOUR HOME TO SUIT YOUR NEEDS ▽
If you spend a lot of time working and entertaining at home, it is
vital that space is used efficiently and effectively. This well-designed
conversion shows how a home office has been made by utilizing the
spacious roof area, while maintaining a light and airy atmosphere.

intrude on your existing living area. Don't be
bound by convention and judge each space,
however unusual, on its own merits.

COLOUR AND LIGHT

Colour has the power to generate different
moods and effects within the home. Use it
to create an inspirational environment and
enhance the function of every room. Before
choosing colours, consider how much light
each room receives and the direction of the
windows. Cool colours, including blue, grey,
and green, are calming but can make shady
rooms appear cold and clinical. You may
want to limit their use to accent colours in
a dark room, or to brighten their effect with
colourful rugs or fabrics. Warm colours,
including pink, yellow, and red, are ideal for
rooms that do not receive much sun and for
areas where you want to offer a welcoming
feel, such as a hallway or family kitchen.

Room schemes can also draw upon the
depth and texture of fabrics and surfaces
for effect. Fine muslins and chenilles teamed
with natural wood flooring and rough plaster
walls are wonderfully tactile, and show that
shades of one colour can be as effective as
several different colours together.

As part of your planning, start a file for
each room to keep paint shade cards, fabric
swatches, and tile and flooring samples. If in
doubt about the effectiveness of your chosen
scheme, opt for simplicity. Neutral blocks of

colour and plain walls provide a dramatic backdrop for a striking piece of furniture, and have as much impact as busy patterns. As the scheme develops, you can add a dash of vibrant colour or pattern as desired.

Thinking about your lighting requirements is vital when planning your interior. It is easy to become confused between all the lighting designs available, so concentrate on the different needs of each area of the house. Work areas and those with changes in level, such as the kitchen and stairs, require good lighting for safety and efficiency. Areas for relaxing, such as the living area or bedrooms, can have lower light levels or mood lighting.

Lighting will also affect the way colour works in your home. A rich red interior that looks warm and inviting in natural daylight, for example, may look harsh under artificial lighting. Above all, the lighting you choose must be flexible, so plan to have at least two different types of lighting in each room, so that they can be used independently or together to achieve a variety of effects as well as providing essential illumination.

RECREATING PERIOD DETAIL

Homes that epitomize a certain architectural style or era pose the dilemma of whether to restore the interior with period detail or opt for a re-design. For many, only authenticity will do, and the work of tracing materials in the correct style is a labour of love. However,

renovation should always be undertaken with caution, as poor judgement can affect both the character and value of your house.

Architectural salvage yards are a useful source of original items and, as a form of recycling, are also a 'green' option. Successful restoration begins with learning about the origins of a building, so ask a local historical society for old photographs and look at similar houses in the area to see if any common features exist to help you establish a more detailed picture of your home.

For those who are not able to rummage through miscellanea in architectural yards or to wait for the right piece to come along, then reproduction pieces are the next best thing. Period wallpaper, fireplaces, tiles,

△ **USING COLOUR**
Large blocks of colour give a geometric quality to walls and units, and create a natural division between the two areas of this room. Colours in the rug tie the scheme together, to create a co-ordinated overall look.

▽ **NATURAL DAYLIGHT**
Sunlight filters in through vertical blinds
that can be set to offer a garden view or
maintain privacy. Creamy colours and
smooth sufaces create a tranquil mood.

▽ PERIOD BATHROOM
Antique and replica sanitaryware and fittings combine the best of traditional craftsmanship with modern technology for a nostalgic but efficient bathroom.

plaster mouldings, and sanitaryware are faithful to the genuine article and have the advantage of being readily available. Use hand-made paints recreated from samples in historic houses for authentic colour and texture. Distemper, limewash, oil-based paints, and glaze will give a surface character as close to the original as possible.

ORGANIZING YOUR HOME

Your character, lifestyle, and who you share your home with all have a bearing on the way you organize the facilities. Individuals

and couples can find it just as difficult to organize their lives and living space as busy households with working parents, children, and pets. There is no simple solution to becoming truly efficient, but an attempt to organize your home will greatly improve the dynamics of your day-to-day life.

Think about the way your rooms interact with each other, how much space is allocated to different activities, and whether you need to improve access between certain areas, such as between a kitchen and dining room. The smooth running of family schedules is

CREATE A COMFORTABLE ENVIRONMENT ▷
Style, colour, and practicality are the essential ingredients
that create a warm and welcoming centre for family life.
Open-plan design, comfortable furniture, and natural wood
add to the relaxed, wholesome simplicity of this kitchen.

for items that will clutter the room or attract dust. Make ancillary areas work for you by providing them with organized storage.

COMFORT, INSIDE AND OUT

In an attempt to transform the interior of your home, do not overlook the importance of the outside. The exterior of your house is the first thing that visitors see on arrival, and an attractive view of a garden or balcony can also transform the rooms inside. A balcony or conservatory creates a link between inside and out, providing both an extra living space in good weather, and a feeling of light and spaciousness when conditions are poor.

Having made an effort to create a home you are happy with, you will also want your friends and family to feel comfortable there too. Keeping your home warm and well ventilated will make it inviting and cosy, and also help to control condensation and damp, which can ruin the fabric of the building.

Rooms really come to life when they are well lived in, and the glow of a flickering fire or a vase of flowers are a simple step to achieving this vital ingredient. A comfortable and cared for home will improve your quality of life and promote a sense of well-being, so take time to plan your surroundings and to make your house work for you.

SUZANNE ARDLEY

△ HOME ORGANIZATION
Storage can look good and still be practical to use. The pitch of the roof is echoed here by a dramatic pyramid of open shelving. Cleverly gradated shelf sections above make an eyecatching feature of everyday bookcases.

essential, particularly at the busiest time of day. Inadequate bathroom facilities can be a source of stress well before work starts. See if it is possible to add an extra w.c. and basin elsewhere in the house, or install a shower in the corner of a bedroom to take pressure off the main bathroom.

Good storage is one of the best ways to improve household efficiency. Items that can be put away easily will also be quick to find. In each room, plan open shelves for everyday belongings and closed storage or cupboards

KITCHEN

INTRODUCTION

△ **DISTINCTIVE SURFACES**
Hand-crafted details, such as this wood door with its "suitcase" handle and inlaid surround, contribute to the atmosphere of a kitchen.

FOR MANY OF US, the kitchen is the most used room in the house. It is not just a refuelling station, but the place where adults congregate and children naturally migrate, and not just for food but company.

I recall with great affection, the small, chaotic family kitchen in our London house where my mother cooked for the seven of us, and where we ate most meals. Although the kitchen was very cramped, low-ceilinged, and dark, and contained a gigantic, noisy fridge that took up about a quarter of the space, mealtimes were memorable for their animated conversations and laughter. To my mind, too few kitchens seem to be able to combine successful planning with the warm atmosphere I remember from my childhood.

Reconciling practical considerations, such as where appliances and furniture should be placed so that they are efficient to use, with comfort is hard, but they are the mainstay of ergonomic design. In this kitchen chapter, I have tried to show you how to achieve a balance that works for you, whether you are designing a brand new kitchen or simply remodelling an existing one.

CREATIVE SPACE ▷
The lived-in appearance of Elizabeth David's kitchen was a source of inspiration to me. Through her, I discovered that kitchens could be comfortably furnished, like any other room in the house.

◁ **CROCKERY STORAGE**
Keep an open mind when choosing kitchen elements. A cupboard for storing crockery may be more in keeping with your design than fitted kitchen units.

appliances, cabinets, and other fittings that look attractive in catalogues and showrooms but do not suit your lifestyle or cooking habits. "A good meal is never expensive but a bad one always is." So the saying goes, and it is these costly mistakes that I intend to help you avoid.

The three major expenses when installing a kitchen are furniture, appliances, and building work. It is important to assess your budget and decide which expenses should be given priority. In my opinion, it is better to have fewer pieces of furniture made to a high standard, with perhaps a make-do cupboard that can be removed at a later date, than a complete kitchen made from cheap, low-quality units that will not last.

KITCHEN ACTIVITIES

Start by deciding what you will be doing and how much time you want to spend in your new kitchen. Do you want to use it just for cooking the occasional meal, for professional cooking, or would you like it to be the main family room in the house? I've found many of my clients prefer kitchens that contain not only a cooking area but an informal dining area, where adults can entertain and children can do their homework, draw, or paint. They also request a "soft" area with a carpet for children to play on, a sofa and television for relaxation, and a kitchen desk for dealing with home administration and telephone calls.

△ **STAINLESS STEEL**
Think carefully before selecting a kitchen cabinet finish. An industrial material such as this is heat- and water-resistant, and reflects light, brightening the room.

Having been involved in kitchen design for the last 18 years, and having come into contact with the needs of many individuals and families, I have developed a great deal of affection for the kitchen as well as knowledge about its design. Early on, much of this enthusiasm came through the influence of my late aunt, the cookery writer Elizabeth David. She was the person who first pointed out to me that kitchens do not need to be plastic laminate boxes, carefully arranged around the perimeter walls. Her kitchen was highly atmospheric, almost a study (she wrote many of her books at its scrubbed pine table) but also a living room, and all this at a time during the 1950s and 1960s when its design was completely out of step with the fashion. Today, we have come full circle. Our idea of the kitchen as a place to live in, relax, and be sociable, as well as cook, would have pleased her.

Designing a kitchen is usually the biggest financial investment after buying a house or flat, and it is all too easy to be seduced into purchasing

COOL STORAGE ▷
Consider a larder for storing fresh produce rather than relying solely on the fridge.

◁ UTENSIL RACK
A wrought-iron rack
above a hob or food
preparation area offers
easy access to kitchen
utensils. It also makes
an attractive display.

In order to produce a successful kitchen design that matches your needs, you have to go back to fundamentals. First establish what you enjoy and what you dislike about your existing kitchen, and use the ideas (*below*) to help build up a picture of your ideal kitchen. Consider how you move about the room: how far do you have to travel from the fridge to the food preparation area? Are storage cupboards difficult to reach?

Are worktops close to the hob? Is it easy to carry in shopping bags from the car?

Once you have worked out how you are going to use the space, research the features that best suit your needs. The pages on essential kitchen elements, such as storage, ovens, and sinks, cover the pros and cons of major kitchen appliances. For example, if you cook with plenty of fresh ingredients you will be able to judge whether a

△ GLASS SPLASHBACK
As an alternative to tiles,
consider using glass to
protect walls near worktops.

WHAT DO YOU WANT FROM YOUR KITCHEN?

Before committing yourself to expensive furniture and equipment, assess your lifestyle
and the kind of non-cooking activities you wish to undertake in your new kitchen.
Use the following options to help you decide what sort of kitchen will suit you best.

❶ A room solely for cooking
meals without interruption.

❷ A family room where light
meals are eaten.

❸ A kitchen that doubles up as
a dining room.

❹ A space for professional
catering on a large scale.

❺ A room for researching,
writing, and planning menus.

❻ An area where children can
play and do homework.

◁ KITCHEN USES
A desk area for organizing
household activities has
been designed into this
family kitchen. One wall
is given over to a desk
with bookshelves above, a
pinboard, and blackboard.

HOW SUITABLE IS YOUR ROOM?

Before you decide to
spend a lot of money
on remodelling an
existing kitchen, or
on designing one from
scratch for a new home,
make sure that the
room you choose to
be the kitchen has the
necessary features or
can be easily adapted.
□ Is the total space big
enough for you or your
family's needs? Could
the room be extended?
□ Does the room have
access to other associated
rooms such as the
pantry, utility room,
and dining room? Is it
possible to add or move
the doors in order to
improve the link?
□ Is the room adjoining
the garden so that you
can have an outdoor
dining area in summer,
watch while your
children play, or keep
the door open for
extra ventilation?
□ Does the room under
consideration have easy
or direct access to the
garage or parking area
for unloading shopping?
□ Is the natural light
good? Could lighting
be improved by adding
a new window?
□ Are there enough
electrical and plumbing
points, and are they
well distributed?

pantry cupboard or a large fridge is a better
investment. Whatever the size of your kitchen,
try to limit the number of elements to keep the
plan simple. In small kitchens, durable items
that offer multi-purpose functions may be better
than specialized features that have only an
occasional use. The same applies to small gadgets
and electrical appliances whose limited purpose
may not justify the amount of space they occupy.

KITCHEN CHARACTER

The personality of a room is determined by the
individual elements. In kitchens, these elements
also have to be functional because they are used
more intensively than other household furniture,
and come into daily contact with heat, steam,
and water. Stainless steel fridges and worktops,
for example, contribute an air of professionalism
to the domestic kitchen as this highly durable

material is frequently used in restaurant kitchens.
Wood cupboards, on the other hand, or cooking
utensils hanging from racks, provide the warm
atmosphere associated with country kitchens.

It is not only kitchen appliances that matter.
Other details, such as your choice of worktops,
lighting, cabinets, wallcoverings, and flooring, all
present an opportunity to influence the character
of the room and to create a comfortable kitchen
environment. When choosing these elements,
bear in mind both aesthetic and practical
considerations. Kitchen flooring, for example,
needs to be hygienic, hardwearing, and "soft"
underfoot, as well as attractive, while a well
thought-out mix of task lights and soft, ambient
lighting can transform working and eating areas.
For kitchen cabinets, the choice of materials and
quality of craftsmanship are vital if they are to
withstand daily wear and tear. Also, by choosing

WHAT COULD YOU CHANGE?

Use the following
checklist to help you
pinpoint what it is
about your kitchen
that you would like
to improve or replace.
☐ Change shape of
existing room.
☐ Alter architectural
features.
☐ Improve access to
natural light.
☐ Reorganize layout
of kitchen cabinets.
☐ Upgrade major
appliances.
☐ Increase number
of electrical points.
☐ Redesign lighting.
☐ Relocate plumbing.
☐ Rationalize available
storage space.
☐ Rethink the size and
height of worktops.
☐ Change worktop
materials.
☐ Replace flooring.
☐ Renew wallcoverings
and splashbacks.
☐ Alter style of cabinets
and door handles.
☐ Rehinge entry doors.
☐ Change furniture.
☐ Update all curtains,
blinds, cushions, and
other soft furnishings.
☐ Decrease noise levels.

ALTERING THE SHAPE ▷
To create a large family
kitchen with space for a
sitting, dining, and desk
area, three smaller rooms
have been combined.

from a range of gloss or matt, pale or dark
cabinet finishes, you can affect how the cabinets
reflect natural light in the kitchen.

KITCHEN LAYOUT

For me, kitchen planning tends to fall into two
categories, fitted and "unfitted". Fitted kitchens,
developed in the 1950s, rely upon units being
placed against the walls, while unfitted types use
a variety of freestanding elements as furnishings.

The "unfitted" approach is an area of kitchen
planning that I have pioneered. It has grown in
popularity, as for many individuals the warm,
comfortable appearance of unfitted kitchens is
both easier to live with, and work in. The Family

Kitchen (*below*), is an example of this planning.
By grouping all the cooking and preparation
facilities together, fewer elements have to be
placed around the walls, leaving space for a table,
a sofa, and doors opening out onto the garden.

Above all, the purpose of this chapter is to
explain how to arrive at an ergonomic kitchen
design where the user feels comfortable. Whether
your kitchen is large or small, it will help you to
choose appliances and furniture according to
your needs, and arrange them for ease of use, in a
way that is not only practical but looks wonderful.

JOHNNY GREY

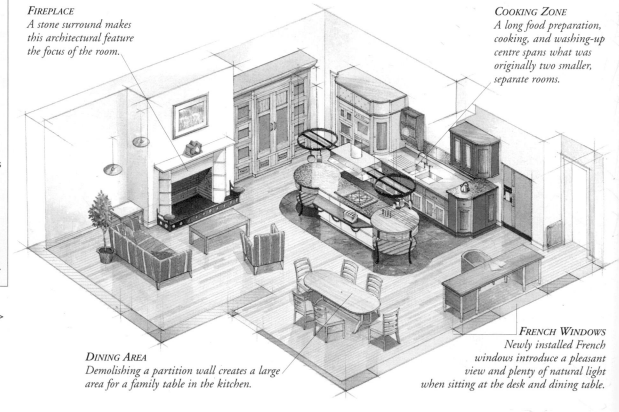

FIREPLACE
A stone surround makes
this architectural feature
the focus of the room.

COOKING ZONE
A long food preparation,
cooking, and washing-up
centre spans what was
originally two smaller,
separate rooms.

DINING AREA
Demolishing a partition wall creates a large
area for a family table in the kitchen.

FRENCH WINDOWS
Newly installed French
windows introduce a pleasant
view and plenty of natural light
when sitting at the desk and dining table.

DUNCAN OF
JORDANSTONE COLLEGE
LIBRARY

PLAN OF ACTION

Before you go ahead with your alterations, use this checklist to ensure that you have not overlooked any requirements. A date for completion and good coordination of plumbers, electricians, and fitters is also important. Consider the following:

☐ Have you received permission from the relevant authorities for structural alterations, such as exposing an old pantry or boiler room?

☐ Can you afford the time to do some of the work yourself?

☐ Will you need to seek professional help?

☐ Have you estimated the costs accurately?

☐ Have you left enough money for decoration?

☐ Is the amount of work within budget or are you happy to retain some features, such as kitchen units?

☐ Have you made other plans for eating when work is in progress?

☐ Will your kitchen plans increase the resale value of the property?

◁ **KITCHEN AFTERCARE**
A finished kitchen needs regular maintenance to keep it looking its best. Here, wood worktops have been oiled, wood floors varnished, and cabinet doors repainted.

ASSESS YOUR NEEDS

THE FOLLOWING questions will help you to focus on your specific kitchen needs, and think about ways to approach kitchen planning so that, as you work through this chapter, you can compile a list of the kitchen elements and designs that suit you best.

STORAGE

The number of people you cater for, how many meals you cook at home, the type of foods you use, how you shop, and who needs access to storage, determine the type and amount of storage space you need in your kitchen.

■ FOOD
☐ Do you cook with a mixture of fresh, frozen, chilled, dried, preserved, or tinned foods, or does one type predominate?
☐ Do you have enough fridge, freezer, and cupboard space to house your preferred choice of cooking ingredients?
☐ If you cook with mainly fresh ingredients, do you have cool, well-ventilated storage for vegetables etc., or do you rely solely on the fridge?
☐ If you like to prepare meals well in advance and freeze them, do you have enough storage space in your freezer?
☐ Do you work all day, live far from the shops, or are without a car so that you need more than the average amount of storage space?
☐ Do you buy essential items in bulk and need additional space to keep large packets, tins, and bottles?
☐ Do you store bottles of good wine and so need an even temperature site away from the oven and hob?
☐ Are your food storage facilities, such as the fridge and larder, within a few steps of food preparation areas to save journeys across the kitchen?
☐ Are items of food well-organized so that they are easy to find, not lost or forgotten at the back of kitchen cupboards?
☐ Do you expend unnecessary energy reaching up to pick cooking ingredients off high shelves, or bending down to reach into units below counter level? If so, could you reorganize your storage cupboards more efficiently so that frequently used items are kept somewhere between knee height and eye level?

☐ If you have young children, do you want some high storage areas to keep certain rationed foods, such as sweets and biscuits, out of reach?

■ EQUIPMENT
☐ Have you accumulated a huge amount of kitchen equipment that needs storing? If so, have you sorted out the equipment to check that every item is useful?
☐ Are there any less frequently used items, such as an ice-cream maker, that could be kept out of the way on high shelves?
☐ Have you allowed room to store everyday food preparation equipment within reach of food preparation worktops?
☐ Is there space for heavy food processors, toasters, and juicers to be kept plugged in at the back of countertops?
☐ Can cooking utensils be stored close to the hob counter?
☐ Can cutting boards and knives be stored within reach of food chopping areas?
☐ Can pans and baking trays be stored near the oven?
☐ Are your day-to-day plates, glasses, and cutlery stored close to the eating area for table laying, or close to the dishwasher?
☐ Have you allowed space to store non-food associated items such as cleaning and shoe-polishing products, in the kitchen?

FOOD PREPARATION

An efficient workspace for food preparation needs careful planning. Think about its location in relation to other activity areas, the type of food you prepare, the amount of people you cook for on a daily basis, and whether you need extra preparation areas for others to share the work.

☐ How much day-to-day wear are your food preparation worktops subjected to? Do you prepare several meals at home daily, or do you often eat out? Do you cook for just yourself, for you and your partner, or do you have a family to feed?
☐ Do you prepare food on your own, or does your partner or children share the work and space with you? If children are involved in food preparation, would a low-level worktop be useful?
☐ Do you cook with mainly fresh food that requires lots of preparation space, or a high proportion of convenience foods that require minimal preparation space?
☐ Would you like worktops made from different materials to suit different cooking activities, such as a cool, smooth slab of marble for pastry-making? Or, would you prefer the same surface material throughout the kitchen?
☐ Are you a sociable cook and prefer facing into the room while you work? Or, do you prefer facing the wall, or looking out of a window while you prepare food?

Cooking

Your preferred style of cooking, be it elaborate cuisine for entertaining, or quick reheating of convenience food, whether you are a solitary or sociable cook, how frequently you cook at home, and the number of people you regularly cook for, determine the type and location of cooking appliances.

☐ Do you want to face into the room while working at the hob? If so, consider a centrally placed cooking area.
☐ Would the type of hob cooking you enjoy benefit from an easy-to-control fuel, such as gas or induction?
☐ Would a wipe-clean ceramic hob surface make kitchen cleaning less of a chore?
☐ If you enjoy gourmet cooking, would you benefit from a hob fitted with extra features, such as a barbecue grill?
☐ Would an extraction system be useful to help dispel cooking smells? If so, would a permanent or retractable hood be more suitable in the space above the hob?
☐ Do you regularly cater for more than five people? If so, is your oven big enough, or would a double oven or heavy-duty range be more suitable?
☐ Would you like to have the capacity to prepare, reheat, or defrost meals in an instant? If so, have you allowed space to accommodate a microwave oven?

Eating

Think carefully about the sort of meals that you would like to eat in the kitchen, whether just breakfasts and snacks, or lunches and suppers, the number of people that sit down to eat at any one time, and how often you entertain. These decisions will help you determine the size and type of table you need, plus the dimensions and best location of the dining area.

☐ Do you want to eat in the kitchen or would you rather eat in a separate room?
☐ What meals do you specifically want to eat in the kitchen?
☐ How many people do you want to be able to seat on a day-to-day basis?
☐ Do you want to entertain in the informal surroundings of the kitchen?
☐ Have you planned the location of the table so that it has a good source of natural light, is draught-free, and sits away from the main kitchen activity areas?
☐ Would a foldaway table or small corner table be more suitable if space is limited?
☐ Would a bar eating area around a central island be sufficient?
☐ Would a built-in window seat or banquette rather than chairs help you fit more seats around a table?
☐ Is a hardwearing tabletop an important requirement?

Washing-up and Waste Disposal

Make washing-up and food recycling simple by choosing the sink, drainage space, and dishwasher on the basis of the amount of work you have to do.

■ Washing-up
☐ If you use a large quantity of plates and glasses on a daily basis, is it worthwhile investing in a dishwasher to save time? If the dishwasher is going to be on while you are in the kitchen, have you checked that it has a quiet operational noise level?
☐ If you use many large pans, do you have a big enough sink to be able to wash them up properly?
☐ While washing-up, do you want to face the wall or have a window view, or perhaps face into the room?

■ Waste
☐ Will you dispose of all kitchen waste, or are you going to recycle some of it?
☐ Do you have the space in the kitchen to store recycling bins for items such as newspapers, bottles, and cans, or will they be stored outside, or in the garage?
☐ Would you like to store food waste for a compost heap? If so, have you a bin next to the preparation area for food scraps?

FRESH FOOD STORAGE

IF YOU COOK with a lot of fresh produce, try to plan well-ventilated storage facilities set away from hot, steamy areas of the kitchen, rather than becoming wholly dependent on the fridge. To avoid unnecessary wastage and for a healthy turnover, ensure all fresh supplies are visible.

LARGE STORAGE

A pantry cupboard is the modern-day solution to the walk-in larder. Its generous storage capacity allows you to house all your foods – with the exception of those that are kept in the fridge-freezer – in one location rather than at a variety of sites above and below the worktops. A successful larder cupboard has shelves with adjustable heights to meet the demands of modern packaging, and a shallow depth so that items at the back do not disappear.

TOP SHELF
Less frequently used items, or those that you have bought in bulk, can be stored at this less accessible height, out of sight.

SHALLOW SHELVES
Avoid over-filling the door shelves with heavy items or they may be difficult to open.

MODERN LARDER △
A storage cupboard with sliding, fold-back doors allows maximum visibility and accessibility, while requiring the minimum clearance when opening. Stainless steel racking shelves allow air to circulate within; walls, floor, and doors are easy to clean.

PULL-OUT DRAWERS
Fresh vegetables, bread, or large goods can be placed in compartments below waist height.

PANTRY CUPBOARD ▽

An attractive piece of furniture that stands away from the main traffic, this cupboard offers cool, dark, well-ventilated storage for a wealth of fresh and non-perishable produce. Half-depth shelves keep items in reach and prevent them from becoming lost and forgotten.

FULL-HEIGHT DOORS
Doors of this size reveal the entire contents of the cupboard when open.

GRANITE SHELF
A cold granite shelf 60cm (24in) deep, keeps cheese and other fresh produce at room temperature.

REMEMBER

■ Work out in advance which foods you prefer to keep in the pantry cupboard and which in the fridge-freezer. If you buy in bulk, you will need additional storage areas in the kitchen.

■ When choosing a pantry cupboard, the central shelf should be about 60cm (24in) deep, while access to mid-height shelves is easiest if these shelves are 15–30cm (6–12in) shallower than the central shelf.

■ If you intend to store a lot of fresh produce in the cupboard, ventilation ducts to the outside may improve conditions. The pantry needs to be dark inside to slow down the deterioration of fresh fruit and vegetables.

STORAGE HEIGHT

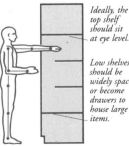

Ideally, the top shelf should sit at eye level.

Low shelves should be widely spaced or become drawers to house large items.

The most accessible storage area sits between knee height and eye level. Store items rarely used above and below this line.

SMALL STORAGE

Certain fresh foods, such as tomatoes, eggs, soft fruits, and baked foods, are damaged by cold refrigeration and taste best if kept at room temperature. Here are some modern and traditional solutions to this problem.

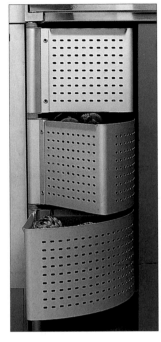

△ **BREAD-BIN DRAWER**
This space-saving alternative to a traditional bread crock has a lift-out drawer for removing crumbs. The wooden lid can double up as a cutting board.

REVOLVING RACK ▷
A modern rack provides dark, well-ventilated conditions to store root vegetables.

MEAT SAFE ▽
A traditional meat safe, with its netted doors, is good for keeping flies off fresh food, while allowing ventilation; central heating and warm summers limit their use to eggs, cheeses, various soft fruits, and tomatoes.

WIRE-MESH DOORS
These keep household dust and insects off fresh foods.

RAISED HEIGHT
A meat safe on legs ensures that food is stored above floor level.

CHILLED FOOD STORAGE

WHEN JUDGING WHICH fridge or freezer best suits your needs, bear in mind the size of your family, your shopping and eating habits, and the position the appliance will occupy in the kitchen. How you organize your food in the space available is the key, so check that the model of your choice has adjustable shelves and see-through drawers to offer the most flexibility.

UNDERCOUNTER FRIDGE-FREEZERS

In a small kitchen, consider an undercounter, side-by-side fridge-freezer that will keep limited worktop space free for food preparation. If the appliance is flush-fitting, the interior space is well-organized, and the appliance is placed directly below a food preparation area, it can work very efficiently. Bear in mind though, that the fridge is one of the most-used items in the kitchen, and frequent bending down to take out or put back food may become irritating.

FRIDGE INTERIOR
Ensure the space inside caters for tall items, such as bottles.

SMALL FRIDGE-FREEZER ▽
Think carefully before deciding to buy a small fridge-freezer. If you enjoy cooking on a regular basis, you may find its limited capacity very inconvenient.

DOOR SHELVES
Store short-term frozen items here, for easy access.

FRIDGE DRAWERS ▽

A recent innovation in cold food storage is fridges and freezers that are compact enough to fit into the space of a drawer. These allow chilled fresh produce to be stored at a number of strategic sites around the kitchen.

EASY ACCESS
Large fridge doors can be difficult to open; single pull-out drawers offer easier access.

FRESH PRODUCE
This section varies between 0.5°C (32°F) and 3°C (37°F), with 50 per cent humidity.

HIGH HUMIDITY
In this drawer, a relative humidity of up to 90 per cent keeps fruit and vegetables fresh and crisp.

REMEMBER

■ Before choosing a chilled storage system, consider how often you prepare and freeze meals in advance. Or does your cooking focus on fresh foods?

■ Other features that may influence your decision are: CFC content, noise level, defrost capability, and energy efficiency rating.

■ When placing your fridge within the room, leave space for access. Specify which way you want the door to hinge, and plan a worktop nearby for loading and unloading food.

■ After a shopping trip, beware of packing the fridge too tightly with food as it takes time to return to a cool temperature.

FREESTANDING MODELS

Designed to stand alone as a kitchen feature, these appliances are not limited by the need to fit within standard cabinetry. Many models sit on wheels and can be easily moved for servicing or to a new location.

DAIRY COMPARTMENT
A transparent lid protects the contents from taste and odour transfer.

◁△ **MODERN STYLE**
Handles the length of the door (*above*) make it easy for adults and children to open the large stainless steel fridge, and gain access to the well-organized contents in easy-clean plastic and glass compartments (*left*).

SPILL-SAVER SHELVES
Raised shelf edges help to contain spills.

DEEP DOOR SPACE
Large items can be stored two-deep, while a high side prevents tall cartons from toppling out.

▽ **TRADITIONAL STYLE**
If you prefer your fridge to be unobtrusive, consider housing it within a cabinet. Vegetables that need ventilation but not refrigeration can be stored in open-weave baskets below.

VENTILATION
Vents at the front enable the unit to have a coil-free back so that it can be fitted flush with the wall.

FRUIT DRAWER
Located in the coolest part of the fridge, see-through fruit and vegetable drawers allow you to see exactly what needs replacing or throwing out.

NON-PERISHABLE FOOD STORAGE

ORGANIZATION OF, and access to, store cupboard supplies is paramount, but because tinned, bottled, and dried foods have fewer environmental needs than fresh foods and location-sensitive appliances, one option is to keep them in slim units and corner carousels that can fill up leftover spaces in the kitchen.

NARROW SOLUTIONS

In larger kitchens, tall, dual-sided pull-out cupboards are an efficient option because items at the back can be easily accessed. Make sure there is room on either side to reach into the pull-out, and that there is a mid-height "fence" to prevent articles from falling out. Place less regularly used, heavier items, on the bottom shelf.

EASY OPENING
A centrally placed handle distributes the weight, making the unit lighter to open, even when it is full.

CLEARANCE HEIGHT
Allow space between each shelf for the easy retrieval and return of taller items.

TALL BOTTLE STORE
Space for tall bottles is created by removing the penultimate shelf divider.

BOTTLE SAFETY
The rail holding bottles in place is thicker for these heavier items.

LAMINATE FINISH
Hardwearing laminates are easy to clean and will withstand knocks.

DIRECT ACCESS
Drawer runners are an integral part of the fence rail, so that access to the shelves is uninterrupted.

CAPACITY
Each shelf is deep and wide enough to hold at least four large bottles.

◁ **PULL-OUT STORAGE**
The success of this store cupboard lies in its flexibility and ease of access. The door slides open and is nudged closed, while shelf heights and compartment sizes can be altered to suit a variety of non-perishable produce.

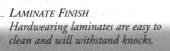

BOTTLE PULL-OUT △
A narrow, below-counter pull-out is useful for cooking oils, vinegars, and cooking wine. It can be tucked into a narrow space adjacent to the hob, oven, or preparation area.

REMEMBER

■ Resolve to sort out your store cupboard supplies and to check "best before" dates periodically, to prevent any old or forgotten packets and jars accumulating and cluttering up space.

■ Pull-outs, smaller cupboards, shelves, and racks all provide an excellent way of organizing your non-perishable items so you can see them. Visibility is a key to ensuring a healthy turnover of supplies. Smaller storage areas, for herbs etc., will also help you to manage and take stock of the huge range of items needed.

■ Unused areas of the kitchen can become non-perishable food storage centres, especially if clever pull-outs make them more accessible. Narrow below-counter pull-outs can be placed near preparation areas without interfering with other elements.

OVER-COUNTER UNITS

Wall-mounted cupboards and racks provide storage space over countertops. They can be useful for stationing spices, oils, and wine, if placed within reach of the food preparation area. In small kitchens where space is at a premium, over-counter units may be the answer, but in order to function ergonomically they should sit at eye level. This height can be a problem because the cupboard may block your view of the counter when working, and also pin your head and shoulders back. For this reason, try not to place cupboards above heavily used worktops or the sink cabinet.

TOP SHELF
Least important jars should be stored on high shelves.

SHELF DEPTH
The shelves should be between 15–30cm (6–12in) deep so that all items are visible.

CHICKEN-WIRE DOOR
A fabric-backed wire door allows air to circulate whilst protecting food items from direct sunlight.

WALL FIXTURE
Ensure wall brackets are securely mounted as the unit is extremely heavy when full.

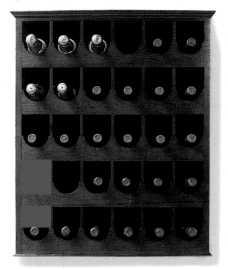

CONDIMENT CUPBOARD ▷
Depending on how tall you are, place the cupboard at a height somewhere between 1.8–2.2m (5ft 10in–7ft 2in). Allow a gap of at least 45cm (18in) between wall units and the worktop below.

◁ WINE RACK
Consider storing your selection of wines on a wall rack to free up floor space. Do not position the rack too close to the oven because wine favours an even temperature around 15.5°C (60°F).

CORNER IDEAS

Even in very small kitchens where space is precious, the corner area where worktops meet is often neglected. This "dead" space can be turned into a useful storage area if a pull-out mechanism is fitted below counter-level. Alternatively, plan a body-height carousel to fit neatly into a corner space, and bridge the gap that may be left between an eye-level oven and a food preparation worktop.

OPEN CAROUSEL
Fixed doors revolve around a pivot and swing shut into place.

REAR SECTION
Once the front section has been pulled out, the rear section slides forward, out of the deep corner space.

◁ BODY-HEIGHT CAROUSEL
Rather than having to delve inside a dark corner cupboard, the doors of this unit fold back to offer access to its contents. Jars, tins, and packets are neatly arranged on four shelves that revolve when nudged. Standing 2m (6ft 6in) high, no effort is required to reach the top shelf.

◁△ TWO-PART PULL-OUT
Contemporary kitchen manufacturers have responded to the challenge of kitchen storage needs by tailoring units to fit into awkward corners. In this two-part unit (*left and above*), frequently used non-perishable foods, such as pasta and noodles sit in the front section (*left*), while items stored in bulk are kept at the back, and can only be accessed once the front unit has been swung to the side (*above*).

FOOD PREPARATION

TO ENSURE COOKING IS enjoyable, the chopping and preparation area needs ample space, a hardwearing worktop, and clever positioning within the room; ensure food and equipment are close at hand, and that you can move with ease to the cooking zone and sink cabinet. To make the task more pleasant, plan an area where you have a view outside, natural light, or you can talk to family or friends at the same time.

BUILT-IN SOLUTIONS

Fixed unit or wall-based preparation areas are an effective way to maximize the limited space on offer in small kitchens, but are much less sociable because you face the wall rather than another person when working. For maximum efficiency, arrange all the equipment used in food preparation, such as knives, adjacent to the activity area. If countertops are especially deep, consider having an appliance "garage" at the back for storing equipment close at hand.

(see pp.52–53)

△ INDIVIDUAL CHOPPING BOARDS
Use portable wooden chopping boards to prepare foods such as garlic and fish, whose strong odours may easily penetrate the wood.
When the task is complete, remove the board and scrub clean in soapy water. Keep several boards in a variety of sizes for preparing different food types.

◁ APPLIANCE "GARAGE"
An elegant solution to storing heavy electrical appliances, such as food processors. When needed, they are slid out onto the counter without being lifted.

CLOSED STORAGE
Equipment is stored out of sight and does not clutter up the worktop. This is a useful feature to include in a small kitchen.

▽ MINI PREPARATION AREA
A small food preparation centre provides enough space to store knives, seasonings, and spices within easy reach of the activity area.

ROLLER SHUTTER
A roll-up mechanism saves space as it does not open outwards like a cupboard door.

CONCEALED SOCKET
Wall sockets inside the "garage" mean appliances are always plugged in, ready for use.

VISIBLE STORAGE
Spices and pulses are attractively displayed in clear bottles and drawers for ease of use.

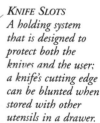

CHOPPING BLOCK
Made from end-grain wood, the block is positioned at the ideal height (see above right); slots in the wood hold sharp knives.

KNIFE SLOTS
A holding system that is designed to protect both the knives and the user; a knife's cutting edge can be blunted when stored with other utensils in a drawer.

PULL-DOWN BOARD
The countertop is saved from wear and tear with an easy-to-access chopping block.

FREESTANDING PREPARATION CENTRES

A central island unit or work table provides a focus in the middle of the room dedicated to food preparation. These freestanding features *(right and below)* enable the cook to face into the space as he or she works and to join in the proceedings. In terms of kitchen planning, they provide a central focus, and a link with the features around the walls, especially in large kitchens. Islands should be placed so that they are within reach of stored food, the sink for rinsing ingredients, and the cooking zone.

WORKTOP HEIGHT

5–10cm (2–4in) below your flexed elbow for food preparation.

17–25cm (7–10in) below elbow-height for small appliances.

The ideal height is dictated by the activity in question.

LARGE WORK TABLE ▷
Working tables are appropriate in kitchens where a solid unit would make the space feel cramped. They can be bought as individual pieces of furniture, and often have a platform below the worktop for storing mixing bowls and pans.

HOB AREA
The hob is set 15cm (6in) below the worktop height so that you can see into pans. The adjacent stainless steel worktop is heatproof and provides "parking" space for heavy items.

HANGING RACK
Oils, garlic, and cooking utensils are stored within reach of the preparation area.

SERVING AREA
A free surface for resting plates of food, between the hob area and a kitchen table, makes serving easy. Crockery can be stored in the cupboard below.

◁ ISLAND UNIT
An island arrangement helps to concentrate key activities into a small area so the cook does not waste time and energy moving about the kitchen. The island is divided up into zones for different activities. The activity determines the worktop height, size, and also material for each zone.

LOW-LEVEL WORKTOP
A low counter is ideal for jobs that require some effort, such as pastry-making, as you can bear down on this marble slab.

FOOD RINSING AND WASTE DISPOSAL

HYGIENIC AND WELL-PLANNED food and waste management are essential to a well-run kitchen. Consider a sink with two basins, where fish, meat, vegetables, and fruit can be cleaned without interrupting other kitchen activities that require water, such as pan-filling. Plan convenient sites beneath food preparation centres for organic waste collection, and storage bins for collecting bottles and cans away from the main activity centres.

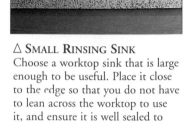

FOOD-RINSING SOLUTIONS

In large kitchens, where the distance between activity zones is greater, a second sink for washing food, close to the preparation area, may be convenient. Alternatively, plan a double sink unit, where food can be rinsed in one half and utensils, pans, and crockery washed in the other.

SPLASHBACK
A high stainless steel guard protects the wall from water splashes.

△ **SMALL RINSING SINK**
Choose a worktop sink that is large enough to be useful. Place it close to the edge so that you do not have to lean across the worktop to use it, and ensure it is well sealed to prevent leakage into units below.

SPRAY-RINSING HEAD
An extendable spray attachment, for cleaning fresh ingredients, is linked to the water supply by a flexible hose.

◁ **DOUBLE SINK**
A double sink enables two people to stand at the sink at once and perform different tasks. As the sink is used intensively, it is manufactured from a durable, water- and rust-resistant material, such as stainless steel.

DOUBLE BASIN
Use one sink to rinse fresh ingredients and the other to soak dirty pans and dishes.

FRONT PANEL
A stainless steel panel prevents water from dripping onto the wood cabinet below.

MULTI-PURPOSE SINK ▽
A well-designed, deep single sink can sometimes offer more flexibility than a double unit with two small sinks. A large sink can accommodate baking trays and pans, while a colander, draining rack, and chopping board can be slotted into the sink to divide up the internal space as required.

WASTE DISPOSAL
Flush food scraps washed off plates down into the waste disposal unit fitted beneath the waste outlet.

SINGLE TAP
Shift the tap to the left or right, depending on the task in hand.

COLANDER BASKET
Drain rinsed foods and the replace the basket with the chopping block, stored belo

DRAINING RACK
Water drains directly into the sink. A separate plate rack or draining board is no longer necessary.

WASTE RECYCLING

Households generate huge quantities of waste materials, much of which can be sorted out and stored for recycling. Before allocating space to recycling in your kitchen, contact the local authority to establish the categories of rubbish that they accept. If you have a garden, consider organic waste.

ODOUR-FREE BINS
Wash out bottles and tin cans before storage, or they will smell.

◁ **STACKING BINS**
Lightweight plastic bins can be easily stacked on top of one other, while lift-up flaps allow the quick deposit of items. Allocate one bin for each category of recycled waste. Store the bins out of sight and plan to empty them regularly.

△ **ORGANIC WASTE HOLE**
A hole or slot carved out of a wood worktop feeds directly into a waste bin below, and is an efficient way of clearing away organic waste matter, such as vegetable peelings. As well as keeping the worktop free, the waste matter can be tipped directly onto a garden compost heap.

△ **RECYCLING COMPARTMENTS**
Here, a pull-out drawer adjacent to the sink holds two recycling bins. Avoid shallow bins that have to be emptied frequently. Make sure the bins are easy to lift out, and that the drawer interior can be wiped clean. Also, check that the drawer is sealed to prevent odour transfer.

REMEMBER

■ Plan organic waste bins or a waste disposal hole close to the food preparation area, to avoid having to transport food scraps across the kitchen.

■ The size of rubbish bins for household waste needs to be in keeping with the size of your family. Emptying a bin several times a day, especially if you live in a block of flats, may become annoying.

■ If you are unhappy about separating out waste materials for recycling, try to recycle just "clean" waste; newspapers and glass bottles are the easiest and cleanest to separate out and store in stacking bins for weekly recycling.

WASTE DISPOSAL

For those who live in small flats or houses, recycling may not be an option because of the space needed to sort out and store the different materials. A waste compactor occupies a small amount of space and will compress all bulky household rubbish into tight bundles. Alternatively, consider a waste disposal unit to dispose of food scraps. A less expensive option is a slim, free-standing pedal bin.

◁ **ELECTRIC COMPACTOR**
All household rubbish is fed in and then compacted at the turn of a switch. This small unit does not need emptying for several weeks at a time.

CHARCOAL FILTER
The filter reduces odours when the door is open.

PEDAL BIN ▷
A flexible unit, as it can be transported to wherever you are working. Its slim shape takes up less floor space than other pedal bins.

PLASTIC BOARD
This creates an extra chopping block above the sink. Organic waste can be swept directly into the waste disposal unit.

WASTE-FREE SINK
Waste does not interfere with sink drainage as it is fed directly into the waste disposal system.

▽ **WASTE-DISPOSAL UNITS**
If you do not intend to recycle organic waste, consider a sink fitted with an electric waste disposer. This feature will grind down food scraps and bones into paste and then wash them away. It can be noisy when the grinder is switched on.

"PARKING" AREA
Place washed items here that are awaiting preparation.

BATCH FEED
The waste disposal unit fits into this section. A safety plug is turned on to start the electric grinder.

HOBS AND EXTRACTORS

THE POSITION AND CHOICE of hob is crucial to the enjoyment and efficiency of the kitchen. Ideally, it should face into the room, have a sink nearby, parking space suitable for resting hot pans, and, wherever possible, a high-performance, well-designed, powerful extractor for removing cooking odours and steam. Task lights built into the extractor hood will help light the hob area.

COMBINATION HOBS

A worktop-mounted gas, halogen, or induction hob and a wall-mounted electric oven offers flexibility of fuel types – quick response from the hob, and even-temperature oven cooking. The variety of hobs has become increasingly specialized. Manufacturers now offer components such as steamers, griddles, or wok burners, so that you can build up hob features to suit your cooking style.

REMEMBER

■ In the life of your kitchen, much cooking time is spent standing at the hob. Arrange your kitchen plan accordingly by placing the hob in a safe, sociable, and convenient location, perhaps forming the central feature in an island arrangement (*see pp.56–57*).

■ When planning a site for your hob, bear in mind the limitations of extractor systems, required to expel steam and cooking smells. Extractors work best when connected to outside walls; hobs on islands require more powerful systems.

■ British and US manufacturers rate extractors according to how many cubic feet per minute (CFM) of air they can process. Work out the volume of your room, to determine the rating you need.

■ A hob must be easy to clean to work efficiently. Many pan grids are now designed to fit into a dishwasher. Check that the rest of the hob is simply designed so that grease cannot collect in awkward corners.

■ Beware of unstable pan grids. If the prongs are short or stand high of the hob, saucepans may accidentally topple off the grid.

■ If your cooking habits demand constant use of the hob, ensure the hob floor and pan grids are made from heavy-duty materials; stainless steel and vitreous enamel are highly suitable.

GAS HOB WITH GRIDDLE ▽
A solid, semi-professional range can be fitted with a combination of different components that suit your cooking habits. Here, a powerful down-draught extractor sits between a griddle and four gas rings.

GAS BURNERS
Cast alloy pan grids surround the two gas burners.

PAN SPACE
A stainless steel surface between the grids avoids overcrowding when four large pans are on the hob.

GRIDDLE PLATE
This flexible system enables food to be grilled on the hob rather than in an oven.

INBUILT EXTRACTION
Food odours and steam are sucked downwards by an internal fan.

CONTROL KNOBS
Easy-grip, giant knobs make gas burners simple to control.

CERAMIC HALOGEN HOB WITH STEAMER ▽
A ceramic hob flanked by two down-draught extractors, a steamer, and a griddle, packs several distinct cooking functions into a small space. The hardwearing granite worktop surrounding the hob can be used as a "parking" area for hot and heavy pans, and is fireproof.

COVERED GRIDDLE
A hinged lid can be pulled down when not in use to form a "parking" space for pans.

STEAMER WITH LID
If you enjoy steamed foods, this component saves valuable pan space on the hob.

CERAMIC HOB
Fitted with halogen rings, this hob compares favourably in versatility to gas.

HOB EXTRACTOR
Extractors on either side of the hob plate ensure steam and odours are removed.

HOBS WITH OVERHEAD EXTRACTION

Condensation can be a problem in many kitchens as pans bubbling away on the hob produce both heat and moisture. To prevent this, and the peeling paint and mould that result, install an extractor. If the extractor has an internal, motorized fan, check that the motor runs quietly when on. If not, see whether the fan can be mounted on an outside wall. If you would rather not have an extractor hood obstructing your headroom, consider a down-draught system (*bottom left*).

▽ **PROFESSIONAL GAS HOB**
Many top-knotch cooks favour gas hobs because they heat up quickly and the temperature is easy to control. Space can be wasted between four burners, but here, the area between pan grids holds two useful pan rests.

LOW-LEVEL HOB ▷
Comparable to gas in flexibility, an induction hob only allows electric energy to be turned into heat inside the cooking pan, so the hob surface remains at a safe, moderate temperature.

PULL-OUT EXTRACTOR
When several pans are on the go, pull out the visor; otherwise tuck it away to maintain clear headroom.

STAINLESS STEEL SIDES
Raised edges improve safety and hygiene, by keeping hot food splashes within the hob area.

PAN STORAGE
Open shelves below the hob are convenient, but grease and dust soon collect on unused pans.

EXTRACTOR HOOD
Ensure task lights are fitted under the hood to light up the hob area.

HOOD HEIGHT
The distance between hood and hob is crucial to the efficiency of the extractor. Take care to follow manufacturer's recommendations.

EXTRACTOR GRILLE
Set against the wall, this system sucks in steam and fumes before they escape into the room.

GAS BURNERS
Unlike electric rings that eventually burn out, gas burners last indefinitely, and the flames are controllable.

HOB HEIGHT

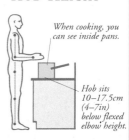

When cooking, you can see inside pans.

Hob sits 10–17.5cm (4–7in) below flexed elbow height.

Place the hob at a lower height than surrounding worktops, to protect the surfaces from fat splashes.

OVEN COOKING

TODAY'S COOK can choose from an extensive range of free-standing and fitted ovens with a choice of cooking options. Some, referred to as "semi-professional", are heavy-duty ovens and resemble those used by restaurant chefs. Beware of being seduced by good looks and list your priorities, such as size, self-cleaning ability, and energy efficiency, before making a decision.

BELOW-DECK OVENS

Many manufacturers produce all-in-one ovens and hobs with either single or double oven facilities. An advantage of combined units is that cooking activities are focused in one part of the kitchen. But if you tend to roast or oven-bake food, you may find bending down to access the oven tiresome. If your kitchen is small, a single oven and hob unit is best but check there is space for the oven door to open.

TRADITIONAL AGA ▷
These enamelled stoves are fired by solid fuels, oil, gas, or electricity, and are constantly hot and ready for use.

FREESTANDING OVEN ▽
A solidly constructed, high-quality appliance such as this features six gas burners, a hot plate and two double ovens. If you cook on a professional basis or have a large family, this oven may be a worthwhile investment.

STAINLESS STEEL SPLASHBACK
A splashback protects kitchen walls from a build-up of grease.

SIMPLE CONTROLS
Easy-grip knobs and pull-down doors make it simple to operate.

STAINLESS STEEL
A durable, brushed stainless steel finish improves with age.

FLAT SIDES
The appliance can be fitted flush to cabinetry if you do not wish it to stand alone.

DOOR VENTILATION
Small vents keep these "child-height" doors cool on the outside.

SEE-THROUGH DOOR
A glass panel helps you check food without opening the door.

STORAGE DRAWER
Baking trays can be neatly stowed away when not in use.

△ SINGLE OVEN AND HOB
A compact appliance for those without the space to house a separate oven at eye level. When switched off, the halogen hob doubles up as an extra worktop.

FOUR LEGS
Short legs raise the oven off the ground so that the floor underneath can be swept.

REMEMBER

■ Decide whether an oven at eye level is a priority. Bear in mind that a separate oven and hob, although convenient, may work out more expensive.

■ If you want to fit a powerful, outdoor extractor motor (*see pp.34–35*), ensure the oven and hob sit against an outside wall.

■ Check whether your floor is solid and can take the weight of a heavy stove.

■ If you wish to turn off your Aga during the summer, provide a back-up oven and hob.

EYE-LEVEL OVENS

Easier and safer to load than below-counter ovens, an eye-level appliance has a simple pull-down oven door. The dish is placed inside without the extra effort of bending down, and you can watch your food as it cooks. If you enjoy catering for large numbers of people, a second oven for warming plates, grilling, or microwaving may be advantageous.

OVEN HEIGHT

Dishes should not have to be lifted above chest height.

Place a single oven, or two ovens housed in a tall unit, somewhere between eye level and waist height for ease of use.

STEAM OVEN COMBINATION ▷
For those who favour healthy, fat-free cooking techniques, a steam oven is the modern-day pressure cooker. By cooking foods such as fresh vegetables and fish in steam, the moisture is retained. Combine a steam oven with a multi-functional electric oven to cover all options.

SLIDE-UP DOOR
One simple action raises the cabinet door that conceals the steamer.

STEAM OVEN
Although costly, consider this type of oven if it suits your eating habits.

SECOND OVEN
For maximum usage, choose a fan-assisted model that can also grill and microwave.

SPACE BELOW
The ovens are fitted at the best height for the user, leaving space for a storage cupboard below.

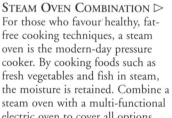

◁ DOUBLE OVENS
For keen cooks who enjoy baking, roasting, and grilling, a double oven combined with a separate worktop-mounted hob is perhaps the answer. Opt for a solidly built appliance with easy to interpret controls and fold-down doors that serve as resting platforms for hot dishes entering or leaving the oven.

MICROWAVE AND OVEN ▷
For people with busy schedules, a microwave and electric oven may be the most useful combination. If cooking is really not your priority, install a dishwasher in the cabinet below the microwave instead of an oven, to save on time spent in the kitchen washing-up (*see Family Kitchen Plan pp.64–65*).

EATING

UNLESS YOU HAVE an exceptionally small kitchen, try to include an eating area in your plan because a table is the linchpin for a sociable kitchen. Above all, it is the gathering place where members of the family and friends naturally congregate. For this reason, the table should occupy the most comfortable space in the room, and have at its disposal the best source of natural light, or a window view.

BUILT-IN TABLES

With careful planning, a small table where you can enjoy breakfast or a light supper can usually be accommodated in even the most compact of kitchens. It can also function as an extra worksurface or a "parking" space for pans in transit.

FOLD-UP TABLE AND CHAIRS ▷
A fold-away table can offer an inexpensive solution for those who wish to eat in the kitchen but do not have the space for a permanent fixture. However, these tables can be unstable and make eating cramped.

FOLDING CHAIRS
Lightweight chairs can be folded away when not in use.

BREAKFAST BAR ▽
Wrapped around the cooking zone of an island hob, a granite breakfast bar offers a spacious, horseshoe-shaped table for informal meals.

△ **BREAKFAST BAR AND SMALL TABLE**
A narrow breakfast bar with bar stools is ideal for informal eating and enjoying quick snacks. Here, a small round table beside the window offers a choice of seating for more relaxed mealtimes.

TABLE SIZE
The table should have at least 30cm (12in) of space per place setting.

LAMINATE SURFACE
Ideal for messy children, this table-top is easy to wipe clean but can scratch.

LOW-MAINTENANCE CHAIRS
Choose hard chairs that can be wiped clean rather than upholstered seating.

RAISED BAR HEIGHT
The counter sits above the hob and hides any cooking mess from view.

LEG ROOM
A good fold-up design has space for uninterrupted leg room.

GRANITE TOP
A hardwearing surface that does not burn or stain.

BAR STOOLS
For extra comfort, choose cushioned stools that support the back and have a foot rest.

REMEMBER

■ The space allocated for a kitchen table is usually that which is left over once all the other fixtures and fittings have been placed. Try to keep the position of the table in mind when starting your design.

■ The aspect of the table is very important. Consider the best source of natural light and ensure the site is draught-free and warm, especially in winter.

■ Try to plan a cupboard near to the table for storing breakfast materials, table linen, china, glasses, cutlery, and any other table-laying equipment.

■ If you have children, the kitchen table becomes a centre for homework, painting, and other table-top activities. If you opt for a wooden kitchen table, choose one with an oiled rather than lacquered finish as it will be much more hardwearing.

TABLE SHAPES

For people who do not have a formal dining room, or for those who simply prefer to eat in the relaxed atmosphere of the kitchen, the shape and size of the table is vital. Bear in mind that kitchen tables are usually round, oval, or rectangular, and each shape determines how people interact with one another. Table size is also worth considering because, although the room may be spacious, a large table may not be in keeping with the mood you wish to create, or how often you entertain.

ELBOW ROOM

Each place setting is 30cm (12in) deep.

Allow a 55cm (22in) width of table space per person for eating without restriction, plus an extra 5cm (2in) on either side of each place, for chair movement without disruption.

ROUND TABLE ▷
Useful for filling a square kitchen floor area, small round tables offer an intimate setting for four people, and are democratic as no one sits at the head. Large round tables are less successful because of their wide diameter, which leaves guests raising their voices to be heard.

FOUR-SEATER TABLE
A table just over 1m (3ft 3in) in diameter seats four comfortably.

OVAL TABLE ▽
An oval is perhaps the most successful shape for seating six people, as everyone can make eye contact. The generous centre space stops the table-top from becoming over crowded.

INSET LEG
Slim legs allow space for two chairs at each end, to seat eight.

SEATING
If you want to save space taken up by separate chairs, build a banquette along one wall.

TABLE SIZE
This oval is 1.6m (5ft 3in) long x 1.3m (4ft 3in) wide at the centre.

RECTANGULAR TABLE ▽
For those who have a large family or who love to entertain, choose a large, rectangular table that seats up to ten people. Here, eating is a communal activity, but of course a dining table of this scale needs a large kitchen.

LONG TABLE
At least 2m (6ft 6in) long, the huge distance between ends can divide guests into two groups.

WASHING-UP

THE WASHING-UP AREA is used more intensively than any other activity zone in the kitchen, so apply careful thought to its arrangement. There are several ergonomic aspects to resolve: the height of the sink; the depth of the washing bowl; the amount of space given over to draining; the proximity of china and cutlery storage; and the position of the sink cabinet to ensure an interesting viewpoint.

REMEMBER

■ Try to keep the distance between the sink, hob, and worktop areas to a minimum as food preparation and cooking involves constant rinsing and cleaning of used utensils.

■ Consider the variety of tasks you wish to perform at the sink before deciding whether one large sink bowl or two or three smaller bowls would best suit your needs. Is the sink to be used solely for pans and oven trays, or for hand-washing crockery and glasses as well?

■ Arrange the sink cabinet so that there is enough space for draining boards on either side, and so that it has a pleasant aspect, perhaps a garden view.

■ If you intend to have a dishwasher, consider installing the appliance at a raised height, to avoid constant stooping down to load the machine.

WASHING-UP BY HAND

Tailor your sink to your washing needs. If you cater for a large family on a regular basis, opt for a heavy-duty sink with long draining boards that is large enough for soaking big pots, oven pans, and chopping boards. A more compact unit will suit those who wash up one or two light meals a day.

TALL TOP SHELF
Although difficult to reach, less regularly used items can be kept here.

CROCKERY STORAGE
Glass-fronted cupboards and a plate rack provide storage within arm's reach.

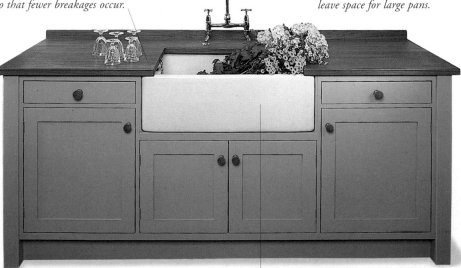

DRAINING BOARD
A wood surface provides more "give" so that fewer breakages occur.

SWAN-NECK TAP
Tall taps with good clearance leave space for large pans.

SINK HEIGHT

Avoid deep basins, as they will put extra strain on your back.

The ideal height for the top of the sink is 5cm (2in) below the base of a flexed elbow. The sink cabinet may sit slightly above waist height but there will be no need to lean over the basin.

BELFAST SINK △
This old-fashioned design has the advantage of being wide, deep, and also robust. It is installed without a frame, which means that the porcelain is visible and there is only a short distance to reach over into the sink. For it to function as a double sink for rinsing and washing, place a small plastic bowl inside the porcelain one.

WHITE PORCELAIN
Porcelain-coated fire clay offers a stain- and heat-resistant surface.

ANGLED WASHING-UP UNIT ▷
In a small kitchen, a wedge-shaped unit with a compact draining area contains this kitchen activity while freeing up space for a greater expanse of worktop.

DOWNLIGHTERS
Built-in task lights above the sink provide a strong light and prevent a shadow being cast over this small area as you work.

COVERED RACK
Plates and cups drain directly into the sink and then, when dry, remain neatly stored behind a hinged door.

CLEANING AGENTS
These are stowed on racks at eye level to keep the sink area uncluttered.

STAINLESS STEEL
Raised sides and a wide overhang prevent water overflowing onto the cabinet and floor below.

CURVED EDGE
For safety and good looks, the cabinet has a curved side rather than a sharp, angular edge.

DISHWASHERS

Research a number of products and compare reliability and life expectancy of the machines. Choose a model with valuable features, such as high energy efficiency, low operating noise levels, two revolving spray arms for a thorough wash, anti-flood sensors, removable racks, and variable-sized plate and glass holders. Bear in mind that smaller, slimline models are available.

▽ **COMBINED APPLIANCE**
Small kitchens quickly become chaotic if dishes are left to pile up unwashed on worktops. Make use of your sink plumbing to install a dishwasher underneath your sink unit at little extra cost.

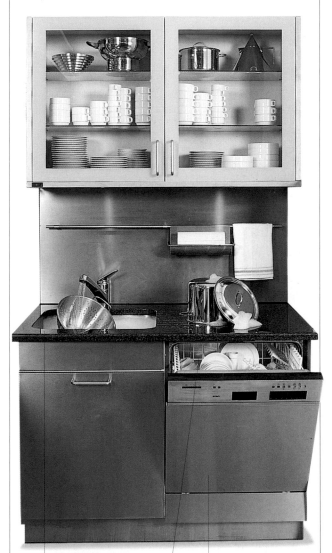

GRANITE SURFACE
A hardwearing granite worktop provides a stain-resistant surface.

DOOR CLEARANCE
If the kitchen is narrow, make sure there is ample space to walk around the door when it is open.

INSIDE THE MACHINE
Stainless steel interiors are more durable and less likely to stain and take on odours.

HARDWARE STORAGE

USER-FRIENDLY CROCKERY, glass, and kitchen equipment storage relies on clever organization, so that items taken out frequently are stored within reach – somewhere between knee height and eye level – and close to the activity area where they are needed. Much of this kitchenware is brought out, washed, and put back several times a day, so proximity to the sink or dishwasher also saves trips across the kitchen.

HIDDEN STORAGE

Kitchen hardware left out in the room on display and not used on a day-to-day basis soon gathers dust or becomes coated in a layer of grease. To avoid extra cleaning, or for those who prefer to keep worktops free of clutter, place items behind closed doors. Order the internal space so that frequently used equipment is near the front, and try to avoid storage systems with deep shelves.

LARGE BOWLS ON DISPLAY
Kitchen pieces add charm, but take them down regularly to clean.

SHELF DEPTH

Store items used daily between knee height and eye level.

To avoid having to stretch, the ideal depth of shelving should not exceed 60cm (24in) to the back of the cupboard. Any deeper would be hard to reach.

COURT CUPBOARD ▷
A 19th-century Irish food cupboard with four doors and two drawers offers both an attractive and practical storage facility. A large cupboard placed against a kitchen wall has a greater storage capacity than does a row of fitted base units and wall units in the same space.

CUPBOARD HEIGHT
The top shelf is within arm's reach, as the full height of the cupboard is only 1.9m (6ft 2in).

UTENSIL DRAWER
Store utensils in compartments to keep them sharp and in good condition.

△ **UTENSILS BELOW HOB**
A shallow drawer, running below the hob, is divided up into nine front and nine back sections to keep smaller utensils in order. Each compartment has a curved base so that you can scoop out a utensil as it is required.

PAN DRAWER
A laminate finish ensures a hardwearing interior.

△ **STORING PANS**
Like other kitchen hardware, pans should be stored close to the activity area. If you prefer your pans to be put away, one option is to install a deep drawer, below the hob, on strong runners that are fully extendable.

VISIBLE STORAGE

All kitchens gain in atmosphere when pots and pans, and other items associated with cooking and eating food, are on view. The most successful open storage systems, whether traditional or contemporary, are those where a sense of order prevails, and practical and aesthetic considerations are well-balanced. For example, plates placed upright (*below*) not only look good but collect less dust on their surface.

SAUCEPAN TREE ▷
If an awkward corner exists close to your hob, a pan stand may be a useful storage feature, although take care, as tall stands can be slightly unstable.

PAN SIZE
Store progressively larger and heavier pans on lower levels.

◁ TRADITIONAL DRESSER
An antique dresser with its open shelves, hooks, drawers, and cupboards, provides a decorative but practical way to store and display cups, plates, cutlery, and glasses.

CUP HOOKS
Hang cups on the front edge of the shelves so that they do not take up valuable shelf space.

CUPBOARD SPACE
Store less decorative, utilitarian items on shelves behind doors.

▽ **OPEN-FRONTED AND GLASS UNIT**
A built-in full-height system for those who like to be able to display decorative crockery and store utilitarian items in the same unit. Fit the unit on a wall linking cooking and eating areas.

CARVED CUPBOARD
Traditional features make the kitchen feel well-furnished, like other rooms.

DOOR WIDTH
Approximately 60cm (24in) wide, the doors are not too obtrusive when open.

DRAWER SPACE
House cutlery, table mats, instruction leaflets, and cut-out recipes in these generous drawers.

DUST-FREE STORAGE
Crockery kept behind closed doors is less susceptible to dust and grease-laden kitchen fumes.

INDIVIDUAL COMPARTMENTS
A separate display space allocated to each item enhances the sense of order.

PULL-OUT DRAWER
Semi-translucent glass removes the tyranny of maintaining a neat display.

SLIDING GLASS DOOR
A good compromise, for even when the door is shut you can quickly locate items.

SMALL KITCHEN PLAN

IN A SMALL ROOM, focus on your primary kitchen needs, mapping out the area for the cooker, the sink, and food preparation. Establish the minimum dimensions you can work within without feeling cramped, and then arrange other appliances and storage around this core. Capitalize on every available space from floor to ceiling, and select durable finishes that can adapt to a variety of uses.

TALL APPLIANCE STACK
Solid floor to ceiling units are placed around a corner to minimize their impact.

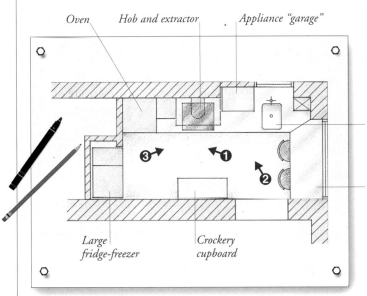

Oven   Hob and extractor   Appliance "garage"

INTERNAL ROOM DIMENSIONS:
1.9m (6ft 2in) WIDE
4.4m (14ft 4in) LONG

Single sink

Bar eating area

FRIDGE-FREEZER
A full-height fridge-freezer is concealed behind cabinetry to make it less obtrusive.

Large fridge-freezer   Crockery cupboard

△ BIRD'S EYE VIEW

The sink and eating areas benefit from the best natural light and window views, and the hob is against an outside wall to ensure good ventilation. Other kitchen appliances sit behind cabinetry so as not to obstruct the flow of traffic.

LARDER CUPBOARD
A pull-out larder sits next to the fridge; fresh and dried produce can be picked up in one trip.

DESIGN POINTS

■ In a small space, the close proximity of tasks is inevitable, but check that you can move about the room freely.

■ Install eye-level appliances in tall cabinets at one end of the room and try to leave the rest open to create a feeling of space in a small room.

■ Check that worktops can double up for other activities. In this kitchen, the eating bar is also used for food preparation.

■ Some appliances have reverse hinging – doors opening in the opposite direction may solve a few of your space problems.

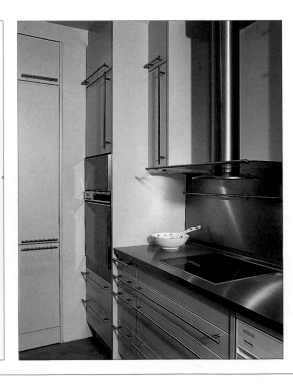

STORAGE CUPBOARD
Storage facilities are designed to fit in above and below major appliances.

EYE-LEVEL OVEN
Hot dishes from the tall oven unit can be set down quickly on the worktop to the right.

GLASS-FRONTED UNIT
Crockery and glassware are stored on view within reach of the dishwasher.

◁ ❶ OPENING UP THE SPACE

The halogen hob sits flush against the worktop, and can serve as a preparation area when not in use. A single cupboard, a slender extractor, and task lights keep this area bright and open.

EXTRACTOR
A slimline extractor removes food odours and steam, which can be a problem in small kitchens.

❷ DURABLE FINISHES ▷
Stainless steel is used on every horizontal surface because it is heat- and water-resistant, while the cabinets below have a tough melamine finish to protect them from knocks in a tight workplace.

APPLIANCE "GARAGE"
This utilizes the full depth of the worktop; an appliance can be stored at the back and pulled out onto the worksurface when needed.

WINDOW VIEW
The sink has a view to make washing-up a more enjoyable task.

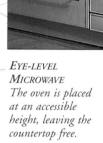

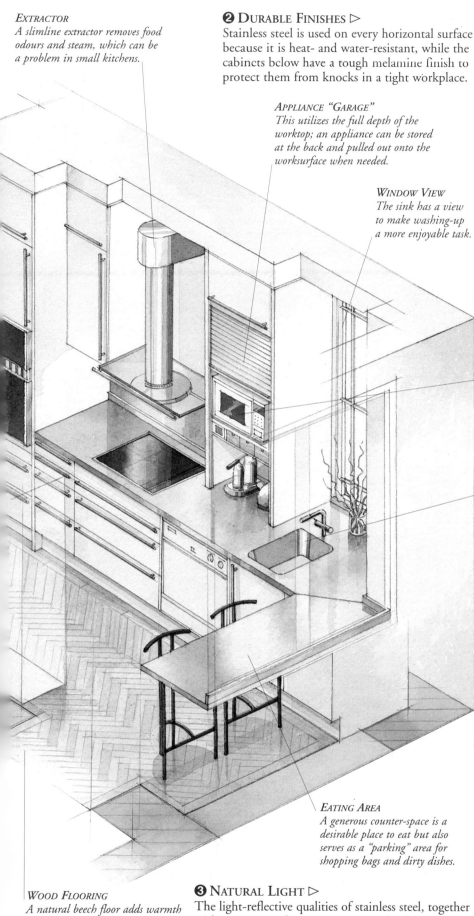

EYE-LEVEL MICROWAVE
The oven is placed at an accessible height, leaving the countertop free.

SINGLE SINK
A small sink saves on precious worktop space. Use it for washing food, and rinsing dishes before placing them in the dishwasher below.

FOR MORE DETAILS...

Appliance "garage" SEE P. 30

Halogen hob SEE P. 34

Eye-level double oven SEE P. 37

Bar eating SEE P. 38

Stainless steel worktops SEE P. 300

EATING AREA
A generous counter-space is a desirable place to eat but also serves as a "parking" area for shopping bags and dirty dishes.

WOOD FLOORING
A natural beech floor adds warmth and offsets the hard, industrial finishes used elsewhere.

❸ NATURAL LIGHT ▷
The light-reflective qualities of stainless steel, together with an open undercounter space and tall windows, make this end of the kitchen feel both light and airy.

SMALL KITCHEN IDEAS

△ MAXIMIZING FLOOR SPACE
A handmade kitchen can be an efficient choice, as furniture can be tailor-made to fit the space. Here, the major appliances sit in a tall stack, while the area beneath the hob is kept free to make the kitchen feel spacious.

FORM FOLLOWS FUNCTION ▷
A straight run of units is arranged in a clear, logical sequence, with the sink between the hob and food preparation area. Above and below counter level, well-designed cupboards offer distinct open and closed storage areas.

◁ KITCHENS WITHOUT WINDOWS
Every available space from floor to ceiling has been filled in this tiny kitchen without windows. Strong task lighting, a simple palette of materials, cool colours, and open shelving produce a calm, well-ordered result.

MOVING IN CIRCLES ▷
A circular kitchen fits comfortably into a room 2.9m (9ft 6in) wide. The centralized arrangement of activities, with the cook in the middle, makes movement between different work stations highly efficient.

UNFITTED KITCHEN PLAN

UNLIKE FITTED KITCHENS in which standard units run from wall to wall, the unfitted kitchen takes a less formal approach. It is home to a collection of hand-crafted pieces that stand alone, and although the sink cabinet is still "technically" fitted, the overall effect is of individual elements with separate tasks, working together to create a smooth-running whole.

COURT CUPBOARD
Decorative cabinetry, mounted on a platform, conceals a raised-height fridge-freezer.

△ ❶ CLOSE PROXIMITY
The cooking and preparation zones occupy their own distinct areas within the kitchen but sit only two steps away from one another, for maximum efficiency.

AGA
Self-contained in its own tiled alcove, this five-door Aga is the main cooking centre.

DESIGN POINTS

■ Imagine activity and storage areas as separate pieces of free-standing furniture. Buy items from a variety of sources and enjoy the differences of shape, height, colour, and finish that each item has to offer.

■ Retain or uncover existing architectural features, such as fireplaces and alcoves, to add character to the room.

■ Where possible, allow space around each piece of furniture, but make sure all the essential facilities are conveniently close to one another. Try to keep the cooking and food preparation areas as the focus of the room.

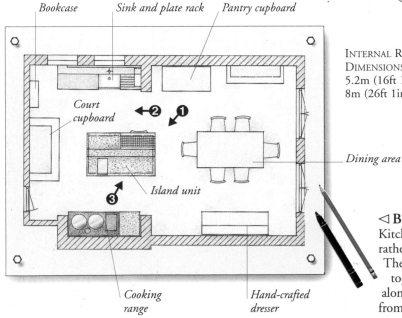

Bookcase   *Sink and plate rack*   *Pantry cupboard*

Court cupboard

Island unit

Cooking range   *Hand-crafted dresser*

INTERNAL ROOM DIMENSIONS:
5.2m (16ft 11in) WIDE
8m (26ft 1in) LONG

DRESSER
Occupying one wall of the dining area, a dresser provides open-shelf storage with cupboards and drawers below.

Dining area

◁ BIRD'S EYE VIEW
Kitchen furniture fills the room, rather than sitting at the edges. The elements are not linked together by worktops but stand alone, and can be approached from more than one direction.

BOOKSHELVES
A wall-mounted bookcase, with a wine rack below utilizes the corner space without making the room feel overcrowded.

❷ CONTRASTING ELEMENTS ▷
Standing side by side, the difference in height, style, and finish between the court cupboard and the bookshelf emphasizes the separate functions of these pieces of furniture, while enhancing the furnished, living-room feel of the room.

CENTRAL ISLAND
The chopping and food preparation area is divided up into granite and end-grain wood surfaces at different heights.

PANTRY CUPBOARD
Space in front of the unit ensures that the wide doors can be left open when re-stocking.

FOR MORE DETAILS...

Pantry cupboard SEE PP. 24–25
Fridge-freezer SEE PP. 26–27
Aga SEE P. 37
Rectangular table SEE P. 39
Tiles SEE PP. 297

PARLOUR CUPBOARD
Wall-mounted to free the floor space around the eating area, this custom-made unit stores china, table linen, and breakfast cereals.

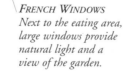

FRENCH WINDOWS
Next to the eating area, large windows provide natural light and a view of the garden.

REFECTORY TABLE
Generous space around the table allows up to ten people to enjoy a meal in comfort.

TERRACOTTA TILES
Large, reclaimed terracotta tiles provide atmosphere and durability.

❸ STORAGE FACILITIES ▷
A tall pantry cupboard rather than a row of base and wall units is an efficient use of space. Everyday crockery sits on a wall-mounted plate rack, and baskets hang on hooks from a gantry.

UNFITTED KITCHEN IDEAS

△ SIMPLE STAND-ALONE FURNITURE

The simplicity of freestanding kitchen furniture is very appealing, and here the combination of painted wood and white walls adds to the effect. The space around each item is important, so avoid continuous runs of units, to prevent cluttering up every wall and corner.

△ ROOM DIVIDERS

In an unfitted kitchen, there is more scope to use old pieces of furniture. The antique pine dresser in the foreground acts as a room divider, separating off the cooking and eating areas. New cabinets provide worktops and storage facilities close to the Aga cooker.

RETAINING ORIGINAL FEATURES ▷

A well-furnished kitchen can combine both freestanding and built-in items successfully. Here, a sitting room was converted to make a large kitchen. Some features were kept intact, such as the ceiling mouldings and the chimney breast; the hob and oven sit in this alcove and use the flue for ventilation.

△ APPLIANCES BEHIND DOORS

A well-proportioned court cupboard can be an attractive and convenient home for large appliances. In this kitchen, a fridge and microwave are built into the cupboard but it could just as easily contain an eye-level oven and a larder for fresh and non-perishable foods.

△ ACCESSIBLE STORAGE

The most useful storage space sits between knee height and eye level; in one large cupboard the space offered at this level is greater than in a series of units above and below worktops. Above all, a tall cupboard is a feature and a relief from the uniformity of similar-height cabinets.

FITTED KITCHEN PLAN

IMAGINATION AND resourcefulness are needed to design a kitchen using standard fitted units. The secret is to be selective, so that your kitchen is not overwhelmed by repetitive cabinetry. Pick doors, drawers, and glass-fronted units from a standard range, and then shop around for worktops, flooring, and lighting to reflect personal taste.

△ ❶ UTILITY CUPBOARD
A tall two-door unit, designed to house a fridge-freezer, has been adapted to create a large storage cupboard for essential cleaning equipment.

DESIGN POINTS

■ Try to create visual interest by avoiding very long runs of similar cabinets with the same door fronts. Break up the monotony by leaving wall space for shelves and pictures.

■ Consider how to balance the horizontal and vertical lines in a unit kitchen. Blocks of tall cabinets, adjacent to the wall, can remove the tyranny of long counters and wall units.

■ To make a fitted kitchen less clinical, try customizing units. Employ a carpenter to build a dresser above base units or, as a cheaper alternative, adapt existing carcasses and paint the insides in bright colours.

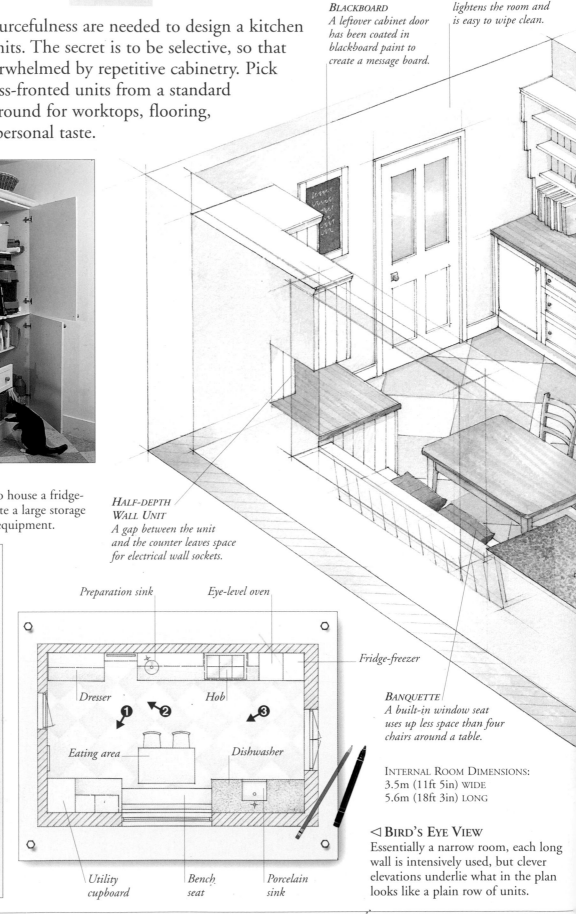

BLACKBOARD
A leftover cabinet door has been coated in blackboard paint to create a message board.

WALLCOVERING
A cream, oil-based paint lightens the room and is easy to wipe clean.

HALF-DEPTH
WALL UNIT
A gap between the unit and the counter leaves space for electrical wall sockets.

Preparation sink

Eye-level oven

Dresser

Hob

Eating area

Utility cupboard

Bench seat

Porcelain sink

Dishwasher

Fridge-freezer

BANQUETTE
A built-in window seat uses up less space than four chairs around a table.

INTERNAL ROOM DIMENSIONS:
3.5m (11ft 5in) WIDE
5.6m (18ft 3in) LONG

◁ BIRD'S EYE VIEW
Essentially a narrow room, each long wall is intensively used, but clever elevations underlie what in the plan looks like a plain row of units.

CUSTOM-MADE DRESSER
The top of the dresser is edged with leftover wood moulding, for decoration.

TEA-TOWEL RACK
A hanging rack is a useful device to fill a wall left intentionally free of units.

VEGETABLE SINK
Fresh ingredients can be rinsed at the preparation site, preventing a journey across the kitchen.

FOR MORE DETAILS...

Vegetable sink SEE P. 32

Lighting SEE P. 290–291

Vinyl flooring SEE P. 292

Lacquered wood worktops SEE P. 301

EXTRACTOR AND HOB
The choice of a stylish aluminium extractor hood and five- rather than four-ring hob helps personalize this fitted kitchen range.

△ **❷ ATTENTION TO DETAIL**
Simple additions can make all the difference. Here, a dresser has been built on top of a standard unit, and thin beech worktops are edged with 40mm (1½ in) strips to make them look more solid.

EYE-LEVEL OVEN
Place a storage cupboard above and drawers below to vary the appearance of the cabinets.

REFRIGERATOR HOUSING
The oven and fridge sit next to one another and must be well insulated to save energy.

LAMINATE DOORS
An inexpensive, hard-wearing finish that withstands knocks.

PET AREA
Place food and water bowls close to the garden door and away from the main activity areas, to avoid spillages.

❸ A COMBINED EFFORT ▷
If the units offered by a manufacturer do not match your needs, commission a handmade piece of kitchen furniture to your specification, as in the case of this space-saving window seat.

SINK CABINET
The sink is fitted into a standard carcass, but durable granite worktops add individuality.

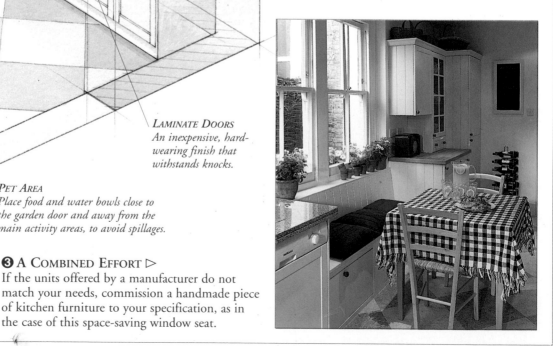

FITTED KITCHEN IDEAS

△ BOLD PLANNING
The design of this kitchen brings the fitted units into the centre of the room rather than placing them around the walls. The hob and sink face one another so that the cook can enjoy two different views when working. Painted plaster walls offset cool stainless steel.

△ STANDARD FITTED UNITS
A low-budget kitchen uses a standard row of base units to create maximum worktop and storage space. The large preparation area has been adapted to suit the cook's needs by adding a small sink for rinsing fresh foods.

QUALITY AND COMFORT ▷
Manufactured to a high specification, using durable, hygienic materials such as ceramic floor tiles, granite, and stainless steel, this fitted kitchen is built to last. It combines high-tech materials with wood, to add the comfort associated with country kitchens.

△ BEHIND CLOSED DOORS
The choice of all-white matching finishes on the fitted cabinetry and walls helps to brighten up this narrow kitchen, which is annexed off a larger room. Eye level, wall-mounted cabinets have been abandoned in favour of floor-to-ceiling cupboards along the entrance corridor.

△ COLOUR VARIATION
The units have been carefully chosen from a standard range so that they fit imaginatively into the room plan. A run of base cabinets surrounds the eating area and doubles up as a serving counter. Their bright painted blue finish adds character to the room, which can be difficult to achieve in fitted kitchens.

ISLAND KITCHEN PLAN

A CENTRAL ISLAND is the key to a large, sociable kitchen because the cook is able to look into the room rather than at a blank wall. In spatial terms, an island arrangement helps to concentrate cooking activities into a small zone so that the cook does not have to waste time travelling backwards and forwards across the entire room.

PLATE RACK
A wall-mounted rack drip-dries and stores wet plates direct from the dishwasher or adjacent sink.

LARGE SINK
A deep sink is suitable for soaking oven pans, while heavy pots need only be carried a short distance from the hob for draining.

Cupboard   Sink   Dishwasher and back-up oven

INTERNAL ROOM DIMENSIONS:
4.7m (15ft 4in) WIDE
6.4m (20ft 10in) LONG

Fridge

Dresser

Island unit

Sofa

Eating area

△ **BIRD'S EYE VIEW**
For an island to be successful, it needs space around it. Allow 1.2m (3ft 10in) between the island and the wall cabinets. If a sink is directly behind the work area, ensure there is at least 1m (3ft 3in) so that two people can work back to back.

DESIGN POINTS

■ Allow space between key activities on the island – the wooden chopping block and gas hob should be 45cm (18in) apart to prevent heat damage and fire risk.

■ Plan a low-level worktop for operating electrical appliances on the island. If finished in cold marble or granite, it can double up as a pastry area.

■ Lighting is important in a kitchen used for both cooking and entertaining. Ensure that the island is well lit from above so that you are not working in shadow, and install lights on dimmer switches to create a soft, ambient light in eating and relaxation areas.

CHOPPING BLOCK
Positioned with a view of the table and garden beyond, the chopping block is within reach of the sink, hob, and fridge.

STORAGE CUPBOARD
Bulky hardware is stored just behind the island.

LOW-LEVEL COUNTER
Built-in electrical sockets make it possible to use food processors and other electrical appliances on the island.

◁ ❶ **SOCIABLE COOKING**
The gas hob and below-deck oven are orientated towards the blue sofa so that the cook can talk to guests. A stainless steel upturn at the back protects the lacquered serving counter from oil and sauces.

DISHWASHER STACK
An eye-level oven sits on top of a raised dishwasher to reduce the need to bend.

❷ EYE-CATCHING CABINETRY ▷
The serving counter cabinet is the most decorative of the four island zones, as it is seen from the table. It hides the hob, making it easier to cook in front of an audience without inhibition.

FULL-HEIGHT FRIDGE
The island plan frees up space around the walls for a large fridge a short distance from the preparation area.

STAINLESS STEEL HOB
The worktops that flank the hob are heatproof. Allow at least 30cm (12in) on either side.

FOR MORE DETAILS...

Centre island unit SEE PP. 30–31

Hobs and extractors SEE PP. 34–35

Storage cupboard SEE P. 42

Lighting SEE PP. 290–291

WINDOWS
A wall of windows, plus glass doors leading to the garden, fill the room with light.

KITCHEN TABLE
Planned in the brightest corner of the kitchen, the family table has an oiled wood surface to make it hardwearing.

SERVING AREA
A free counter for serving food, between the cooking zone and the table, makes entertaining easy.

RELAXATION AREA
Space for a sitting area is made possible by focusing appliances and worktops in the centre of the kitchen.

❸ FULL PARTICIPATION ▷
Trips back to the hob mid-meal to perform the finishing touches to a dish are no longer a chore as the cook is not excluded from round-table talks.

ISLAND KITCHEN IDEAS

△ MINIMALIST ISLAND FITTING
A brushed stainless steel island unit with a small, moulded sink, gives the extrovert cook the necessary facilities to wash and prepare fresh ingredients while entertaining guests, who can perch on stools at the other side.

VARIABLE-HEIGHT ISLAND ▷
A central island works best if it has been divided into four key activity zones, each arranged at the most efficient height to perform the required tasks. Unlike most fitted kitchens, where long runs of worktops are arranged around the kitchen walls, the island enables you to occupy centre stage.

△ MULTI-FUNCTIONAL PENINSULAR UNIT
In a small kitchen, where worktop space is limited and there is no room for a table, consider a circular half end-grain wood and half granite peninsular unit. The purpose-built fitting doubles up as a food preparation and eating area without taking up valuable floor space.

△ CENTRAL WASHING-UP AREA
If your kitchen has no spectacular window view, build the sink into an island unit so that you can face the room rather than a blank wall when performing this mundane task. Here, the sink is thoughtfully placed so that you simply turn around to use the hob.

△ SLENDER ISLAND WORKING TABLE WITH RAISED-HEIGHT PLATFORM
A narrow kitchen can accommodate a long modern or traditional working table that acts as a central workspace for several people at once. A removable preparation platform at one end of the table allows you to stand and prepare meals while supervising children's activities.

IMPROVISED KITCHEN PLAN

ONCE YOU UNDERSTAND the principles of ergonomic kitchen design, it is possible to assemble a comfortable and easy-to-use kitchen on a tight budget. The secret is to improvise, so rather than just settling for low-cost units, scour junk shops and auctions for furniture that can be adapted for kitchen use, and bring inherited items, which you may have placed elsewhere in your home, into the kitchen.

APOTHECARY DRAWERS
Drawers picked up at auction store spices, candles, and other household items.

PORCELAIN SINK
Inherited intact, this porcelain sink with drainer attached is built into a homemade kitchen cabinet.

△ ❶ CONTAINED SPACE
As space is limited, the sink, cooker, and preparation area butt up against one another, but this compact arrangement works well.

DESIGN POINTS

■ Thoughtful selection of items is necessary; ensure that they are functional and measure each piece of furniture to check that there is room for them.

■ The most problematic area is around the sink. Think about the amount of draining board space – allow 60cm (24in) on either side. Consider how the worktop joins up to the basin – it needs a high-performance seal. Also, the area behind the sink needs protecting from watersplashes (see pp.296–297).

■ Finding furniture with hardwearing worktops may be difficult. Assess your priorities to see whether you can install new worktops (see pp.300–301).

INTERNAL ROOM DIMENSIONS:
1.9m (6ft 2in) WIDE
4.7m (15ft 4in) LONG

Spice drawers

Cooker unit   *Food preparation area*

Sink cabinet   *Bench*

Small cupboard

Waist-height storage cupboard

HARDWARE STORAGE
A china cupboard and cutlery drawer below the sink allow items to be put away as soon as they have been washed up.

WOODEN BENCH
With no room for a table, a bench provides a place for guests to sit.

Wood-burning stove

◁ BIRD'S EYE VIEW
The sink, cooker, and a long food preparation counter form an L-shape of fitted cabinetry, while unfitted cupboards and a bench sit up close, leaving space for the sink cabinet doors to open.

FREESTANDING GAS COOKER
This upright gas appliance has a fold-away grill at eye level. Easy-to-watch, eye-level grills are only found on old cookers.

UNDERCOUNTER FRIDGE
Fitted below the preparation area, a small fridge squeezes into a narrow space, and is cheap to buy secondhand.

FOR MORE DETAILS...

Undercounter fridge SEE P. 26

Oven cooking SEE P. 36

Sink cabinet SEE P. 40

Wallcoverings SEE PP. 296–297

STORAGE SHELF
An old pine shelf provides open storage above the counter for utensils and equipment, and keeps the worktop space free.

△ ❷ PROTECTIVE MEASURES
In this narrow kitchen, the wood counter butts up against the cooker. To keep the wood surface intact, hot pans are always put down on heatproof mats.

ASPECT
Clever planning means that the worktop sits between two windows and is flooded with natural light.

WOOD-BURNING STOVE
A cast-iron stove provides extra "parking" space for items close to the food preparation counter.

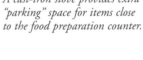

TERRACOTTA TILES
Tiles, bought from an old farmhouse and cleaned, make a durable flooring.

LARDER CUPBOARD
A waist-height unit makes an improvised larder cupboard.

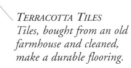

❸ LOW-COST MATERIALS ▷
Painted wood boarding is employed to great effect to cover up an uneven ceiling. It is also used to build low-cost fitted cabinetry below the sink unit and the wood worktops.

IMPROVISED KITCHEN IDEAS

△ AFFORDABLE STAINLESS STEEL
If you like the qualities of stainless steel but cannot afford new units, try a catering auction where secondhand professional kitchen fittings are sold. Try to purchase a stainless steel workbench and a sink to provide a basic washing-up, food preparation, and bar eating area.

△ INEXPENSIVE FACELIFT
If it is not within your budget to alter the plan of your kitchen to suit your specific needs, transform its appearance by painting the cabinets in a strong colour and changing the door handles. On a bigger budget, new worktops and lighting make a huge difference.

△ EQUIPMENT RACKS
Utensils hanging on the wall not only look attractive but are stored within easy reach of the counter. Here, three stainless steel towel rails have been installed to make a hanging device. For a longer worktop, try using a coat rail taken from an old wardrobe.

WALL DISPLAY ▷
In small, narrow kitchens, there is often not the room for a desk in which to store meal plans or lists of household tasks. Instead, put up a noticeboard and attach favourite recipes, food lists, and bills for safe keeping.

△ DO-IT-YOURSELF SHELVING
Open shelves fitted with hooks are relatively easy to construct and have the capacity to store a variety of kitchen equipment above counter level. Although a less expensive alternative to purpose-built cabinets, items stored in this way will gather dust and need to be brought down regularly for cleaning.

FAMILY KITCHEN PLAN

A FAMILY KITCHEN is more than just a place for cooking food, and here lies the challenge. It is the centre of family life and should be arranged accordingly. Divide the room into distinct zones: an island cooking area, where the cook faces into the room as he or she works; an informal eating area; and a play and relaxation area with a large sofa.

DESIGN POINTS

■ Make sure that you are happy cooking in front of an audience before you opt for an open-plan family kitchen.

■ Use soft furnishings, such as sofas and rugs, to absorb sound and so help to reduce noise levels in a large family kitchen.

■ A long island works best if you plan two circular food preparation areas at either end.

■ Position the sink and hob opposite one another, to minimize walking distances.

■ Allow room for plenty of storage space and ensure that it is in easy reach of activity areas.

CEILING LIGHTS
Disc lights hang down on stems from the ceiling, helping to lower the ceiling height and so create a more intimate atmosphere at night.

SITTING AREA
Sofa and chair are grouped around the fireplace to create a "soft" area for relaxing and playing.

FIREPLACE
As units and appliances are not spread around the whole room, a fireplace can be integrated into the plan.

PANTRY CUPBOARD
A full-height food storage cupboard – rather than storage above and below the counter – caters for family needs.

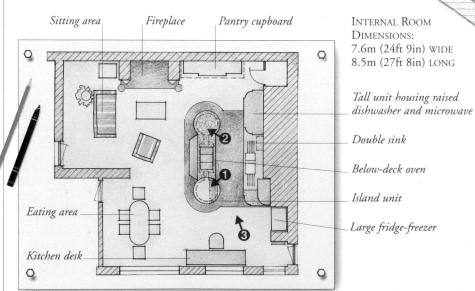

INTERNAL ROOM DIMENSIONS:
7.6m (24ft 9in) WIDE
8.5m (27ft 8in) LONG

Tall unit housing raised dishwasher and microwave

Double sink

Below-deck oven

Island unit

Large fridge-freezer

Sitting area   Fireplace   Pantry cupboard

Eating area

Kitchen desk

△ BIRD'S EYE VIEW
Appliances are confined to the island and sink cabinet to keep cooking activities close together, while freeing up space elsewhere for an eating and sitting area.

❶ SUPERVISED ACTIVITIES ▷
An unobstructed view from the island to the oval table means that homework, drawing, and other table-top activities can be supervised while food is prepared.

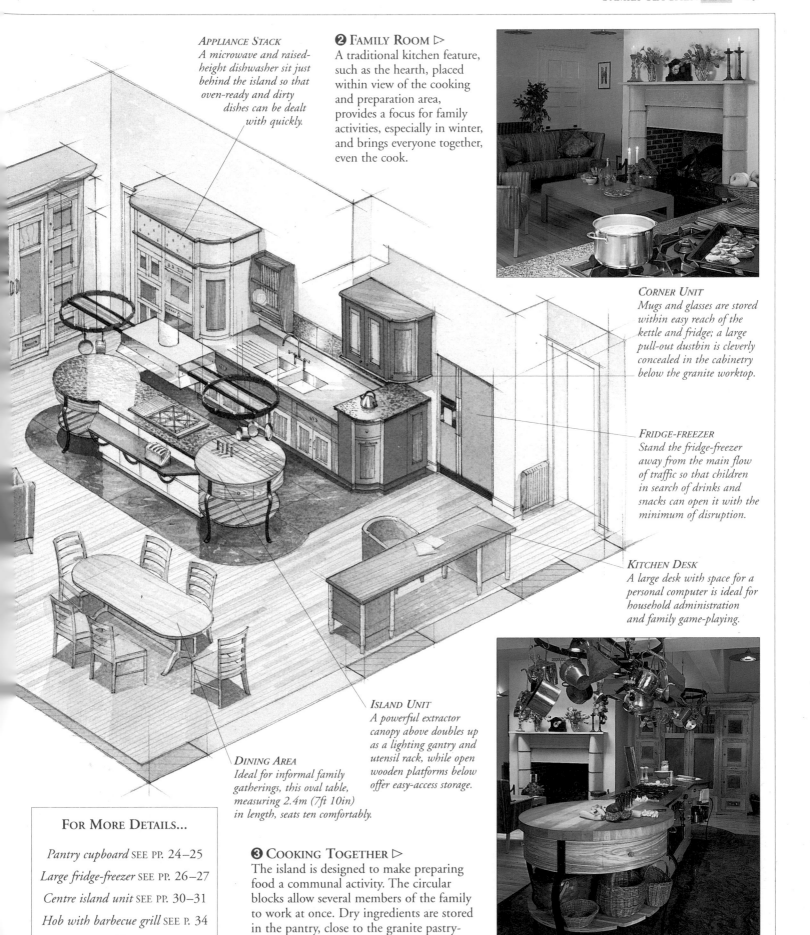

APPLIANCE STACK
A microwave and raised-height dishwasher sit just behind the island so that oven-ready and dirty dishes can be dealt with quickly.

❷ FAMILY ROOM ▷
A traditional kitchen feature, such as the hearth, placed within view of the cooking and preparation area, provides a focus for family activities, especially in winter, and brings everyone together, even the cook.

CORNER UNIT
Mugs and glasses are stored within easy reach of the kettle and fridge; a large pull-out dustbin is cleverly concealed in the cabinetry below the granite worktop.

FRIDGE-FREEZER
Stand the fridge-freezer away from the main flow of traffic so that children in search of drinks and snacks can open it with the minimum of disruption.

KITCHEN DESK
A large desk with space for a personal computer is ideal for household administration and family game-playing.

ISLAND UNIT
A powerful extractor canopy above doubles up as a lighting gantry and utensil rack, while open wooden platforms below offer easy-access storage.

DINING AREA
Ideal for informal family gatherings, this oval table, measuring 2.4m (7ft 10in) in length, seats ten comfortably.

FOR MORE DETAILS...

Pantry cupboard SEE PP. 24–25

Large fridge-freezer SEE PP. 26–27

Centre island unit SEE PP. 30–31

Hob with barbecue grill SEE P. 34

Oval table SEE P. 39

❸ COOKING TOGETHER ▷
The island is designed to make preparing food a communal activity. The circular blocks allow several members of the family to work at once. Dry ingredients are stored in the pantry, close to the granite pastry-making block. Fresh food is kept in the fridge, a few paces from the end-grain block.

FAMILY KITCHEN IDEAS

△ **CHILDREN'S COOKING SHELF**
The low slate shelf that runs along the front edge of the island provides an indestructible child-height counter for younger members of the family who enjoy cooking. At other times, it functions as a preparation centre for operating electrical appliances, and a breakfast bar.

△ **EATING TOGETHER**
The kitchen table is the focal point of family life, so even when space is limited, try to include a table in your plan. A small, round table, 1.2m (3ft 10in) in diameter seats four. When not in use, the chairs can be tucked in closer to the table.

CREATIVE ACTIVITIES ▷
A family kitchen table is not only used at mealtimes but for a variety of activities, such as painting, drawing, and model-making. Choose an old pine table where blemishes will not be too obvious, or cover the table with a waterproof tablecloth for protection.

△ **TOY DRAWER**
Toys scattered all over the floor are likely to cause accidents, so plan a pull-out drawer where toys can be quickly stowed away as mealtime approaches. A hygienic floor covering, such as linoleum, is also advisable.

△ **KITCHEN OFFICE**
A desk area in the kitchen can be useful for organizing both household administration and helping children with their homework while you are involved in kitchen tasks. A pinboard and blackboard for notes and shopping lists also help your household to run smoothly.

LIVING AREA

INTRODUCTION

THE LIVING AREA is usually a focus for leisure activities in the home, whether you like to spend relaxing evenings in front of the television, need a play space for children, or a room for entertaining. Careful planning is required to create a space that can adapt easily to a variety of functions, and to ensure that different activities do not conflict. Think about who will use the space and how they will spend their time. Consider how you move around the room, and plan the layout so that the main door, windows, and furniture are easily accessible. Place occasional furniture where it can be fully utilized, such as next to a sofa, but avoid flow areas that need to be clear for access. A mixture of cupboards and open shelves can provide a range of storage options for books, games, CDs and other accessories, as well as for large items, such as a music system or television.

A quiet corner with a table and task light will provide an ideal spot for reading or studying, while comfortable sofas and chairs and adaptable lighting are essential for relaxing and watching television. Most importantly, your living space must reflect your own leisure needs and interests, with fixtures and furniture chosen accordingly.

DISPLAY AREA

The living area is often the largest space in the house and also the most public room – a reception area, where visitors can be entertained. As such, this room has traditionally been used for formal display – a place where valuable items, such as paintings, antiques, and expensive furniture can create an impressive setting. To maximize the use of your living space, try to make sure that its decoration and function are compatible. Stylish formality may suit a room

△ ARMCHAIR
A design that is easy to get in and out of, offers head support and arm rests is ideal for relaxing, reading, or watching television.

GRAND LIVING ▷
Richly furnished with antiques, tapestries, and ornate plasterwork, this room offers style on an impressive scale. Seating and activity areas radiate from the huge fireplace, which forms a dominant centrepiece for the room.

that is not used on a daily basis, but will not create a relaxed gathering place for family and friends if expensive furnishings are endangered by everyday activites. Accept that a certain amount of wear is inevitable if the room is to be fully appreciated. If you use your living room only infrequently, consider allocating a smaller room or space for the purpose.

ADJOINING SPACES

Many living areas are open plan, or comprise a number of linked spaces with different functions, such as a dining area, conservatory, or balcony. If this is the case, aim to reflect the style and colours of the main room in the secondary spaces to create a cohesive look. If you want to draw an invisible line between areas, it is possible to do so in several ways. Lighting can be planned to isolate spaces or particular features, or flooring changed

△ OPEN-PLAN LIVING
Sofas, armchairs, and tables form two interconnecting groups of seating from which to enjoy warmth from the open fire or a view of the terrace and pool. Neutral tones and natural flooring create a calm, restful scheme.

WHAT DO YOU WANT FROM YOUR LIVING ROOM?

Living areas are often a hive of activity, with different family members busy with their own pursuits. The room must be versatile, to suit everyone's requirements. Use the following options to establish your needs before purchasing expensive furniture and fittings.

❶ A family room with areas for dining and relaxing.

❷ A music and television room for audio-visual entertainment.

❸ A cosy space for relaxation, with comfortable seating.

▽ FLOODED WITH LIGHT
Glazed doors without curtains expand this living space, giving easy access to the balcony dining area and an uninterrupted view from inside. Ample daylight makes the room appear large and bright.

HOW CAN THIS SPACE WORK FOR YOU?

Whatever the shape or size of your living area, you must ensure that its layout and design will adapt easily to your leisure activities.

☐ Is the room spacious enough for different activites to take place at the same time, or would it be simpler to convert a room elsewhere in the house?

☐ Would modular sofas and chairs better suit changing needs by offering more flexible seating arrangements than a standard three-piece suite?

☐ By removing a wall, could two rooms be changed into an open plan area, providing a better use of space and a lighter more airy environment?

△ VISUAL FOCUS
A fireplace can be a focal point all year round. Fill it with flowers when it is too warm to appreciate the glow of an open fire.

between areas to create a subtle division. Screens and blinds also make effective room dividers. Alternatively, the back of a long, low sofa or a table can be positioned to separate areas.

FOCAL POINTS

All rooms benefit from a focal point, and this can be particularly important in a living area that fulfils different functions. A fireplace or television are obvious choices for this space, so consider how well they can be seen from different parts of the room. Or if you do not want the television to become the focal point,

hide it in a decorative cabinet that is a focus in it its own right. Plan your seating to emphasize your chosen feature. Windows with an interesting skyline or a leafy outlook offer an everchanging focal point if the room has no particular features of interest. Large expanses of wall can also create a blank canvas to display wall hangings or a collection of pictures, providing a plain background where there is nothing to compete with their colours or design.

SUZANNE ARDLEY

ASSESS YOUR NEEDS

THE FOLLOWING questions will help you focus on what you want from your living area, and start you thinking about ways to plan this space so that, as you work through this chapter, you will be able to compile a list of the living room furniture and designs that best suit you and your lifestyle.

FURNITURE

The number of people who will use the living area and the frequency of use are major considerations when choosing furniture and furnishings. Style is very much a case of personal taste, and as long as furnishings can withstand everyday wear and tear, you can achieve a room that has lasting good looks.

☐ Consider whether your living area will be used regularly by people of different age groups. If so, will your choice of seating be flexible enough to cater for their differing needs?
☐ If you enjoy entertaining, do you want to invest in furniture that can be moved around easily and seating that can be changed around to suit the occasion?
☐ Would one or two adjustable tables be adequate for your needs, or do you require a range of different tables or units for books, trays, lamps, and entertaining?
☐ Do you prefer to sink into a soft, capacious sofa, or to sit well-supported by firm upholstery?
☐ Is there any member of the household who might have difficulty sitting down and getting up from a low sofa or chair?
☐ If you allow your pets to sit on the furniture, would machine washable covers be more practical than a fully upholstered sofa?
☐ Do you want to have your television and music centre on permanent display, or would you prefer to conceal them?
☐ Do you want to make the television the focal point in the room? If so, can your seating be positioned so that people watching can see the screen easily?
☐ Do you need to plan your living area round existing pieces of furniture, which will influence your choice of new items, or are you starting afresh?
☐ Would an additional heating facility, such as an open fire or heater, which can be controlled independently of the central heating system, improve your use of the living area during colder months?
☐ Do you spend sufficient time relaxing stretched out to warrant the additional space a lounger requires, or would a comfortable armchair be more practical?

SPACE

Planning a living area from scratch gives you maximum opportunity to ensure that the room fulfils your requirements. However, even small alterations, such as buying a screen, can substantially improve your use of this living space.

☐ Do you want to use your living area for entertaining, watching television, listening to music, working, or hobbies?
☐ If you are using your living room for a range of activities, would you prefer to split the room into clearly defined zones, or to create an open-plan space?
☐ Would wall-mounted cupboards or shelves free up enough space for an extra chair or table?
☐ Do you need to choose a floor covering that children can play on safely, that can be cleaned easily, and that can be walked on barefoot in comfort?
☐ Does your flooring have to cope with a lot of wear and tear? Would rugs placed on heavy wear areas help to maintain the flooring's appearance and extend its life?
☐ Would either a moveable screen or a static room divider help you to carry out more than one activity at a time in your living room without interruption?
☐ Does your living area have access to a garden? If so, can the flooring withstand marks or damage from people walking in and out.
☐ Would your use of the living room benefit from improved access to other rooms, such as the dining room and kitchen, or to the garden? Could you install an additional door or knock through a wall?

LIGHT

There are few households where lighting and the use of natural light cannot be improved. Consider what activities take place in your living area, and how these would benefit from changes in lighting.

☐ Can you organize the living area to fully utilize natural daylight?
☐ Would you prefer versatile, rather than fixed light sources, so that lighting can be moved or angled to illuminate different areas of the room?
☐ If your living area has small windows or limited natural light, could you choose a pale colour scheme to make the room appear brighter?
☐ Do you prefer curtains or blinds? Will your choice provide adequate privacy yet allow sufficient daylight to enter?

SEATING

CAREFULLY SELECTED SEATING is a key factor in achieving a relaxed and comfortable living room. The way in which each piece is arranged in relation to others plays an important part, creating areas of privacy, or a gathering place where family and friends sit and talk, focus on the television, or radiate around a cosy fireplace.

SOFAS

Bringing an informal and intimate feel to living areas, sofas are ideal for two or more to sit in comfort or an individual to stretch out easily. Two-seat and three-seat sofas or a combination of both can utilise space more effectively than individual chairs. Modular sofas offer flexible seating arrangements and are ideal for awkwardly shaped rooms.

△ **MODULAR SEATING**
A choice of sofa length and corner sections makes modular seating a viable option when planning for an irregularly shaped room. It can be used to divide or link different areas and makes a strong feature in large rooms.

FILLINGS
Cushions contain natural and man-made fibres

△ **SOFA WITH LOOSE COVERS**
Choose a sofa with loose covers for an informal look. Machine-washable covers are ideal if the fabric is pale, or the sofa is likely to receive heavy wear and tear from children or pets.

SOLID FRAME
This model is made from a beech frame, rubberized hair, coil springs, and cotton felt.

△ **UPHOLSTERED SOFA**
Traditional details on an upholstered sofa create a formal style. Treat the covers with a fabric protector, because they cannot be removed for cleaning.

TAPERED BACK
Upholstered back is softly padded and tapered to the foot.

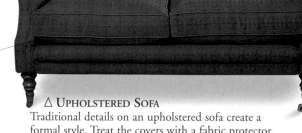

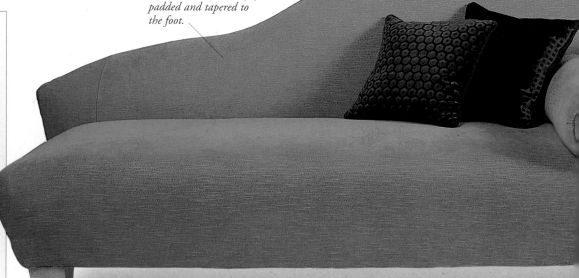

REMEMBER

■ A well-designed sofa will be a pleasure to use, but try to find out what is beneath the fabric to ensure the frame and filling meet your expectations. Run your hand over the sofa. At no point should the frame, springs, or fixings be detectable immediately under the fabric cover as this will eventually cause areas of wear.

■ The frame of the sofa forms its "skeleton" to which the various parts of upholstery are held in place. Look for a solid hardwood frame which is glued, screwed, and dowelled for sturdiness and rigidity.

CORRECT POSTURE

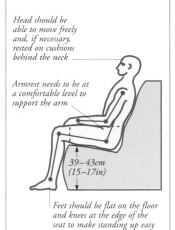

Head should be able to move freely and, if necessary, rested on cushions behind the neck

Armrest needs to be at a comfortable level to support the arm

39–43cm (15–17in)

Feet should be flat on the floor and knees at the edge of the seat to make standing up easy

When sitting for long periods on a sofa or soft chair, the body's posture can be more relaxed than when eating or working at a table.

▽ CHAISE LONGUE
This contemporary chaise longue offers a place to recline during the day, with a coiled arm and neck rest and firm bolster cushion for comfort. Placed apart from other furniture, it provides an ideal seat for undisturbed reading or resting.

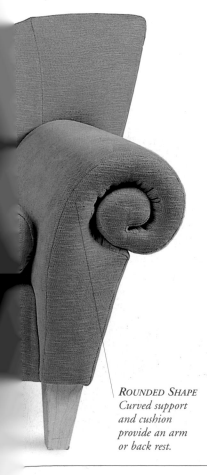

*ROUNDED SHAPE
Curved support and cushion provide an arm or back rest.*

CHAIRS
Tub chairs, arm chairs, recliner chairs, and beanbags are the perfect complement to sofas. As well as adding interest to a room, occasional chairs make effective use of areas too small to place a sofa. Before you buy a chair, test that the filling supports your weight as you sit, stretch out, or curl up. The cushions should recover their shape easily once you have stood up to ensure that the whoever uses the chair next will also find it comfortable and supportive.

*NECK REST
The bolster can move to support the head and neck.*

*LEATHER COVER
The upholstery is easy to clean and hardwearing.*

ARMCHAIRS AND BEANBAG ▷
Wingchairs are a traditional and formal addition to living areas and provide a high back and head rests for greater comfort. Beanbags filled with polystyrene beads mould themselves to any shape, making them perfect for children to lie on while watching television or playing games.

△ FOOTSTOOL
This footstool features a strong metal frame with castors. Its deep canvas-covered cushion doubles as a place to sit, as well as to keep feet raised up from the floor.

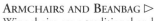

△ ARMCHAIRS
These chairs are small enough to be moved and grouped together easily. The same design but choice of different fabrics and the addition of a pleated skirt to one adds an element of interest.

*FOOT REST
The foot support has a removable pad and can be raised and lowered as desired.*

◁ RECLINING CHAIR
Designed for the maximum choice of postures, reclining chairs can be operated electrically or by a manual lever. Measure the chair to check the area required when fully reclined, and whether there is sufficient space to move comfortably between it and adjacent furniture.

OCCASIONAL TABLES

UNLESS YOU HAVE A particularly small living area, try to include at least two types of occasional table in the room to facilitate entertainment and relaxation. Choose tables of different heights to carry essential lighting and accessories. A lamp can be placed on a tall table to shed light on adjacent furniture, while drinks on a low coffee table can be reached easily from the sofa.

COFFEE TABLES

A central table is useful for putting down cups, snacks, and magazines or books, or for displaying cut flowers. Coffee tables come in a range of shapes and sizes, but all are under 50cm in height, so they can be reached easily while sitting on a chair or sofa. A shelf or rack under the table-top will provide useful extra storage for items that you use regularly but do not want to display.

CHEST ▷
A wooden chest with a decorative lock and craftsmen-made joints adds character to a room. It also serves to hide away functional items that would otherwise clutter up valuable space. With regular polishing and care the wood will develop an attractive patina.

SURFACE AREA
Drinks and snacks can be rested handily on the large surface.

LOWER SHELF
Items can be kept to hand on the lower shelf.

△ TROLLEY
The sleek lines of this contemporary chrome and frosted glass trolley table make it an ideal choice for homes where guests are entertained regularly. The smooth glass surface is durable, will not stain or warp, and is easy to wipe clean and buff to a shine. The glass also enables daylight to illuminate items placed on the lower shelf, and maintains a look of spaciousness and simplicity.

CHUNKY WHEELS
Easy to move round the living area, the wheels can also be locked into position.

SIDE TABLES

As their name implies, side tables stand to the side of the room, or next to a chair or sofa, and are taller than coffee tables. Placed next to seating, they will provide a useful site for a reading lamp. Accessories, ornaments, or flowers can also be displayed on a side table to best advantage, so that they can be seen from every part of the room. A table lamp will ensure that light falls onto the surrounding table surface to illuminate items of interest.

TABLE LAMP
Placed within easy reach of seating, the lamp can be turned on without stretching.

DRAWER SPACE
A useful storage space for pens, writing paper, and spectacles.

LAMP TABLE ▷
Lamp tables or stands tend to have a small surface area, providing just enough space for a lamp base and perhaps a couple of books or miniature picture frames. Use them next to a chair, or to light up a dark corner of the room.

△ STORAGE TABLE
Small odds and ends that could be mislaid are kept to hand in this small but well-designed table. It has open and closed storage, leaving the top free to display decorative accessories.

NARROW WIDTH
The slim top will not obstruct movement around the sofa.

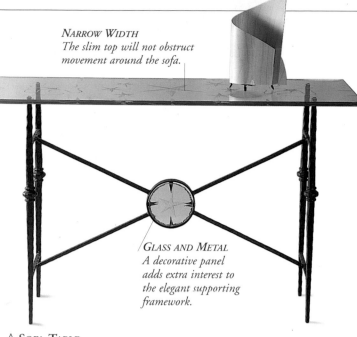

GLASS AND METAL
A decorative panel adds extra interest to the elegant supporting framework.

△ **SOFA TABLE**
The back of many sofas are placed unseen against a wall. However, those situated in the middle of a room can benefit from a narrow sofa table to improve the sofa's featureless back. Primarily decorative, the table can also provide a useful space for a few accessories or a lamp for background light.

△ **TABLE IMPROVISATION**
A small filing cabinet is a functional and interesting alternative to a table. Useful papers and accessories are kept close to hand but out of sight in this well-organised system. The bright blue finish adds a dash of colour and has the advantage of resisting stains and scratches better than wood. Ensure that the cabinet is level with the sofa arms so items on top can be accessed easily.

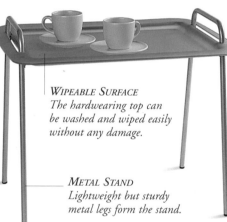

◁ **TRAY TABLE**
A table with a moveable tray top is a practical solution to carrying food and drinks from the kitchen to the living area. When the tray is taken off, the stand folds flat for easy storage.

WIPEABLE SURFACE
The hardwearing top can be washed and wiped easily without any damage.

METAL STAND
Lightweight but sturdy metal legs form the stand.

MULTIPLE CHOICE
Three sizes of table provide optimum flexibility and tables to cater for a range of different occasions.

TAPERED EDGE
The table edges are tapered to allow your hand to grip each one firmly for removal.

NEST OF TABLES ▷
Tables that fit together neatly in a nest are an ideal choice for living areas with limited space. They are particularly useful for entertaining, when more tables than usual are needed for guests. Glider feet ensure the tables move smoothly in and out from underneath one another. Place the stack where there is sufficient space at the front to remove each table easily.

REMEMBER

■ Choose tables that you can maintain easily and that will cope with the expected amount of wear and tear.

■ Central heating can dry out wood, making joints loose and glue weak. If you have a valuable or antique table, make sure it is kept well away from heat sources, such as radiators and fires, and treat it regularly with a nourishing wood polish.

■ Avoid coffee tables with sharp corners, which could be accidently walked into or knocked against.

■ Glass tables or those with glass insets should be made from tempered glass that will shatter into tiny pieces on impact, causing little damage. Check the glass on older tables, and, if necessary, fit new glass that meets safety regulations.

ENTERTAINMENT

RELAXATION INCLUDES the active pursuit of hobbies and games, as well as passive entertainment offered by television and sound systems. As a result, living rooms often have to contain a disparate combination of old-fashioned adult games and hi-tech equipment. Flexible storage is helpful for maintaining a sense of uncluttered space. Mobile pieces can be moved around to suit different demands and occasions.

GAMES AND PASTIMES STORAGE

Living rooms often have to accommodate a wide ranging selection of hobby-related or leisure materials – games for children and adults, CDs, books, and home crafts. Clutter is not conducive to a relaxing environment, so while these items need to be readily accessible, they must also be easy to put away out of sight when no longer in use.

DRAWERS
Small drawers are perfect for storing packs of cards, dice, and pads of paper.

RECESS
Boxed games and leather accessories fit neatly into the central recess.

DISPLAY OPTION
With the door open and the collection of glasses on show, this mobile unit becomes a multi-coloured display cabinet.

▽ COLOURFUL CUBE
Based on the principle of a fridge door, the door of this unusual drinks cabinet interlocks with the interior, creating additional storage space. The unit is mounted on five castors, one of which is on the base of the door to support the contents securely when open.

MOBILE TABLE-TOP
The unit can be moved into position to provide additional surface space.

REMEMBER

■ Store your television and sound system near power and aerial points, away from direct heat and sunlight. Because of their magnetic fields, do not place televisions next to unshielded speakers or cast-iron or steel radiators.

■ If you choose to hide your sound system or television in a cupboard, ensure it is well ventilated. Remote-control systems require a glass-fronted door, as they do not work through solid panels.

■ A beautiful piece of furniture with compartments can offer storage for many hobby and craft items, as well as provide a decorative focus in the room.

■ If you do not have a special piece of furniture for your games or video cassettes, store them in attractive fabric-covered boxes on open shelves.

■ Modern sound systems are now so compact they fit more easily into a room than older models.

FLAP DOOR
Open flap becomes a playing surface for board games.

CUPBOARD SPACE
Lockable cupboard beneath stores larger items securely.

◁ GAMES CHEST
This elegant early nineteenth-century secretaire has proved an ideal place to store boxed games, playing cards, and score pads. It has a large flap which, when closed, completely conceals its contents. It opens to reveal a number of drawers and alcoves for small items as well as providing a handy flat surface.

△ STORAGE AS SCULPTURE
A wide and imaginative range of CD racks are now available, from slot-together systems to tall free-standing towers. This simple and elegant model in natural wood turns CD storage into a wall-mounted work of art.

AUDIO-VISUAL ENTERTAINMENT

The attractive and efficient storage of audio-visual equipment calls for ingenious solutions. Wall brackets, designed for televisions and loudspeakers, free valuable floor space, while mobile television and video trolleys allow the equipment to be wheeled out of sight.

ALL-ROUND VIEWING △
This well-made, wall-mounted steel and alloy television support, with secure fixings, has a tilt and swivel action that allows the set to be viewed from any angle.

SWIVELLING SHELF
The swivelling top section increases the versatility of this television and video trolley.

DOUBLE-SIDED
Accessible from both sides, the shelf spaces of this unit can be used for CD or video storage.

△ MOBILE TELEVISION TROLLEY
Mobile pieces of furniture, such as this solid beech storage unit, are particularly useful in restricted living spaces, where it is often convenient to move items out of the way when they are not being used. This unit, although designed for television or sound-system storage, could equally well be used for work storage or as a handy bedside cabinet. The unit is mounted on rubber-tyred castors for easy movement.

COLLECTIONS

THE LIVING AREA is the obvious setting for displaying collections, as objects can be enjoyed at leisure by household members and guests. Whether your collection is large or small, books, shells, pictures, clocks, or fine porcelain all have an intrinsic display value that will enhance your living space, providing a decorative focus and contributing to the style and mood of the room.

DISPLAYING OBJECTS

Give careful thought to the best way of displaying objects, taking account of the size of your collection and living area, and whether valuable items require special storage conditions. Even commonplace objects can earn aesthetic status if they are displayed well – wooden spoons in a jar are utilitarian, but they can be decorative when arranged on a wall.

RECESSED ALCOVES
Building a false wall creates alcoves, a visually effective way of framing objects.

BRACKET SHELVES
Wall-mounted shelves highlight individual pieces or small groupings.

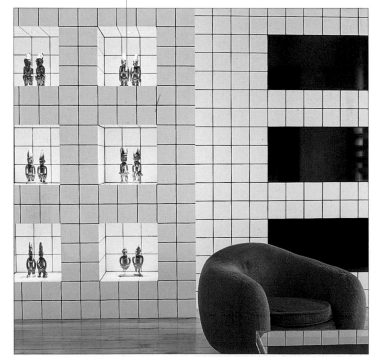

△ MINIMALIST DISPLAY
The strong geometric severity of these alcoves, which owe something of their style to shop displays, encourages a changing selection of objects. Alcoves are particularly suitable for single items, or graphic groups, but they require effective accent lighting. In this display, low-voltage downlighters draw the eye to the small figures in the niches.

ROOM OF VASES ▷
The collector of this British studio pottery of the late nineteenth and early twentieth century designed his living area around the vases, using a combination of antique freestanding cabinets and wall-mounted shelves. The style of furniture should complement the collection as much as possible: here, the cabinets and vases date from the same period.

BOOKS

Most homes accumulate huge numbers of books, which can be extremely heavy. Ensure that your living room shelves are attached securely to structurally sound walls, with supports at regular intervals. If you are using freestanding cabinets, ensure that the floor is load-bearing. Never expose books to damp or excessive heat.

▽ WALL-TO-WALL DISPLAY
Built-in shelves must fit in with architectural features: here, shallow shelves on either side of the deeper central shelves do not obstruct the window. Keep a set of steps on hand for access to books on the high shelves.

ATLAS SHELF
A closely spaced shelf is designed to accommodate a world atlas.

BUILT-IN CABINETS
Low cabinets store drinks, games, and a sound system.

SHALLOWER SHELVES
Shallow shelves are ideal for small books, such as paperbacks.

REMEMBER

■ Collections do not remain static: allow for expansion by providing up to 50 per cent more space than you estimate is needed initially.

■ If you cannot afford built-in lighting, consider other ways to enhance objects: painting the interiors of niches is effective.

■ Books and objects to be displayed vary greatly in size: adjustable shelves or niches of differing dimensions are more flexible than fixed units.

■ Store books upright – it damages them if they are too crowded or too loose. As a rough guide, allow 2.5cm (1in) between the top of the books and the next shelf. If you only have a few outsize books, stack them horizontally.

△ FREESTANDING CABINETS
The advantage of freestanding bookcases is that, unlike built-in shelves, you can take them with you if and when you move. They may be quite dominant, so they should fit in stylistically with the architecture of the living room. Glass fronts are ideal, as they protect books from dust.

FAMILY ROOM PLAN

FAMILY LIVING AREAS are more than just a place for sitting down to talk or watch television, they are centres of activity used by different age groups for different things. To satisfy everyone's needs, create an environment with distinct zones, so that a range of leisure activities can be pursued unhindered. If the living area will be used by children and pets, combine function with style, and avoid furniture and furnishings that cannot be cleaned or replaced.

Recessed fireplace   *Tub chair*   *Music area*

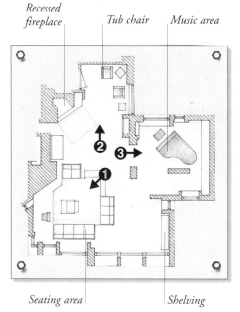

INTERNAL ROOM
DIMENSIONS:
10m (33ft) wide
10.5m (49ft 6in) long

Seating area   *Shelving*

△ BIRD'S EYE VIEW
This open-plan room includes areas for music practice, entertaining, or watching television, and offers a quiet corner for reading. A sunken seating space and narrow dividing partitions create subtle breaks between the zones.

DESIGN CLASSIC
Leather and chrome surfaces are durable and comfortable.

INSET FIREPLACE
A real fire creates a focal point for the room.

SCULPTURAL ACCESSORIES
Strong shapes, such as the tied reeds, stand out against the large expanses of pale wall.

◁ ❶ BUILT-IN SEATING
The sunken area of the room has fitted seating to maximize the available space. The ledges are covered with carpet, providing a seamless link with the rest of the room and making steps soft enough to walk on barefoot. Full-length windows flood the living area with natural light, and pale walls, furnishings, and glass tables achieve a restful, spacious look.

◁ ❷ PEACEFUL RETREAT

This quiet corner of the room makes an ideal area for reading or gazing at the fire. Full-length windows allow natural light to keep it bright all day, while at night, the sleek halogen uplight creates a subtle look. The group of pictures provides a focus for the corner and successfully combines contemporary and traditional styles.

FOR MORE DETAILS...

Armchairs SEE P .75

Nesting tables SEE P. 77

Displaying collections SEE PP. 80–81

Soft flooring SEE PP. 292–293

GRAND PIANO
The piano is angled towards the window to enjoy maximum benefit from natural daylight.

DIVIDING WALL
A partition encloses the space and reduces noise levels in the adjacent area.

PRACTICE ROOM ❸ △

Practising a musical instrument, including hours of perfecting scales, can be excrutiating for others nearby. This semi-enclosed corner of the family living area keeps noise levels to a minimum without being totally shut off, allowing others in the room to concentrate on other activities. For times when everyone wants to join in, there is space to perch on the deep sill round the wall, or to appreciate the music from the seating area.

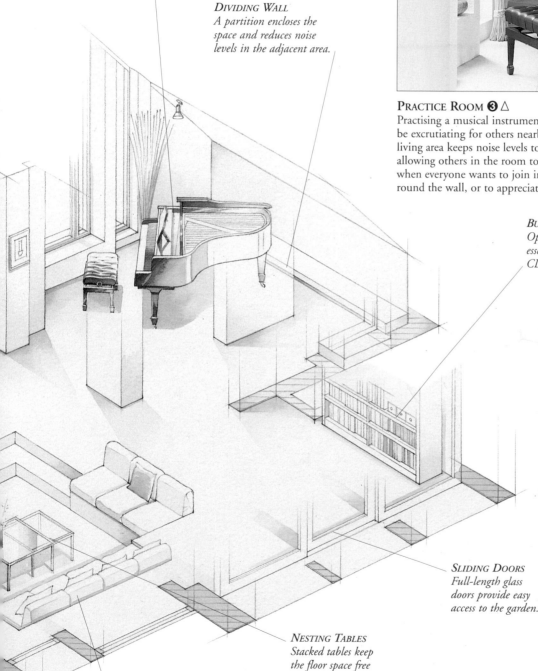

BUILT-IN SHELVES
Open shelving provides essential storage for books, CDs, tapes, and videos.

DESIGN POINTS

■ Using a different colour scheme in each zone of the living area can look disjointed. Opt for subtle differences, such as in flooring texture or in lighting, to separate one area from another.

■ Make sure that all electrical work has been undertaken before decorating or installing built-in shelving or cupboards. Each activity zone must have sufficient lighting and enough electrical sockets for your various appliances.

■ To maximize use of your living space and avoid conflict, group together or screen off areas for "quiet" activities, such as reading or homework, and space for "voluble" activities, such as music practice or television viewing.

SLIDING DOORS
Full-length glass doors provide easy access to the garden.

NESTING TABLES
Stacked tables keep the floor space free for movement.

SOFT SEATING
The sofas are supported by the raised floor level.

LIVING AREA PLANS

YOUR STORAGE SHOULD contribute to the aesthetics of your living areas, so plan it carefully, and buy the best you can afford. Built-in cabinets can actually improve existing proportions, for example by making a long, narrow room shorter and by concealing unwanted alcoves or irregularities. Shelving can accentuate the character of a room: if you have a low ceiling, visually strong uprights and shelf dividers may give the illusion of more vertical space. Conversely, you may actually choose to emphasize the horizontality of a room by playing down the vertical supports and using a shelving system with thicker shelves.

DESIGN POINTS

■ Avoid placing furniture only around the edges of the room. Storage used as room dividers gives the feeling of more space rather than less.

■ Shelves to accommodate different sizes of books should vary in depth from 23–40cm (9–15¾in). Sound systems and televisions require deep shelves: allow for sockets and tolerance for wiring and plugs.

■ Provide adequate lighting for your storage, such as directional lights over bookcases and slim-line fluorescents inside cabinets.

LIVING ROOM

The living room should be a place of relaxation and comfort. To achieve this, you have to plan the layout of the room carefully, and consider the practicalities of storage – you need somewhere to keep books, a place to house the television, and a surface on which to put down your drink. A combination of built-in shelving and cupboards allows you to display your favourite objects and to conceal others, but they must be designed carefully to complement the architecture of the room.

RECESSED SHELVING
An alcove is built out to make the shelves look as if they are set into the thickness of the wall.

CUPBOARDS
Elegantly panelled cupboards are built around and above the doorway.

MANTELPIECE
A carefully styled mantelpiece gives focus to the room.

TELEVISION CUPBOARD
A swivel arm angles the set towards viewers and retracts for concealment.

SIDE TABLE
Small tables close to seating are essential for putting down drinks or books.

DINING ROOM

Nowadays, a room dedicated solely to dining is an increasingly rare phenomenon. There are many advantages to having a separate dining room, particularly from the point of view of storage, as it can take the overspill from the kitchen, such as precious china and cutlery and large serving dishes. If the room is at a distance from the kitchen, it makes sense to choose storage with a low, flat surface for resting cleared-away dishes during the meal. A modern version of the old-fashioned sideboard is ideal.

BUILT-IN HOT PLATE
A hot plate keeps food warm and saves unnecessary trips back and forth to the kitchen.

TRAY STORE
Keep a selection of trays in the dining room, for transporting dirty dishes to the kitchen.

BUILT-IN SIDEBOARD
A combination of cabinets, open shelves, and drawers houses a range of accessories for the table.

TRADITIONAL SIDEBOARD
A dinner service is stored in the sideboard; plates are displayed along the back.

DUAL-FUNCTION ROOM

In modern homes, a separate dining room is rarely an option. If the kitchen is small, the living room will also have to accommodate the dining table – an arrangement that well-planned storage can ease. Establish the best places for different activities – a convenient spot for eating, a non-focal point for the television, a desk area – and choose storage that can demarcate different areas.

MAGAZINE RACK
Dual-function rooms must remain tidy – a rack keeps magazines at hand.

MOBILE TROLLEY
Useful for table accessories, a trolley can be wheeled away when not needed.

CONVERTED CUPBOARD
An old cabinet converted to house a sound system and CDs doubles as a television stand.

COFFEE TABLE
Choose a tiered coffee table that offers storage as well as a top surface.

PARTITION SHELVING
Backed up against a sofa, low shelving acts as a room divider and a store for crockery.

WRITING DESK
Dedicate a corner of the room to personal correspondence and household accounts.

LIVING AREA IDEAS

△ **CONSERVATORY LIVING ROOM**
With thermal conservatory blinds and underfloor heating, this bright and airy room is used throughout the year. Scenic views of the garden can be enjoyed in all directions.

◁ **FLASHES OF COLOUR**
Bring life to natural wood flooring and pale walls or furniture with bright colours and contemporary patterns. Floor and scatter cushions give the room a softer look.

△ **COMFORT AND GRANDEUR**
Formality and fun combine to create a relaxed, stylish living space. Seating areas are linked by the clever use of colour, and the table soccer game is played in the space beneath the gallery.

WALK-IN ROOM ▷
Removing part of the dividing wall that separates the narrow hall and small living area has created a large, light, and airy open-plan room. A degree of privacy has been maintained by keeping a small section of the original wall near the sofa.

BEDROOM

INTRODUCTION

The bedroom is the first room you see in the morning and the last one you see at night so its style and atmosphere should promote a sense of wellbeing at all times. Unlike other communal areas, the bedroom is one room not on general view, where you can choose furniture and furnishings to please yourself.

Most of the time spent in a bedroom takes place during sleeping hours when you are oblivious to your surroundings. However, it is still important to create a room that ensures you enjoy every moment spent there.

A century ago, it was not uncommon for several children to share the same bed in top-to-toe fashion, or for parents to make provision in their room when the need arose. For the masses, bedrooms were simply furnished and functional with perhaps an open fire, chamber pot, and wash stand the only concessions to comfort.

△ BED DESIGN
A high-quality bed is essential if you are to enjoy a good night's sleep. This contemporary model has a sturdy frame with a softly contoured headboard and sprung mattress for support.

TAPESTRY BEDROOM ▷
A four poster Goanese bed, swathed in heavy embroidered panels creates the focal point of this sumptuous 16th century English bed chamber.

Expectations are different now and the bedroom is considered a personal domain in which the highest standards of comfort and privacy are demanded. Space for fitted storage, en-suite bathrooms, and dressing areas are sought after in many homes, and the value of these extras, even in budget housing is increasingly appreciated.

CHOOSING FIXTURES AND FITTINGS

Whatever the quality of the interior design, the bed itself is by far the most important element in the room. The quality of the bed will affect how well you sleep so give priority to your choice of bed and opt for the best you can afford.

Once you have made that decision, you can base other decisions around it, such as the type of flooring. Bedrooms are considered "light wear" areas, so whether you prefer the warmth of natural wood flooring or the softness of deep pile carpet, is simply a matter of choice. Remember that pale shades will make a room appear larger and dark shades will make it look smaller. Where there is an abundance of space to fill, bedrooms can be furnished equally well in either opulent or minimalist style. If the room lacks space avoid fussy designs, busy patterns and dark shades.

BEDROOM STORAGE

Plan storage facilities carefully, and design the layout to enable easy access to the bed from either side. Clothes, shoes, cosmetics, books, and bedding will clutter up a bedroom quickly if there is insufficient storage or if the space is badly designed. Good storage enables you to keep possessions where they can be found in a hurry.

WHAT DO YOU WANT FROM YOUR BEDROOM?

Before deciding on the layout, furniture, and furnishings of your bedroom you will need to analyze your needs and consider all the facilities you may want to include, such as an en-suite shower room, work area, or walk-in wardrobes.

❶ A bedroom with en-suite facilities for easy bathing.

❷ A bedroom that doubles up as a breakfast room.

❸ Ample space for hanging clothes and storing belongings.

HOW CAN THIS SPACE WORK FOR YOU?

The shape and size of your bedroom will dictate the proportions of the furniture and fittings you can fit into your plans. Decide if minor alterations could improve your options allowing you to derive the maximum benefit from the bedroom and its fittings.

☐ Are there alcoves or recesses where wardrobes could be fitted to give a flush finish to the wall?

☐ Is the ceiling in your room high enough to allow a raised platform on which to place the bed, giving space for storage or an en-suite shower room beneath?

☐ Could extra space be created by installing a wall bed that can be recessed into the wall units when not in use?

☐ Is the room big enough to incorporate a relaxation area with sofa and coffee table?

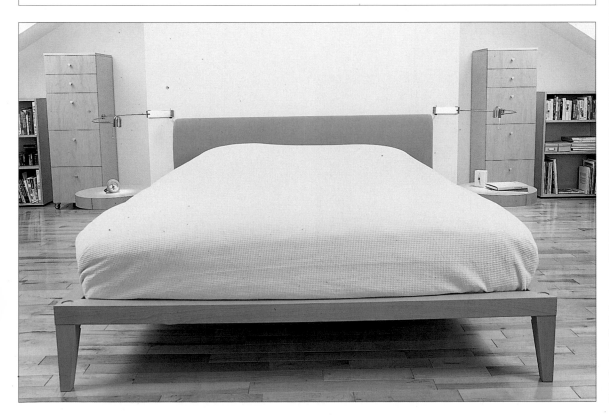

◁ CREATE A RETREAT
A roof space conversion offers many possibilities for spacious accomodation. In this newly created bedroom, natural wood flooring and simple storage are the minimalist backdrop to the large, predominant bed.

△ COORDINATED LINENS
Country cottage charm is
created by blending floral,
gingham, and plain prints.
Spring colours bathed in
natural light create a sunny
and fresh look.

▽ WARM GLOW
Soft lighting and earthy
colours work to make this
bedroom look cosy and
inviting. Plain walls offset
the contemporary wrought
iron bed frame.

HEAT AND LIGHT

The role of heating and lighting is vital to the
atmosphere of the room. You can create different
effects at different times of day and by selecting
accent lighting to highlight a special feature,
mood lighting to create a relaxed atmosphere,
or functional lighting for a bedroom that you
occasionally work in. Design in a combination
so you can change the mood to suit the moment.

Adequate heating can make all the difference to
your comfort when sleeping, getting undressed,
or walking about barefoot.

CHILDREN'S ROOMS

Children's rooms can be fun to plan, using the
colourful, innovative designs for furniture and
furnishings now widely available through

▽ MULTI-PURPOSE BED
A practical and compact unit for a child's room,
this design provides a comfortable, lofty bed, a
desk, and a sofa that converts into spare bed.

specialist shops and mail order. When planning
the room, take into account how the child will
spend his or her time, whether the room will be
used solely as a bedroom or as a bedroom and
playroom, and if so, what type of games and
activities are popular.

It is essential to look for durable floorings,
wallcoverings, and furnishings that can withstand
all the wear and tear busy children inflict on
their surroundings. If at all possible, incorporate
a child's favourite colours to make the room
especially inviting.

Manufacturers have to ensure their products
conform to safety standards but it is up to you
to guard against exposed sockets, unsafe
windows, or hot radiators at child level in a
children's room. Check the room thoroughly
and note all the potential hazards. It may seem
like an expensive option to buy safety gadgets
that may never be needed, but it is a small price
to pay for peace of mind.

SUZANNE ARDLEY

ASSESS YOUR NEEDS

THE FOLLOWING questions will help you to create a bedroom that best suits you and your lifestyle by prompting you to consider the main issues affecting the type of bed you require, your choice of bedroom furniture, and the layout of the room.

BEDS

Your choice of bed will determine how well you sleep and, ultimately, how good you feel during the day. Put considerations of comfort and support before those of style, and lie on the bed with your partner before buying it to be sure it suits you both.

☐ Do you have space in the bedroom for a larger or non-standard bed shape that will give you room to stretch and move without disturbing your partner?
☐ Would you prefer to have separate twin beds or would a double bed with two single mattresses linked together cater for your different weights and heights?
☐ If it is important for you to be able to sit up in bed and watch television or read, would an adjustable bed with raised head or feet be better than pillows?
☐ Do you have any recurring back or neck problems that could be helped by choosing more substantial support than just a mattress and base?
☐ Do you or your partner suffer from dust-mite allergies that would warrant choosing a bed with alternative fillings, such as foam, polyester, or latex?
☐ If space is limited, are you able to introduce a headboard with storage in the style and size you prefer or would you consider having one specially made?
☐ Are you choosing a bed for a child whose body weight and length will change during the life of the bed? Also, could the design you like be outgrown before it really needs replacing?

FURNITURE

Investing in well-designed bedroom furniture will make the room a pleasurable as well as a practical place to use. Consider how much space you need to move around and dress freely and choose furniture that does not have hard edges or sharp corners.

☐ Would fitted furniture with floor-to-ceiling storage give you extra space to introduce another item, such as a table?
☐ Are you able to keep infrequently used belongings, such as suitcases somewhere other than the bedroom to free up valuable storage space?
☐ If you intend to watch television in bed have you placed the set where it can be watched without having to stretch your neck or sit at an awkward angle?
☐ Do you like to take tea and coffee in the bedroom or have breakfast in bed

and if so, do you require a larger bedside table or one that can be moved to a more convenient position?
☐ Do you require individual cupboards and small drawers for storage or would one or two large cupboards with shelving provide enough space for everyday items?
☐ Have you made adequate provision for books, magazines and other items to be kept in or on your bedside table?
☐ Can you incorporate a small sofa or armchair in the room so that you can sit somewhere other than the bed to relax?

LIGHT AND HEAT

Good lighting and heating will greatly enhance the comfort of your bedroom. The right lighting will make various tasks easier and create a pleasing environment. You should be able to sustain a comfortable room temperature for both sleeping and dressing.

☐ Would mirror-fronted cupboard units reflect light back into the room from a window, making the room brighter and appear more spacious?
☐ Would you benefit from having more than one source of light in the room to highlight areas, such as a dressing table where you need to see clearly?
☐ Do you intend to add another facility to the room, such as an en-suite that might obstruct natural daylight, making it necessary to install additional light sources?
☐ If you and your partner like to be able to read in bed without disturbing each other, is the lighting by the bed independent and operated separately?
☐ If noise from nearby traffic disturbs your sleep, have you considered replacing the window with a design that gives extra sound and heat insulation?
☐ Could better use be made of space if the radiator was changed to a tall narrow design that utilizes space above waist height?

BEDS

A BED IS THE MOST IMPORTANT piece of furniture you will ever own. A high-quality bed will provide an excellent night's sleep, leaving you feeling bright and refreshed in the morning. Comfort and support are more important than shape and style although, given the choice of models available, you should not have to compromise on either. Invest in the best bed you can afford – you will soon appreciate the benefits.

DOUBLE BEDS

It is advisable to try out the bed of your choice with your partner before buying it. Whether you want a four-poster or a contemporary wrought iron frame, it is the type of bed and mattress that really matters, making all the difference to the quality of both of your sleep. Sharing a bed should be a pleasure. If space in your bedroom permits, buy a bed larger than the minimum for your sizes. That way, whether you wish to stretch out alone or curl up together, you can do so in comfortable harmony.

*DUAL-ACTION
Mechanism works
each side of the
bed independently.*

△ **ADJUSTABLE COMFORT**
Individual adjustable beds can be positioned to allow you to sleep, read, or watch television independently of your partner. Some remote-controlled models offer variable-speed massage options with a timer.

PRACTICAL STYLE
*Independent light sources
on both sides can be easily
reached without disturbing
either partner's sleep.*

BRIGHT FABRIC
*Covered headboard adds
colour and interest.*

△ **CARVED WOODEN ELEGANCE**
An antique or traditional-style wooden bed can form the focal point of a bedroom. A bed with panel sides may have a slatted base to support the mattress, or the divan may sit inside the frame. Measure old bed frames before buying, as a standard-sized mattress and base may not fit.

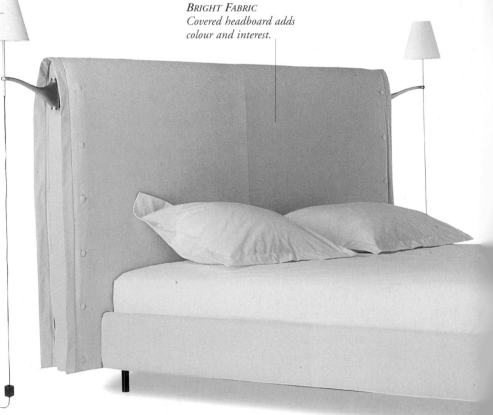

SINGLE BEDS

Suitable for children, or for those who prefer the cosiness of their narrow dimensions, single beds are also useful for guest rooms, where space is often limited. When choosing the right bed for a child, do not be tempted to settle for an inferior-quality mattress. Childrens' growing bodies, particularly their backs, need just as much support as adults'.

COLOURFUL FRAME
The metal framework is painted in a bright and hardwearing finish.

△ **SINGLE STYLE**
A single bed should be at least 15cm (6in) longer than the occupant and at least 90cm (36in) wide. This light tubular steel bed has rounded corners, making it ideal for a child's room.

△ **FOUR-POSTER BED**
Combining romantic style with practicality, four-poster beds were originally shrouded in thick tapestries to keep out the cold. Modern four-posters are mostly decorative, but decked with swathes of netting, they are also effective for keeping out mosquitoes.

◁ **CONTEMPORARY COMBINATION**
Padded sides and a duvet-style headboard are the fun but functional assets of this bed frame. The covers are removable and swivel-arm side lamps remove the need for bedside tables.

PLAIN COLOUR
A simple shade accentuates the minimalist style.

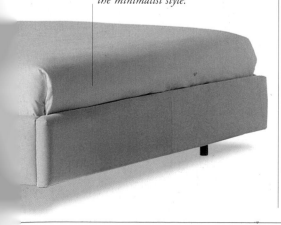

STORED FLAT
The legs fold under to enable the lower bed to fit neatly under the top one.

ADDED COMFORT
The mattresses are pocket sprung.

△ **STACKING BEDS**
There is no reason why spare beds should be any less comfortable than those already in use. Stacking beds can be left as single beds or joined together to make a double.

BED SIZE

You cannot expect a good night's sleep if your bed is too short or narrow. Look for a bed at least 15cm (6in) longer than the tallest occupant. Its width must allow you to bend your elbows without either touching your partner or hanging over the edge.

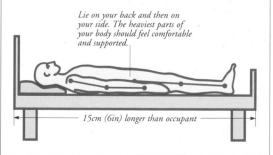

Lie on your back and then on your side. The heaviest parts of your body should feel comfortable and supported.

15cm (6in) longer than occupant

REMEMBER

■ However good the bed you buy, it is only expected to last ten years. A bed absorbs huge amounts of human sweat and discarded skin which gradually deteriorate the springs and allow dust mites to thrive.

■ Do not be tempted to swap the old mattress for a new one and keep the original base. Old, worn bases will greatly reduce the lifespan of a new mattress and will transfer old skin cells and dust mites.

BEDSIDE STORAGE

YOUR CHOICE OF BEDSIDE furniture will depend on which items you like to have to hand. Open cabinets or small tables are adequate for a simple lamp and a few books. If you prefer to have access to a clock, light, radio, tissues, toiletries, and medicines, or want to keep valuables nearby, then a bedside chest or cupboard is more suitable, with drawers and doors to keep possessions out of sight and prevent a build-up of dust. Whatever you choose, bedside storage should be sturdy, easy to access, and the same height as your bed.

CHESTS AND CUPBOARDS

Neat and practical bedside storage for accessories, small items, or linen can be provided by chests with regular or graduated drawers, cupboard space, or a combination of all three. Chests with several compartments will allow you to store items of differing sizes, leaving the top free for a bedside lamp or clock. Avoid overcrowding the top as it is likely that items will get knocked over in the dark.

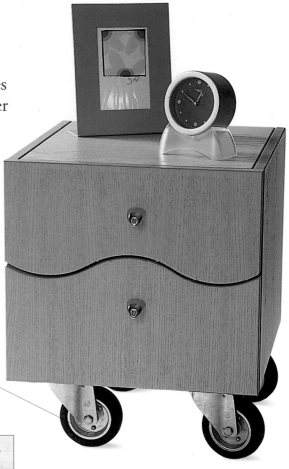

Wheels can be unlocked to move chest around.

△ **BEDSIDE TROLLEY CHEST**
A chest on wheels provides flexible storage that can be moved round the room and is easy to access. It also offers a good surface for a bedroom television, as the chest can be pulled out and angled to face the bed as required. Spacious drawers with curved detailing create strong lines in this simple but versatile chest unit.

SMOOTH OPERATION
The chest drawers should glide open and shut smoothly.

△ **CHEST WITH DRAWER STORAGE**
If you have limited cupboard space in your bedroom, or need to reach a range of belongings from the bed, a chest of drawers is invaluable. Keep smaller items in the top, heavier items in the bottom and avoid overfilling the drawers, which could make them difficult to open.

SURFACE LEVEL

Choose a bedside chest or table that allows you to see your clock or radio from a lying position. It should be possible to turn a bedside lamp on or off, or reach for a glass of water easily, whether sitting up or lying down.

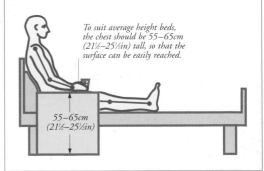

To suit average height beds, the chest should be 55–65cm (21½–25½in) tall, so that the surface can be easily reached.

55–65cm
(21½–25½in)

△ BED-END STORAGE
If you feel the cold, it can be useful to store extra blankets or duvets near the bed for easy access. This chest has removable shelving to accommodate bulky items such as spare blankets and pillows, or fresh bedlinen.

REMEMBER

■ When choosing your bedside storage, consider the items you regularly use and need near the bed and whether you prefer to display or conceal them.

■ If you intend to keep cash, credit cards, or jewellery in your bedside cabinet, look for one that can be locked to deter opportunist thieves.

■ Two-door cupboards provide easy access to items next to a double bed, as a door can be opened away from you from either side of the bed.

■ Built-in bedside storage can be more practical than a free-standing unit in a small room.

△ DECORATIVE CABINET
Scrolled fretwork panels enclose the inner shelving, concealing the contents, and making this bedside cabinet a decorative feature of the bedroom. The practical paint finish can be retouched easily if the pale surface becomes marked or damaged by spillages.

FROSTED GLASS
The opaque glass lid is wipeable and obscures items stored in the cavity beneath.

◁ SWING-OUT LID
Unobstrusive drawer handles and a cylindrical shape give this cabinet a distinctive style and the advantage of no corners or hard edges to catch on bedlinen or to knock bare feet in the dark. The curved drawers can be accessed from any angle, and the swing-out lid slides across near the bed.

BEDSIDE TABLES
When space in your bedroom is limited, furniture that is adaptable, or can be moved around when needed, is a practical choice. Any small table can be used next to the bed, providing it is well-balanced and can hold a lamp, clock, and drink. Less bulky and heavy than a solid cupboard, tables can maintain a feeling of light and spaciousness if the open area beneath is kept free from belongings. Use baskets or boxes for storage, to keep clutter to a minimum.

IN PLACE
The fixed lamp cannot be knocked from the table top.

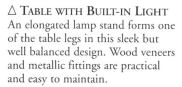

△ SIMPLE TABLE
A small folding table takes up the minimum of space and can be stored flat when not required. Simple trestle supports are strong enough to stand firm and hold the weight of everyday items on top.

△ TABLE WITH BUILT-IN LIGHT
An elongated lamp stand forms one of the table legs in this sleek but well balanced design. Wood veneers and metallic fittings are practical and easy to maintain.

▽ FOLD-DOWN TABLE
To preserve the smooth outline of the units, a discreet fold-down table has been built in for occasional use.

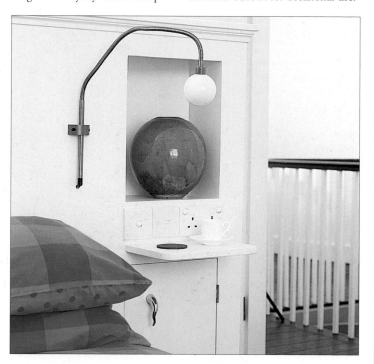

CLOTHES STORAGE

PROVIDING GOOD STORAGE for your clothes will ensure that they look better and last longer. There should be adequate hanging space in wardrobes so that the garments are well ventilated, and shoulders and sleeves do not rub against cupboard surfaces or get caught in doors. A combination of long and short hanging space, shelves, and drawers is ideal.

BUILT-IN OPTIONS

Integrated clothes storage tends to make better use of space and is easier to tailor to your personal requirements than freestanding alternatives. However, built-in cupboards can be expensive, and must fit in with the proportions and architecture of your bedroom.

CONCEALING CURTAIN
The draping quality of the fabric suits the decorative style of this bedroom.

◁ IMPROVISED WARDROBE
Curtaining off an alcove or section of your bedroom to hide a clothes rail is an inexpensive way to provide basic storage. A clothes rail on its own is cheaper still, but does not have the benefit of dust protection. This is probably the most flexible of the "built-in" options, as it is easy to dismantle.

REMEMBER

■ Contoured wooden hangers are better for your clothes than wire ones, which bend easily and can catch on garments.

■ Drawers are more expensive than shelves. Allow for different depths of shelving.

■ Good lighting is essential for clothes selection. For deep wardrobes, interior fluorescents are useful. Consider lighting that comes on automatically when the door opens.

■ For seasonal storage, place clean clothes in sealed bags or lidded boxes. Cedar balls or shavings will deter moths.

FREESTANDING OPTIONS

A well-designed freestanding wardrobe can provide a striking focal point in a bedroom, and of course can go with you if you move. However, it is rarely big enough to hold more than one person's clothes, and interior fittings tend not to be as flexible as for built-in furniture.

ARMOIRE ▷
This ornate wardrobe was specially designed to supplement a couple's dressing room, and so was fitted only with shelves for folded clothes and accessories such as shoes, hats, and bags. The fretwork doors are lined with fabric – a similar decorative effect can be achieved with a grille and pleated fabric.

DOUBLE DOORS
Fabric-lined doors protect clothes inside from dust.

OUTER COVER
The cover fits neatly over the internal frame to protect the clothes.

TIE-BACKS
Fabric strips hold back the "doors" for easy access.

SHELVES
Looped at the top, fabric shelves for clothes and shoes hang from a central rail.

△ BUILT-IN CUPBOARD

Simple sliding doors glide open to reveal the inside of the wardrobe. When closed, they form an abstract background perfectly in keeping with the architecture of the room. There is ample storage for clothes and luggage, with a narrow recess designed to hold a briefcase or bag. The shallow drawers are ideal for underwear and scarves.

◁ WALK-IN CLOSET

If you have the luxury of space, a walk-in cupboard fitted out like a small storage room with drawers, hanging rails, and shelves is ideal. Transparent drawers allow instant visibility for accessories, and high-level shelves can be used for out-of-season storage. An absence of windows means less exposure to dust, but lighting must be good.

HANGING SPACE

Short hanging for jackets and shirts

Long hanging for coats, long skirts, and dresses

1m (3ft 3in)

1m (3ft 3in)

1.3–1.5m (4ft 3in–4ft 11in)

Short hanging for trousers and short skirts

Extra space beneath for shoes on rails

A variety of single and double hanging makes the best use of space. A wardrobe should be a minimum of 60cm (23½in) deep to hold adult clothes.

△ CLOTHES TENT

Reminiscent of old "campaign" styles of furniture, several versions of these fabric wardrobes are available. The internal structure is a chrome or wooden frame from which to hang clothes and shelves. A canvas tent fits over the frame, with flaps at the front instead of doors.

ACCESSORIES

WHEN PLANNING YOUR BEDROOM storage, remember the array of accessories that supplement your basic wardrobe – everything from earrings to shoes. Such items often have to be stored in a specialized way to facilitate easy retrieval and provide protection. In recent years, manufacturers have designed numerous ingenious solutions specifically for the efficient storage and management of accessories.

SMALL ITEMS

It is extremely frustrating to waste precious time rummaging through crammed drawers and bags to locate small accessories such as jewellery, gloves, and underwear. Make sure that you sort and store them in a highly organized fashion. The key to successful storage of these items is good lighting and the ability to see everything at a glance for instant selection. Seek out small pockets of space and use the backs of doors – large cupboards and deep drawers are not appropriate for small items.

REMEMBER

■ Try to have all your accessories instantly visible – not stacked, so that items at the bottom are never used. Look for the many specialist products on the market that help organize the insides of cupboards and drawers.

■ Numerous small drawers are useful for the organization of accessories. It is crucial that the depth of drawer is exactly right, so that you do not have to dig for your belongings.

■ An inexpensive way of protecting shoes is to keep them in their original boxes. Cut a window at the end for easy identification, or attach a photograph of the contents of each box.

■ Try to keep pairs of objects together so that you do not have to search for the missing item every time.

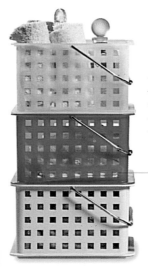

HANGING SPACE
Accessories like ties and belts can be hung up to save drawer space for smaller, more bulky items.

INEXPENSIVE CRATES
These plastic crates provide a practical way to store items that need ventilation, such as towels and linen.

△ **PLASTIC CONTAINERS**
Plastic storage units range from inexpensive stacking crates to mobile trolley units with plastic trays that can be added on as required. These offer a flexible method of storing anything from toiletries to clothing or shoes.

△ **TIE RACKS**
Various types of tie rack are available that either hang from the rail inside the wardrobe or, to save space, on the back of a door, as shown above. All prevent ties from becoming creased and allow easy selection.

ACCESSORIES RAIL ▷
Gloves rival socks in their ability to lose their partners. This system of pegs and small pouches looped over a rail keeps gloves in pairs and scarves together for easy retrieval.

POUCH
Scarves are easy to find in small bags.

PEG CLIP
Gloves are pegged together in pairs.

DRAWER ORGANIZER ▷
A creative solution to the problem of chaotic underwear drawers, this expandable plastic drawer insert separates and sorts underwear, socks, and scarves. The entire contents of the drawer are visible at a glance, so you are more likely to use all of the items on a frequent basis.

ADJUSTABLE INSERTS
Rows of dividers clip together and can be cut to fit snugly inside the drawer.

▽ **BUILT-IN SOLUTION**
Extra storage is squeezed out of a small bedroom by framing the door with a selection of different-sized cupboards and numerous narrow drawers. Small drawers are ideal for storing accessories such as scarves, underwear, and hosiery.

SHOES

Most people have numerous pairs of shoes, from everyday footwear to shoes worn only occasionally. They are often kept at the bottom of a wardrobe, where they take up considerable space and tend to collect dust. Consider these other options.

△ **SHOE CABINET**
Specially designed deep drawers, fitted with metal rods, are ideal for storing shoes. To extend the life of good leather shoes, protect them from dust and keep them spaced apart so that they are not touching; shoetrees ensure they keep their shape.

DOOR HOOKS
Three metal hooks attach the fabric shoe pockets to the back of a door.

SHOE POUCHES
Small pockets separate and protect shoes from rubbing against one another.

△ **FABRIC POCKETS**
A space-saving shoe organizer that hangs on the back of a door can store a large number of indoor shoes and accessories, but is less practical for heavily used outdoor shoes, which will quickly soil the fabric.

CHILDREN'S STORAGE

BEDROOM STORAGE MUST be able to adapt and grow with the child to fulfil a variety of different functions and needs. Up to the age of about ten, most children will use the bedroom floor as a play space, after that they will be more oriented towards desk or table-top activities. Storage should be organized to simplify the unpopular task of tidying up.

TOYS AND GAMES

Display is an essential ingredient of storage for children – what the eye doesn't see, the hand doesn't play with. For this reason, shelves are better than cupboards, but it is good to have a variety of methods, including baskets and drawers, to adapt to the changing requirements of the growing child.

CHILDREN'S SHELVING

30cm (11¾in) deep for books and valuables

45cm (17¾in) deep for crates and larger toys

A mixture of deep shelves at a low height for play and shallow shelving out of reach is ideal, especially in a shared bedroom.

HIGH SHELF
Keep fragile toys and old books on a top shelf so that they are on display but are not damaged.

REMEMBER

■ Toys for younger children should be at a low level to encourage play, but ensure that potentially hazardous toys and small pieces are out of the reach of babies and toddlers.

■ Do not display toys all at once: put some away and rotate them periodically so that they do not lose their novelty value.

■ Old-fashioned toy boxes look pretty, but their depth makes locating toys difficult and their heavy lids can trap tiny fingers.

■ Allow for a variety of storage systems to cater for everything from bulky toys and large books to small bricks and tiny plastic play people.

△ TOY STORAGE
Junk shops make good hunting grounds for versatile pieces like this old pine unit, which acts almost as a toy filing system. It has plenty of space for books, display shelves at different heights for soft toys, and drawers of varying sizes – some labelled – for special treasures.

SHELVING
The system is adjustable, so the shelves can be raised and lowered as required.

HIGH BED ▷
In a small room, a bed with storage – in this case adjustable shelving – and/or a study area underneath provides the best use of floor space, and gives a sense of enclosure and privacy which becomes more of a priority as the child gets older.

HAMMOCK ▷
Soft toys harbour
dust, which can trigger
asthma in vulnerable
children. It is hard to banish them
entirely, but a hammock will keep
them suspended within view.

BOOK BASKET
High beds do not have the
advantage of bedside tables, so
attach a basket to the side for books.

PAINT TRAY
Embed paint
pots in a sponge-
lined tray to
hold them firm.

SMALL DRAWERS
Keep collections
of tiny objects in
small drawers.

PLASTIC CRATES
Transparent boxes
obviate the need
for labels.

MOBILE UNIT
Crates on castors
transport bricks
around the room.

TEENAGERS' BEDROOMS

Untidiness seems to be an essential rite of passage
in adolescence, but a teenager is more likely to tidy up
if provided with stylish and easy-to-use bedroom storage.
Before investing in expensive units, however, steel yourself
to seeing them "customized" by their teenage owners.

△ **STORAGE CUBES**
A full wall of units specially designed for a teenager provides bedroom
storage for many diverse objects, including provision for a television and
a selection of open display shelves. The various compartments open in
different ways as their doors are hinged at the side, top, and bottom.

△ **STUDY AREA**
A quiet place to study is essential for older children. This bedroom for a
teenage student makes use of a top-lit alcove, benefitting from the view
and natural light. Open shelves and drawers in the pedestal unit keep
study items tidy and separate from clothes storage and the sleeping area.

ADULT BEDROOM PLAN

FAR FROM PRESENTING a problem, this irregular roof space has been fully exploited to create a roomy, practical adults' bedroom. Careful consideration has been given to each of the three staggered sections that form the room, taking into account factors such as natural light and areas of restricted headroom, to create separate spaces for sleeping, clothes storage, and breakfasting.

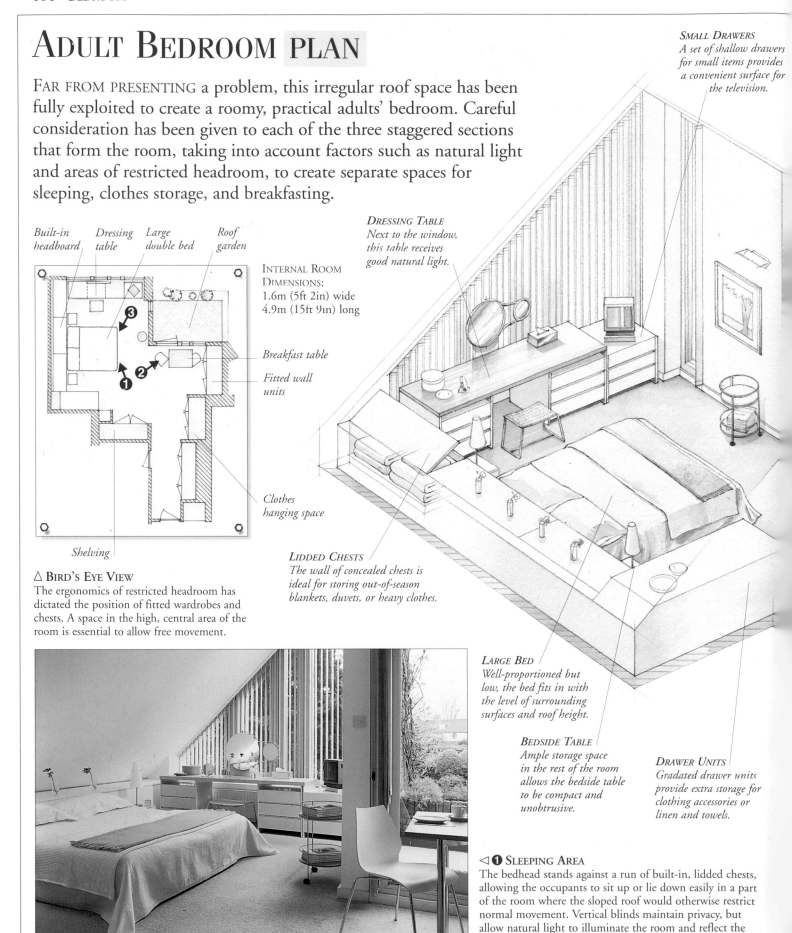

Built-in headboard *Dressing table* *Large double bed* *Roof garden*

INTERNAL ROOM DIMENSIONS:
1.6m (5ft 2in) wide
4.9m (15ft 9in) long

Breakfast table

Fitted wall units

Clothes hanging space

Shelving

SMALL DRAWERS
A set of shallow drawers for small items provides a convenient surface for the television.

DRESSING TABLE
Next to the window, this table receives good natural light.

LIDDED CHESTS
The wall of concealed chests is ideal for storing out-of-season blankets, duvets, or heavy clothes.

LARGE BED
Well-proportioned but low, the bed fits in with the level of surrounding surfaces and roof height.

BEDSIDE TABLE
Ample storage space in the rest of the room allows the bedside table to be compact and unobtrusive.

DRAWER UNITS
Gradated drawer units provide extra storage for clothing accessories or linen and towels.

△ **BIRD'S EYE VIEW**
The ergonomics of restricted headroom has dictated the position of fitted wardrobes and chests. A space in the high, central area of the room is essential to allow free movement.

◁ ❶ **SLEEPING AREA**
The bedhead stands against a run of built-in, lidded chests, allowing the occupants to sit up or lie down easily in a part of the room where the sloped roof would otherwise restrict normal movement. Vertical blinds maintain privacy, but allow natural light to illuminate the room and reflect the white paintwork, creating a sense of tranquility and space. The moveable trolley can be pushed to the table or bedside.

❷ ROOM WITH A VIEW ▷

Sitting at the table to eat breakfast, read, or simply admire the view from the bedroom is greatly enhanced by the glass doors and full-length windows. On bright sunny days the small table can be moved out onto the roof patio, where leafy shrubs, trees, and lush flowering plants provide a fresh, crisp outlook from every possible angle.

SHELVING
Floor-to-ceiling cupboards provide neat storage for bedlinen and laundry, and make good use of the sloping, triangular roof space.

BUILT-IN WARDROBE
Divided hanging space means that everyday items can be separated from special items.

SMOOTH DOORS
The neutral finish and uniform design of the cupboard doors create a clean, uncluttered feel.

NEAT HANDLES
Full-length "strip" handles and magnetic catches allow the large doors to be opened and closed easily.

FITTED CARPET
Easy on bare feet, the pale fitted carpet enhances the calm, restful colour scheme.

ADJUSTABLE SHELVES
The height of the shelves can be altered to accommodate shoe and hat boxes, and folded clothing.

FOR MORE DETAILS...

Beds SEE PP. 94–95

Lighting SEE PP. 288–291

Soft flooring SEE PP. 292–293

Concealed storage SEE PP. 302–303

◁ ❸ LIGHT AND SPACE

The deep, built in chest-space behind the bed provides the low headboard with practical storage and a surface for displaying small items. It also serves to project the bed forward, giving more room for movement when sitting up in bed to read or watch television. The roof window allows the best of the early morning sunlight to flood onto the bed, while maintaining privacy.

DESIGN POINTS

■ Overhead storage is ideal for light but bulky items, such as suitcases or hat boxes, and for the seasonal storage of winter or summer clothing.

■ If the main bedroom has an unattractive outlook or faces a noisy road, consider moving to a smaller room and storing less-used items elsewhere.

■ Atmosphere is all important for bedrooms. Dimmer switches will allow you to adjust the light levels to suit your mood.

ADULT STORAGE PLANS

SLEEPING MAKES VERY LITTLE demand on storage capacity, so it is well worth exploiting the bedroom as much as possible for other purposes. Although it was considered unhygienic by many in the early twentieth century to keep clothes in the bedroom – "It is not a clean thing to do, and makes the room horribly untidy", opined the French architect Le Corbusier – for most people today it is often the only option. There is no doubt that a dressing room or walk-in cupboard is ideal, but because the space for these is often carved out of an existing bedroom, you do have to be careful not to ruin the room's proportions.

BEDROOM WITH DRESSING ROOM

A separate dressing room reduces the pressure for storage in the bedroom itself, so that the sleeping area stays reasonably uncluttered. It also allows for one partner to dress without disturbing the other. Unlike a walk-in wardrobe, a dressing room should ideally have natural light, a mirror for grooming, and sufficient space in which to dress. A door to the room is not necessary, as the clothes are protected behind the cupboard fronts.

DESIGN POINTS

■ Before investing in a wardrobe, measure your clothes by the linear metre, in order to gauge how much space is needed. Allow for expansion.

■ Consider your current bedroom: can it be divided, or will it seem too small? For a dressing room, allow a minimum of 3.5m² (38ft²); for a single walk-in wardrobe, you will need at least 3m² (32ft²).

■ Allow a minimum clearance of 60–75cm (23½–29½in) between the front of wardrobe doors and other furniture; each person requires 1.5m (4ft 11in) clearance space for dressing.

CLOTHES DRAWERS
A chest of small and shallow drawers divides wardrobe territory and is useful for underwear and accessories.

HIGH CUPBOARDS
Areas that are difficult to access can be used for medium-term storage of out-of-season clothes.

WINDOW
A window to the side provides welcome natural light in a dressing room.

CHEST OF DRAWERS
Useful for small items and as a surface for personal display, a chest of drawers also gives focus to the room.

BUILT-IN WARDROBES
Segregated hanging space is provided by built-in wardrobes on either side of the mirror.

DOORWAY
An open doorway leading into the dressing room provides a feeling of spaciousness, and the wall offers extra storage space.

BEDSIDE TABLE
Positioned on either side of the bed, a table is needed for books and other bedside items.

BEDROOM WITH WALK-IN WARDROBE

A walk-in wardrobe is the most efficient way to store clothes, as there are no doors once you are inside, and you can see everything at a glance. Because the garments need to be kept free from dust, a walk-in wardrobe must have a main door and preferably no windows. Ideally, each partner should have a closet, tailored to his or her specific needs.

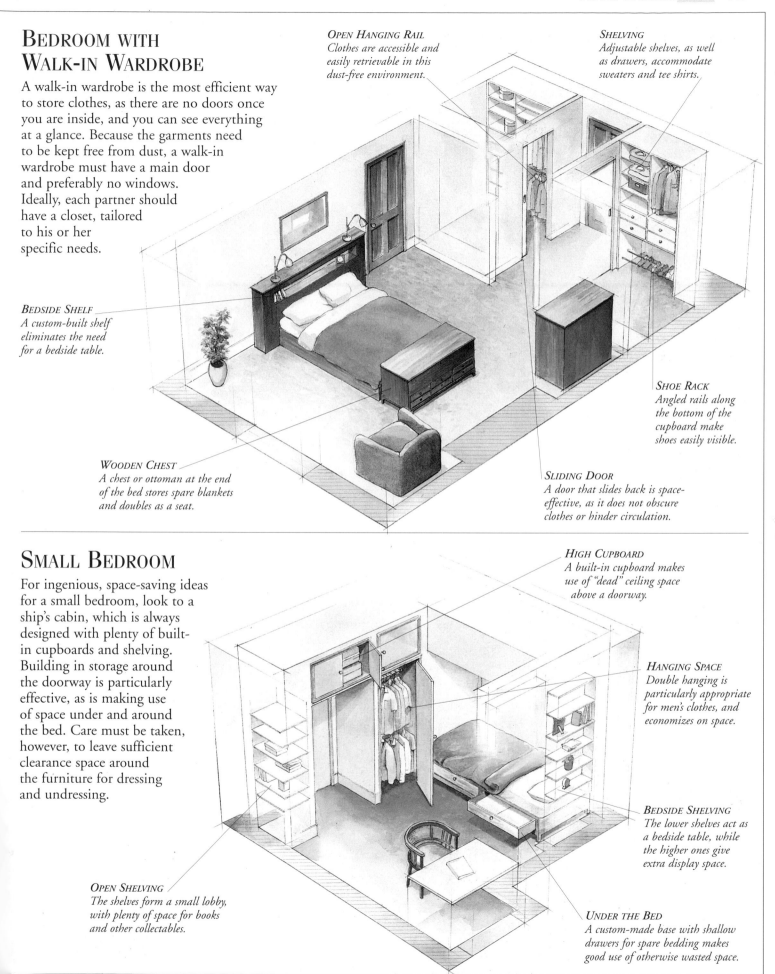

OPEN HANGING RAIL
Clothes are accessible and easily retrievable in this dust-free environment.

SHELVING
Adjustable shelves, as well as drawers, accommodate sweaters and tee shirts.

BEDSIDE SHELF
A custom-built shelf eliminates the need for a bedside table.

SHOE RACK
Angled rails along the bottom of the cupboard make shoes easily visible.

WOODEN CHEST
A chest or ottoman at the end of the bed stores spare blankets and doubles as a seat.

SLIDING DOOR
A door that slides back is space-effective, as it does not obscure clothes or hinder circulation.

SMALL BEDROOM

For ingenious, space-saving ideas for a small bedroom, look to a ship's cabin, which is always designed with plenty of built-in cupboards and shelving. Building in storage around the doorway is particularly effective, as is making use of space under and around the bed. Care must be taken, however, to leave sufficient clearance space around the furniture for dressing and undressing.

HIGH CUPBOARD
A built-in cupboard makes use of "dead" ceiling space above a doorway.

HANGING SPACE
Double hanging is particularly appropriate for men's clothes, and economizes on space.

BEDSIDE SHELVING
The lower shelves act as a bedside table, while the higher ones give extra display space.

OPEN SHELVING
The shelves form a small lobby, with plenty of space for books and other collectables.

UNDER THE BED
A custom-made base with shallow drawers for spare bedding makes good use of otherwise wasted space.

ADULT BEDROOM IDEAS

△ **ECLECTIC COLLECTION**
Rich colour and texture perfectly complement period timbers and furniture in this quiet hideaway. The unusual collection of free-standing pieces, such as the country-style blanket box, combine to create a lived-in uncontrived feel.

△ **CO-ORDINATED CHOICE**
It is possible to blend just two colours for a simple, delicate room theme, as in this classic toile de joy print. Even in a limited space, the bedlinen, furnishings, and wallpaper are matched to striking effect without looking oppressive.

△ **CLOSET COLOUR**
Fitted wardrobes utilize space efficiently, but standard finishes can be uninspiring. Here, bright lemon yellow provides a splash of colour and a look of continuity throughout this young and vibrant room.

△ **RELAXATION ZONE**
Where space permits, a sofa can cradle you more comfortably than piles of pillows stacked against a headboard. Place it where daylight will shine on a book or allow you to contemplate a pleasant view.

CLEAN LINES ▷
Natural wood tones, warm earth colours, and crisp linen add a tactile feel to this neat and orderly room. An adjacent dressing area with a dressing table and mirror frees up valuable space in the bedroom.

CHILDREN'S BEDROOM PLANS

CHILDREN ARE OFTEN ALLOCATED small, irregularly shaped rooms that no-one else wants. However, unless you have the luxury of a separate playroom, consider sacrificing a larger room for younger children to share, providing them with plenty of floor space for play, then moving them to smaller rooms when they are older. Children's storage should be flexible to cater for their changing needs – modular furniture is ideal. Take care not to fill every nook and cranny with fixed storage: for young children, idiosyncratic spaces are important places for pretend play.

NURSERY

Comfort, practicality, and, above all, safety are essential in a nursery. A baby will spend a considerable amount of time high up on a changing mat, and cannot be left alone, so this area in particular must be well planned, with all the equipment you need close at hand. Too much freestanding furniture will obstruct the floor space when the baby is mobile, but sturdy, adjustable shelves for toys can be used later for books and games.

HANGING TOY ORGANIZER
Fabric pockets provide overflow accommodation for soft toys, and are a decorative wall feature.

SEATING AREA
A comfortable window seat for an adult or older child also provides useful storage space beneath for toys.

CHANGING AREA
For safety reasons, nappies, wipes, and creams must be kept within easy reach of the mat.

WICKER BASKET
A large basket or box is useful for a quick tidy-up of toys before bedtime.

UNDER THE COT
Make use of the space beneath the cot to accommodate extra boxes for toys or accessories.

ADJUSTABLE SHELVING
Shelf or drawer space is required for babies' tiny clothes; hanging space is not yet necessary.

SHARED BEDROOM

A room of their own is not a priority for most children under the age of ten – younger children often prefer company. As they get older, however, sharing a bedroom can lead to tensions if the space is not planned to give each sibling some sense of their own "territory". Bunk beds may be the answer; otherwise, shelves or a screen can act as a partition between two beds. Allocate shelf and cupboard space, and separate noticeboards on which they can express themselves individually.

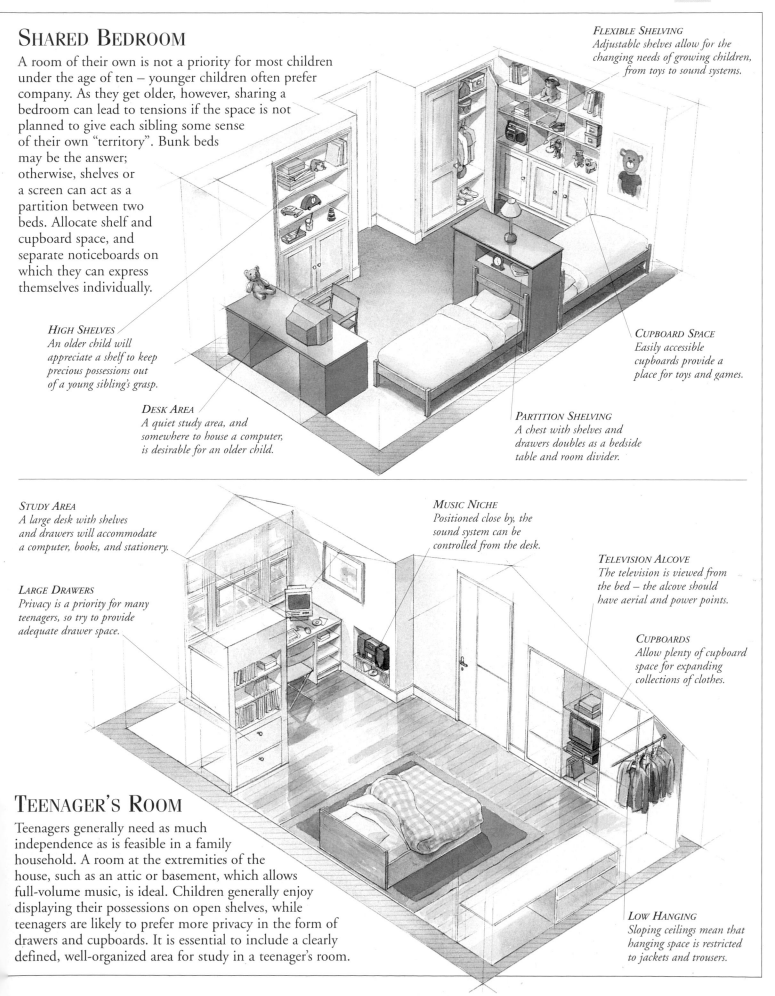

FLEXIBLE SHELVING
Adjustable shelves allow for the changing needs of growing children, from toys to sound systems.

HIGH SHELVES
An older child will appreciate a shelf to keep precious possessions out of a young sibling's grasp.

DESK AREA
A quiet study area, and somewhere to house a computer, is desirable for an older child.

CUPBOARD SPACE
Easily accessible cupboards provide a place for toys and games.

PARTITION SHELVING
A chest with shelves and drawers doubles as a bedside table and room divider.

STUDY AREA
A large desk with shelves and drawers will accommodate a computer, books, and stationery.

LARGE DRAWERS
Privacy is a priority for many teenagers, so try to provide adequate drawer space.

MUSIC NICHE
Positioned close by, the sound system can be controlled from the desk.

TELEVISION ALCOVE
The television is viewed from the bed – the alcove should have aerial and power points.

CUPBOARDS
Allow plenty of cupboard space for expanding collections of clothes.

TEENAGER'S ROOM

Teenagers generally need as much independence as is feasible in a family household. A room at the extremities of the house, such as an attic or basement, which allows full-volume music, is ideal. Children generally enjoy displaying their possessions on open shelves, while teenagers are likely to prefer more privacy in the form of drawers and cupboards. It is essential to include a clearly defined, well-organized area for study in a teenager's room.

LOW HANGING
Sloping ceilings mean that hanging space is restricted to jackets and trousers.

CHILDREN'S BEDROOM IDEAS

△ WORK AND PLAY
Children are attracted to colour, so rooms that are bright and fun will be loved and well-used. Encourage play in stimulating surroundings with rounded, child-sized furniture.

▽ APPLIQUÉ BEDSPREAD
A plain bedspread covered with appliqué animals offers an improptu start for numerous bedtime stories. Large cushions encourage use of the bed as a soft play area.

△ DIVIDING BLINDS
This corner alcove maximizes space with cupboards, seating, and shelves full of children's belongings. Plain cotton blinds can be lowered to conceal everything from view.

FILING CABINET STORAGE ▷
Old office cabinets are updated with splashes of colour to match the rug. The spacious drawers operate easily, even when filled with heavy books. Built to last, the cabinets can be re-sprayed as the child grows up.

BATHROOM

INTRODUCTION

THE BATHROOM is probably the most personal and private room in the house, and one which is in frequent use. The success of a bathroom design relies on taking into account the demands that will be made on the room. Will it be a functional bathroom for a busy family or a luxurious room, purely for one's own use, in which to relax. Bathrooms are no longer regarded simply as utilitarian washrooms where cleansing rituals are performed out of sight behind closed doors. They are congenial spaces where you can surround yourself with well-designed, practical, and aesthetic objects that reflect both your lifestyle and taste.

More than ever, people expect bathrooms to fulfil a range of functions, and are happy to re-fit the existing bathroom, convert a spare room into a bathroom, or add a bathroom ensuite so that they can indulge in everything from a bracing wake-up shower or soothing hot spa, to the exclusivity of a bathroom-cum-dressing-room. Even where space is tight, clever planning and positioning of sanitaryware can ensure time spent in the bathroom is truly pleasurable.

BATHROOM INFLUENCES

My initial interest in bathroom design was awakened by a visit to Fiji some years ago when visiting old family friends in the Nausoris. Their remote Colonial-style house had a wonderfully simple but effective shower system. Fed by a rainwater tank hidden in the treetops, ice-cold water coursed through a hosepipe to a colossal shower head towering above the cubicle. No half-way measures here: plunging into the deluge, you

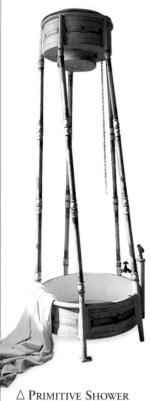

△ **PRIMITIVE SHOWER**
Taking a shower rather than a bath was considered eccentric when this portable shower was made in the 1800s. The innovative design has a tank supported by mock-bamboo poles and, on pulling the lever, water is released through the fixed shower head, and collects in the foot bowl.

▽ **BATHING IN GRANDEUR**
Kingston Lacy was one of the first stately homes in England to install a bathroom on a grand scale. Before plumbing was fitted in the 1920s, servants filled the bath and washstand with hot water.

◁ **BOLD AND SIMPLE**
Simple lines and uncluttered surfaces are the mainstay of modern bathroom design. Durable, low-maintenance materials cater for busy people with limited time for keeping the bathroom spotlessly clean.

were left gasping and drenched in cold water from head to toe. Having experienced my first invigorating "power shower", I was convinced that showers were as therapeutic as they were cleansing and, on my return to England, tried to recreate the same showering experience.

EARLY WASHING FACILITIES

In stark contrast to the old saying "cleanliness is next to Godliness", early domestic washing facilities were as basic, but less effective, than my shower in Fiji, and consisted of a bowl and a pitcher of water placed in a corner of the bedroom. There were no bathrooms but, on occasion, a portable bath tub was brought into the room and filled by hand with water heated on the fire. Family members would take it in turns to bathe in the same water. It was impractical to take a bath on a daily basis so odours were masked with scents, such as lavender, bergamot, and rosemary.

1930s BATHROOM ▷
Demand for bathroom
facilities grew in the 1930s
which led to a wider choice
of sanitaryware including
this type of pedestal basin;
coloured suites rather than
white suites were considered
to be luxury items.

△ RETRO LOOK
Modern technology joins
forces here with classic
1930s style to give a heated
towel rail that looks good
and works efficiently.

By the mid-1800s, purpose-built bathrooms
began to be installed, but only in grander houses.
These bathrooms were furnished comfortably
like other rooms in the house, but instead of
displaying elegant bureaus and dining tables,
they had ornate washstands, dressing tables, and
baths. These early bathrooms helped the rich
distinguish themselves from the "great unwashed",
at a time when people began to understand that
dirt carried germs and potentially fatal diseases.

FORM AND STYLE

In time, soft furnishings and ornate details were
considered inappropriate for bathrooms as they
gather dirt and dust, and so the room evolved
a colder, more clinical appearance. Plain white
tubs, tiling, and metal fixtures became the norm.
By the 1940s, pressed steel baths with hand-
held showers were being mass-produced, enabling
more homes to own a bath, but apart from some
patterned porcelain and plain-coloured suites,
bathrooms remained functional and hidden away.

BATHROOM COLOURS

The 1970s and 1980s saw a growth in the range
of coloured suites and unusual bath shapes
fuelled by a desire for exclusivity, while in the
late 1990's minimalist metal, glass, and mosaic
designs gained pre-eminence. Despite the hi-tech
movement, traditional sanitaryware and fittings
have undergone a revival with roll-top baths,
classic brass shower roses, deep mahogany

panelling, and ornate furnishings becoming increasingly popular. Modern reproductions abound, but for lovers of authenticity, original sanitaryware is available, restored to its former glory by specialist retailers. Taps and fittings, ball-jointed radiators, and wrought-iron clothes horses complete this nostalgic dip into the past, recreating its own distinct and decadent style.

ADDITIONAL FACILITIES

Today, a comfortable bathroom is taken for granted, and now in family homes we have come to expect a second bathroom or a separate shower room to prevent a bottleneck of users at peak times. House builders appreciate this trend and second bathrooms, particularly an ensuite bathroom or shower room leading off the master bedroom, are fast becoming a standard specification in new-build homes. Property developers and estate agents agree that an extra bathroom increases both the desirability and value of your home.

The popularity of the second bathroom has also been fuelled by the development of space-saving sanitaryware designs and ventilation systems. It is now possible to fit ensuite facilities into the smallest of spaces – a feat that would have been impossible in the past.

INNOVATIVE DESIGN

Bathroom design has now become a state-of-the-art industry, combining form and function with the latest technology. In addition to a huge choice of baths and showers, and bath/shower modules, a spectacular range of sanitaryware

◁ **NEEDLE SHOWER 1910**
Early enthusiasts of showers would have been impressed by this striking design with its overhead shower rose and a series of body sprays from the circular tubes that created the first all-round shower.

▽ **JACUZZI SHOWER**
Showers over baths are not new, but Jacuzzi's all-in-one system is designed to fit into the space of a standard bath. The power shower capsule and sleek bath shape make bathing highly enjoyable.

products offer hydrotherapy, steam cleansing, lymph stimulation, and body toning systems. The introduction to the industry of ceramic disc technology now enables a single-lever mixer (with just one handle and spout) to deliver an even temperature and flow of water. The ceramic disc creates an ultra-smooth action as you turn the tap on and off, the mixer does not drip, and it resists limescale build-up in hardwater areas. Booster pumps have also had their part to play by improving water pressure and overall shower performance. Water temperatures can now

▽ CONTEMPORARY TAP
Ceramic disc technology has led to single lever taps that control both the flow rate and temperature mix of the water smoothly and effortlessly.

be pre-set for adults and children, while as an additional safety measure, unbearably hot water from the shower head will cut out instantly to prevent scalding. These small but highly significant developments in bathroom technology have transformed the face of the ordinary bathroom, making it more efficient, safe, and fun to use.

ENVIRONMENTAL CONCERNS

In response to the arrival of new bathroom materials, finishes, and fittings, manufacturers have developed a host of cleaning chemicals to keep your bathroom in pristine condition. There are products that prevent and remove limescale deposits, chemicals that dissolve residue left by soaps and oils, and substances to irradicate stubborn mildew. But the use of these harsh chemicals, combined with the dramatic increase in the amount of water required by each household to sustain more than one bathroom, is creating serious environmental problems. Responsible manufacturers are addressing these issues by developing products, especially wc cisterns, that use less water to flush than models currently in production. At present, 7.5 litres (1.6 gallons) of water are needed to flush the wc but with design improvements being researched by manufacturers, this is likely to be reduced.

Much can be done by individuals to save water when using the bathroom on a daily basis. Remember, a shower uses up much less water than running a full bath so, if possible, try to take more showers. Another small but important step is to remember to turn off the tap rather than leaving it running while cleaning your teeth. Also ensure that taps do not drip, a huge amount of water can be wasted this way.

PLANNING YOUR BATHROOM

Many bathrooms are as intensively planned and as expensive to install as kitchens; the plumbing and drainage pipes, electrical points, and heating and ventilation systems all need to be accurately placed within the room, and must comply with health and safety regulations.

When designing the space, aim to arrive at a solution that suits your lifestyle. Consider what demands will be made on the bathroom, how much time will be spent in it, and who will use it. The time you devote to this and to assessing the advantages and disadvantages of bathroom hardware will be rewarded when you emerge from a room that leaves you feeling a hundred times better than when you went in.

△ MODERN MATERIALS
This well-considered wc design with a hidden cistern combines durable stainless steel with the beauty of a clear acrylic seat which is warm to the touch.

WHAT DO YOU WANT FROM YOUR BATHROOM?

Before purchasing a range of expensive sanitaryware and fittings, analyse your lifestyle and bathing habits, and decide which family members are going to use the new bathroom. To help you arrive at a solution, compare the benefits of the bathroom facilities below.

❶ A space that can be shared with others.

❷ A bathroom equipped with child safety features.

❸ A room that doubles up as a dressing room.

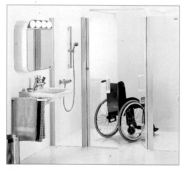

❹ Facilities that less-abled people can easily use.

❺ A comfortably furnished bathroom in which to relax.

❻ A fitted bathroom where everything can be put away.

❼ A bathroom that makes the best use of a small area.

❽ A shower room rather than a bathroom.

❾ Maximum comfort from existing facilities.

HOW CAN THIS SPACE WORK FOR YOU?

Whatever the shape or size of your existing bathroom you will want to get the most from the products you choose. Decide how suitable the room is for the items you wish to include and what alterations, if any, will be required.

☐ Is your present bathroom big enough for you and your family's needs or would converting a spare bedroom into a large bathroom be a better planning solution?

☐ Would choosing compact sanitaryware designs enable you to squeeze a shower, bath, and other items of sanitaryware into a limited space, or would a separate shower room be a better solution?

☐ Is the bathroom lighting good enough to see when shaving or applying cosmetics, or could it be improved by a second window or specialist lighting around the mirror or basin area?

CHOOSING A STYLE ▷
This fresh white bathroom combines a range of style details that are subtlely co-ordinated. Little touches, such as an ethnic terracotta pot holding lavatory paper, family photos, and fresh flowers present an elegant but well-furnished look.

△ FORM AND FUNCTION
High-quality fittings will enhance both the look and the performance of an otherwise ordinary item of sanitaryware. Choose an attractive design with a simple, smooth operation.

The style choices you make for your bathroom are personal and need to be carefully thought through. Your selection of products is crucial. Fixtures and fittings must last well, and still look good after several years' wear and tear. To help you decide what elements you wish to include in your brand-new or re-modelled bathroom, establish what you like and dislike about the existing room. Ask yourself questions, such as: How easy is it to step in and out of the bath? How warm is the bathroom on cold winter mornings? Is the sanitaryware easy to clean? Is the shower powerful enough? Also, consider the

architectural features in the room itself, such as decorative plasterwork and the windows, and how they will affect the finished look. Before pulling everything out and starting from scratch, stop to ask whether some of the existing elements might fit equally well with the style of your new bathroom plan.

STYLE PREFERENCES

As regards my own personal style, as much as I love the simplicity of contemporary bathroom design and innovative new materials, I feel most comfortable in rooms that have an informal,

◁ CHOOSING THE ELEMENTS
Look for attractive designs that also help with
your storage. This modern pedestal basin has a
compartment for storing towels and a ledge on
which to rest soaps when washing your hands.

them out of reach of young children. If you
choose a back-to-wall wc, the cistern will be
boxed in behind a half-height false wall, or
tongue and groove panelling, creating a display
shelf on top for attractive bottles and jars.

CHARACTER AND FUNCTION

Once you have decided what style you favour,
look for sanitaryware, materials, and fittings that
will add the desired character but are, above all,
functional. Collect manufacturers' brochures
outlining the specification of each product to
help you make informed decisions. To help you
choose, the advantages and disadvantages of the
major bathroom products are outlined in the
following pages. For example, if you have young
children you will be able to judge whether
ceramic tiles or rubber flooring is best. Whatever
element you are considering, take into account

lived-in atmosphere. Objects that are displayed
because you like them or simply because they
have been handed down to you, achieve a warm
personal look that others, selected merely to
present an image, often lack. In the same way,
a clever blend of contemporary and traditional
pieces can produce spectacular results, so even
if your bathroom is in an old house, do not feel
limited to furnishing it with period pieces.

Whatever your style preferences, try to plan
as much storage space as possible in your new
bathroom so that items do not clutter up
countertops and other activity areas. Place only
attractive objects on display, and keep utilitarian
items hidden behind closed doors. Toiletries,
lavatory paper, cleaning materials, medicines,
and first aid boxes take up a considerable space.
Installing a semi-countertop basin with storage
units beneath, is one solution. Shelves around
the walls at shoulder-height can be used to
display decorative accessories, while keeping

◁ CHOOSING DETAILS
Most bathroom bottles,
pots, containers, and tubes
are small. Plan separate shelf
compartments so items can
be stored and found easily.
Mirror-fronted cabinets
also reflect light. Choose a
lockable design to protect
children from danger.

WHAT COULD YOU CHANGE?

Use the following
checklist to help you
pinpoint what it is
about your bathroom
that you would like
to improve or replace.
□ Change shape of
existing room.
□ Alter architectural
features.
□ Improve access to
natural light.
□ Upgrade sanitaryware
and fittings.
□ Renew tiling and
waterproof seals.
□ Replace flooring.
□ Redesign lighting.
□ Add shaving sockets.
□ Improve ventilation
and heating.
□ Reorganize plumbing.
□ Reduce noise levels.
□ Increase privacy.
□ Reorganize available
storage space.
□ Rethink the size,
height, and position
of sanitaryware.
□ Change furniture.
□ Update all curtains,
blinds and other soft
furnishings.

PROFESSIONAL DESIGN ▷
Set out to use available space efficiently, this bathroom has custom-made fittings with walls and floor clad in stainless steel to create a waterproof capsule that needs no separate shower.

PLAN OF ACTION

Having decided on the style and elements you wish to include, use this checklist before starting alterations to ensure that nothing has been overlooked.

☐ Have you received permission from the relevant authorities for additional plumbing fixtures?

☐ Will you need the help of professional plumbers, builders, and electricians, or will you be able to do most of the work yourself?

☐ Are you planning to renovate or re-enamel items of sanitaryware, for example, a cast iron bath? Do you need help having it taken out?

☐ Have you costed the total job and received quotes for plumbing or other work you cannot do yourself?

☐ Have you allowed a little extra money in the budget for finishing decoration and soft furnishings?

its practicality in a bathroom environment as daily contact with heat, steam, and splashes of water soon cause inferior materials to deteriorate.

It is not just the sanitaryware that needs to be attractive and functional in bathrooms, but also details such as lighting, wallcoverings, window treatments, furniture, and cabinet surfaces. Good lighting makes a bathroom safer to use, well-chosen flooring must be both hardwearing and comfortable underfoot, and the right cabinet finish can transform the look of the bathroom and offer a water-resistant surface. These considerations present an opportunity to influence the look of the room while achieving a comfortable bathroom that is simple to maintain.

IDEAS INTO REALITY

This chapter is intended to help you to arrive at an ergonomic bathroom design with items arranged for ease of use and visual pleasure.

If your bathroom plans are ambitious – for example, if the room needs to be extended to accommodate the sanitaryware or you are adding a second bathroom in the attic – you should also consult a qualified architect. An architect will want to look at your proposed bathroom before start of work so that he or she can advise you on building regulations and on the important rules about wiring and electricity in the bathroom. Architects will also be able to recommend a good team of plumbers and fitters. If you want to create a bathroom that satisfies all your needs, however, your input is vital, so use the ideas on the following pages to help you formulate your designs before putting them into practice.

SUZANNE ARDLEY

ASSESS YOUR NEEDS

THE FOLLOWING questions will help you focus on your specific bathroom needs and think about ways to approach bathroom planning so that, as you work through the book, you will be able to compile a list of the bathroom elements and designs that best suit you and your lifestyle.

BATHS AND FITTINGS

Consider the amount of time you like to spend in the bath and whether you prefer a quick dip, a long soak, or a bath that doubles up as a shower. Think about the needs of other members of the family, and whether you would like a bath that is large enough to share. These decisions will help you decide on the size and type of bath you need, plus the best fittings, and a suitable location.

■ BATHS
☐ Would fitting a corner, tapered, or compact bath free up much-needed space along one wall for an extra item of sanitaryware, such as a bidet?
☐ Do you like to spend time lying back and relaxing in the bath? If so, have you considered bath designs that will cradle your head, neck, and back in comfort?
☐ If you do a strenuous job that leaves you with aching muscles, would a spa bath system be a good idea?
☐ Do you enjoy taking a long time in the bath? If so, would you like to be sure that your chosen bath material retains the heat incredibly well? Or would a heated bath panel be useful?
☐ Would you like the bath to double up as a shower? Does the base of the bath have an anti-slip surface for safety?
☐ Is easy maintenance important to you? Remember, baths in dark colours lose their looks quickly in hardwater areas as limescale deposits mark the surface.
☐ Would you like to share a larger double bath with your partner? If so, would any structural alterations be necessary to strengthen the bathroom floor?
☐ Do you have young children or less-able family members who would find climbing in and out of a bath difficult? Would they benefit from safety features, such as grab rails?

■ BATH FITTINGS
☐ Are your children likely to pull out the bath plug? Would a pop-up waste be more practical than a plug and chain?
☐ When different members of the family take it in turns to use the bath as a shower, would a bath/shower mixer with thermostatic limiter be a wise choice to avoid possible scalding from hot water?
☐ Do you want to be able to wash your hair over the bath? If so, have you chosen a bath/shower mixer that will suit the rim of your chosen bath?
☐ Do you have young or elderly family members who find it difficult to operate standard taps? Have you considered lever taps that are easier to use?

SHOWERS

An effective shower needs to be carefully planned to work with your existing plumbing system. Consider how many times a day you want to shower, and whether you would like to have different showering options, such as a massage setting. Think about the people who will use the shower, and whether you need safety features for the young or elderly. Also, weigh up whether it is easier to house the shower in a separate room.

☐ Do you want the convenience of instant hot water for showers at any time of the day or night or do your showering times correspond with the availability of hot water from the hot water cylinder?
☐ Do you prefer a powerful shower? If so, is it possible to install a shower pump to improve the shower's performance?
☐ If there is sufficient space, would a large, double shower, enabling you to bend and stretch without touching the sides when washing, appeal to you?
☐ Would a shower that can double up as a relaxing steam room suit your lifestyle?
☐ If you opt for a shower with body jets, can the position of the jets be altered to suit all the family members who may use it?
☐ Are there less-able members of the family who would find stepping in and out of the shower difficult, and see a built-in shower seat as a practical addition?
☐ Have you dismissed fitting a shower cubicle because space in the bathroom is restricted? Did you know that shower cubicles can be fitted with a choice of inward and sliding doors that only use space within the shower cubicle to open?
☐ Would you prefer an invigorating shower with needle jets of water, a relaxing shower with massage and pulse options, or one that offers a choice of functions to suit all members of the family?

☐ Do you like to be drenched from head to toe in water, or would an adjustable shower head be more useful that can be raised or lowered to target different parts of your body without getting your hair wet each time ?

☐ Do you like to keep soap and shampoo within the shower enclosure? Would a shower cubicle with a space designed to hold these items be useful?

BASINS AND FITTINGS

Make your choice of washbasin and fittings simple by considering the people who will be using the basin on a daily basis. Decide whether more than one person will want to have access to a basin at the same time. Will you be carrying out other activities, such as shaving and hair-washing? This will influence the height of the basin and position of the fittings.

☐ Will two people want to wash in the bathroom at the same time? Have you the space to fit twin sinks with enough elbow room for two people?
☐ Do you require space under the basin to store items? Would a wall-mounted basin help to free-up this floor area?
☐ Are you taller or smaller than average? Would it be more comfortable to fit a wall-mounted basin at a height that suits you? If so, have you checked that the wall basin you have chosen can be fitted with a syphon cover to hide the pipework or recess the supply pipes in the wall?
☐ Do you have young children who tend to overfill the basin or splash water onto the floor? Would a basin with inward-sloping edges be a good idea?
☐ Do you want to wash your hair in the basin? If so, can the spout be turned to one side so that your head can fit quite comfortably over the basin?

WCs AND BIDETS

Think carefully about who will use the wc and bidet, how often, and for how long. The most important factors are comfort and cleanliness. Other points worth considering when selecting a wc, are how easy is it to operate the flush mechanism, how much water the wc needs to flush, and whether you want a close-coupled, low-level, or high cistern wc.

☐ If you want an old-fashioned, high-level cistern, does the bathroom have tall walls to enable the cistern to sit high above the pan so that the force of water is strong enough to flush the wc properly?
☐ Does the lavatory seat rest against the cistern or wall when open to prevent it falling shut at an inconvenient moment?
☐ Will both young and old members of the household be able to sit down and stand up from the wc with ease?
☐ Would you prefer to mount the wc bowl on the wall so that the seat can be higher or lower than average?
☐ Are the contours of the wc bowl, seat hinges, water inlet, and rim easy to clean?
☐ Do you want to conserve water? Is there a choice of different flushing modes with the cistern, for example, a half press for a short flush or a full press for a long flush of water?

STORAGE

Make a mental list of the type of items you would like to keep in the bathroom. If it is a family bathroom, take account of products that will have to be stored out of reach of children. The type and amount of storage space you need to design into your bathroom will be determined by the number of products you and your family use and who requires access to these products.

☐ Do you have enough cupboard space to house your beauty and cleaning products?
☐ Could the storage of everyday items be better planned so that less-used items do not obstruct access to those you use regularly?
☐ Do you want storage cupboards that are easy to maintain in a bathroom? If so, have you checked that the cabinet finishes are steam-proof and the hinges rust-proof?
☐ Do you want a bathroom cabinet that can be locked so that medicines and cleaning chemicals can be kept away from children?
☐ Do you need a container for storing children's bathtime toys?

BATH SHAPES

CHOOSING A BATH that is a pleasure to use is just as important as finding one that looks good. Before coming to a decision, ask permission to climb in and out of the baths you like on your showroom visits; although you may feel ridiculous, it is the only way to make a practical choice. Once in a bath, see that it suits your body shape by stretching out your legs and reaching for the taps. Check also that fittings, such as grab rails, are well placed.

POPULAR SHAPES

The rectangular bath is still the most popular shape, partly because it fits neatly into a bathroom corner, and also because of its practical lines which enable the occupant to stretch out and lie down. From this basic shape, a range of modern space-saving designs have evolved, such as the tapered bath. For a traditional style, the old-fashioned slipper bath (*below*) or double-ended bath (*below right*) are comfortable and good-looking designs.

△ STANDARD BATH
The addition of a non-slip step, grab rail, and shelf unit to a standard rectangular bath are useful features in a family bathroom.

▽ SLIPPER BATH
Position freestanding baths so that there is plenty of space around them to show off their contours, and to enable you to step in and out of the bath from either side.

BATH RACK
Essential for holding washing items where wall-mounted dishes are impractical.

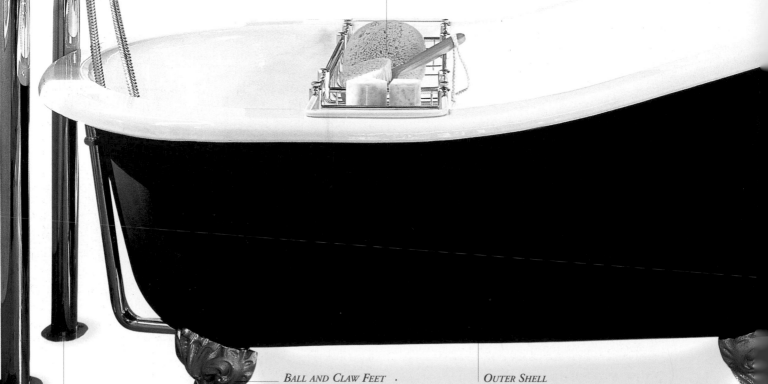

METAL SHROUDS
Tall metal cylinders conceal pipework.

BALL AND CLAW FEET
Decorative ball and claw feet hide the sturdy bolts securing the slipper bath to the floor.

OUTER SHELL
Most baths can be painted with a water-resistant paint so that they co-ordinate with the bathroom colour scheme.

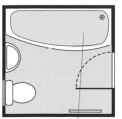

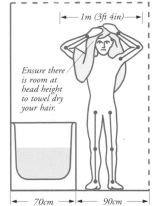

A tapered end creates space for other elements.

◁ **TAPERED BATH**
A clever and practical solution to cramped bathroom conditions is to install a tapered bath which gives more space where it is needed – at the end where you stand up and shower. Meanwhile, the narrow end allows space beside it for a full-size basin with elbow room; the sink can be used in comfort without hitting the bath edge.

INNER SURFACE
Enamelled surfaces are durable but colder to touch than acrylic.

ELBOW ROOM

←1m (3ft 4in)→

Ensure there is room at head height to towel dry your hair.

←70cm→ ←90cm→

Plan a floor area at least 90cm (36in) wide alongside the bath so that you can towel dry both the upper and lower half of your body in total comfort.

REMEMBER

■ Access to all sanitaryware plumbing is essential. Ensure that panelled bath surrounds on all types of bath can be opened quickly in an emergency by fitting either magnetic catches or hinges.

■ Abrasive cleaning liquids and chemicals can damage acrylic and enamelled bath surfaces and shorten their life. Only use products recommended by the sanitaryware manufacturer.

■ To make the bath safe for young and old people, install grab rails and non-slip mats.

△ **DOUBLE-ENDED BATH**
Comfortable ends and centred taps and waste are essential if the bath is for more than one. The bath should be deep enough to prevent displaced water from overflowing.

ALTERNATIVE SHAPES

Manufacturers also produce baths in circular shapes. A round or corner bath may be more in keeping with your bathing needs, especially if you enjoy sharing a bath with your partner or tend to bathe several children at once. It may fit more successfully into your room plan than a rectangular bath.

△▷ **FULL CIRCLE**
Most round baths have a greater water capacity than standard shapes so they take longer to fill up and are less economical. They are usually manufactured from acrylic or resin which makes them light, while a shelf-seat is often moulded into the design for comfort and ease of use.

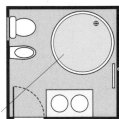

A round bath leaves space for other sanitaryware.

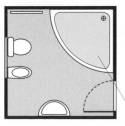

◁△ **CORNER BATH**
A bath tucked into a corner occupies a similar floor area to a standard bath but fills the space differently, which can be an advantage when planning a bathroom layout; a corner bath is shorter than a standard bath so an extra item can be placed next to it along one wall.

This design leaves space for a radiator to warm towels.

SPECIALIST BATHS

FOR THOSE WHO PERCEIVE bathing as a special time to indulge in the therapeutic effects of water, there are a whole host of sophisticated spa systems that can both stimulate and relax you. Alternatively, you may prefer to plunge into a gleaming copper bath, or submerge yourself in a deep tub of water.

TONING AND RELAXING

The therapeutic properties of spa baths, soak tubs, and whirlpools are undeniable. They offer a perfect way to unwind at the end of the day. A stream of water mixed with air is pumped out of jets to pummel the neck, back, thighs, and feet, and encourage good circulation.

△ HYDROTHERAPY
A sculptured head rest and sloping back gently support the body, aiding the jets of aerated water to massage directly along the length of the spine. A touch-control pad, within arm's reach, can alter the waterflow and also the temperature to maintain comfort levels throughout the treatment.

SPA BATH AND SHOWER UNIT ▷
Combining a relaxing spa bath with an invigorating shower in one compact unit makes good use of limited space. It also eliminates the need for extra pipe runs that two self-contained systems require. The circular end provides room to shower in comfort with shelves for shampoo and soaps.

WATER THERAPY
The speed of the jets can be altered for a relaxing or an invigorating body massage.

◁ SPA BATH
To ensure the muscles really benefit and relax, the water in the spa bath should be deep enough to lightly support the weight of the body. The water should be warm, not uncomfortably hot, to encourage a total sense of well-being.

TEMPERATURE CONTROL
A thermostat keeps the temperature constant.

MULTI-SPRAY HEAD
Delivers a soothing pulse of water or energizing jets.

NEAT PROFILE
Unobtrusive tap-heads with neat contours are less likely to be knocked.

WATER MOVEMENT
Variable water speeds ease
joints and relax muscles.

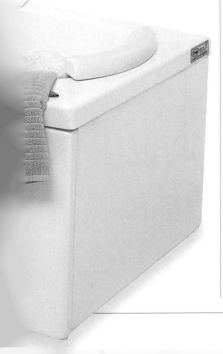

SIT BATHS

Sit baths take up less floor space than standard baths but keep you in an upright bathing position. Although this sounds awkward, it can be very soothing as these baths are often so deep that you can submerge yourself up to your neck. Taller than standard baths, they can be tricky to fit in small spaces under sloping roofs and windowsills. Choose a traditional sit bath shape if room cannot be found for the new deeper models.

GRAB RAIL
Handle allows
the bather to
sit down safely.

STEP DETAIL
Natural wood steps
help you climb over
the steep side.

DEEP TUB ▷
Two people can sit comfortably on the recessed seat in this deep tub. Finished in natural wood, the resin construction is strong and lightweight, and the fittings are neat. The wide rim allows bath products to be kept within easy reach of anyone seated in the bath.

SPECIALIST BATH MATERIALS

Stainless steel, copper, marble, and wood can make exciting alternative materials for baths but are expensive. Unlike acrylic or resin that are warm to the touch, materials such as stainless steel, copper, and marble will feel cold, and some absorb heat from the water, reducing its temperature. Baths can also be made from quality hardwoods. As well as being warm, they retain their heat well.

MAINTENANCE
Use a non-abrasive
cleaner and soft cloth.

STAINLESS
STEEL
Satin or
mirror
finishes are
available.

△ WOODEN BATH
Planks of solid hardwood are bonded together and protected with polyurethane varnish to provide a watertight seal. The moist conditions prevent the timber from drying out and so hold the planks together.

NATURAL WOOD
Clean lines and
beautiful graining
make a feature of
this simple bath.

△ STAINLESS STEEL BATH
Stainless steel bath interiors are easy to keep clean, hygienic, and hardwearing. The outer panel has been painted to give the illusion of solid veined marble.

SURFACE DETAIL
A roll top and deep sides
show off the copper's gleam.

COPPER BATH ▷
The distinctive slipper shape and copper interior have classic style. The copper is protected with a lacquer finish but care must be taken not to scratch off the surface finish as blue-green staining can result.

SHOWER SYSTEMS

A GOOD SHOWER IS UNBEATABLE, whether you prefer invigorating needle jets of water or a relaxing massage spray. Showers use up less water than a bath, take up little space, and can be fitted into the smallest of rooms, making them ideal for busy households and as en-suite facilities. A variety of trays, together with a huge choice of enclosures and fittings, offer an infinite range of systems from which to choose.

SINGLE SHOWERS

A shower can be tailored to suit your exact requirements, from the shape and fittings to the temperature and speed at which water is delivered. Most showers are designed for one occupant with one shower head and one set of controls. Cubicle sizes vary though, so it is worth stepping inside one to bend and stretch and check that you, and other members of your family, can shower in comfort.

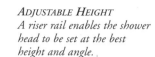

ADJUSTABLE HEIGHT
A riser rail enables the shower head to be set at the best height and angle.

BODY JETS
Jets of water massage shoulders and legs.

TEMPERATURE CONTROLS
A pre-selected temperature stays constant when showering.

SHOWER FINISH
Low-maintenance acrylic is hardwearing and simple to wipe clean.

▽ CIRCULAR SHOWER
An all-in-one shower unit can eliminate the need for additional plumbing, ceramic tiling, and electrical work. Here, an overhead spray, two pairs of body jets, integral lighting, and storage for shampoos and soaps provide luxury in one compact unit.

WASHING AND DRYING

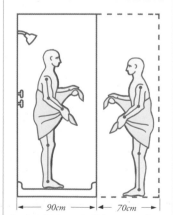

← 90cm → ← 70cm →

It should be possible to partly dry yourself within the confines of the shower unit. You will need space to raise your arms and to bend to reach your feet.

△ STANDARD UNIT
A standard square shower tray will fit easily into the smallest of bathroom corners. A single shower head or combined shower head with body jets can be fitted to offer a range of showering options. Unless you choose a complete shower surround, a waterproof covering such as ceramic tiles must be used on the bathroom walls to prevent water penetration.

DOUBLE SHOWERS

For sharing a shower or for the luxury of having more room in which to move around, a double shower unit offers extra comfort. Most are rectangular, though round, square, and tapered designs offer flexibility when planning the layout. Plan to fit the shower head and jets centrally so that when sharing, both occupants are deluged equally and able to wash simultaneously.

ANGLED SHOWER ▷ ▽
The diagonally aligned shower door fills the same area as a standard door, but makes access easier in confined spaces. A roomy shower interior with multi-jet shower head, separate hand spray, and a seat showers one or two adults.

SHOWER HOSE
Insulation around the hose stops it becoming too hot.

Doors have room to open even where space is limited.

WOODEN SEAT
A seat is useful for the less able, and for those taking a long shower. Polyurethane finish is water resistant.

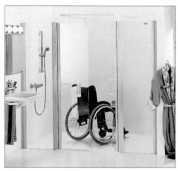

△ SHOWERS FOR THE LESS ABLE
Watertight seals around the shower doors at floor level mean that less-abled users can move in and out of the shower enclosure without flooding the floor. The double doors, grab rails, and thermostatic controls facilitate easy wheelchair access, privacy and above all, a safe environment for the user.

REMEMBER

■ Where space is limited, showers can be fitted under the stairs or on a landing.

■ Arrange quotes for the plumbing, tiling, and electrical work, and include these in your budget when working out the total price of the installation.

■ Check first with your installer that the system you intend to buy is compatible with your water supply.

■ Shower trays are made in four main materials: steel, acrylic, resin or composite, and ceramic. Run your hand over the materials to decide which one you prefer the feel of.

■ Clean the showerhead often to remove limescale build-up.

SHOWER SURROUNDS

Keeping the rest of the room dry and enjoying the benefits of an effective shower relies on containing the water within the showering space by means of a screen, door, or curtain. The least expensive option is a waterproof curtain, while the most expensive is a toughened glass surround.

△ SHOWER CURTAINS
PVC and plasticized fabrics used for modern shower curtains are impregnated with fungicide to prevent mildew.

SHOWER DOORS ▷
In the event of breakage, shower doors manufactured from tough safety glass shatter like a car windscreen into thousands of pieces that cause little harm.

△ STANDARD
Hinged on the left or right, the doors open into the bathroom.

△ INFOLD
Made in two sections, the door folds into the shower cubicle so that it does not take up any floor space.

△ PIVOT
Partly opening into the unit, the door occupies little space.

◁ ▽ SHOWER POD
Space and light are the main features of this spectacular shower room, constructed from toughened frosted glass. Stainless steel handles are used to slide the doors open and closed. A wood floor and central shower rose add to the pleasure of the experience.

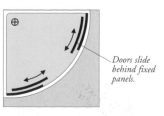

Doors slide behind fixed panels.

SHOWER AND BATH FITTINGS

GOOD QUALITY FITTINGS are as important as the sanitaryware itself. Many bathrooms are bought with the taps and wastes included in the price. As well as complementing the bathroom style, they should be durable and easy to operate – even with soapy hands. Shower, bath, and tap fittings are used many times throughout the day, so invest time choosing the right details to ensure that even the most economic of bathrooms is a pleasure to use.

◁ **FIXED SHOWER**
A decorative swan-neck riser with a fixed shower rose is ideal if you prefer a total soak rather than a light shower. The slender pipework remains static once in place, so you must supply a precise measurement for the shower height, to ensure that you will be able to stand upright under the shower rose.

FIXED ROSE
The jet of water cannot be adjusted.

BATH SHOWER MIXERS

Bath shower mixers are fitted with a "divertor" handle that can be switched over to fill the bath or to operate the shower. They are ideal for washing your hair and rinsing out the bath after use, and are indispensable if there is no room in the house for a self-contained shower unit.

SHOWER CRADLE
The hand-held shower allows freedom of movement.

△ **RETRACTABLE HANDSET**
These telescopic hoses fit neatly within the bath surround and slide in and out for use. They are less likely to catch against other fittings as the shower hose is tidied away. Not all bath shower mixers are available with retractable handsets.

SHOWER HOSE
Flexible for a full-height shower or for rinsing the bath.

"DIVERTOR" HANDLE
Choose a handle that automatically returns to fill the bath after a shower to prevent accidental scalding.

TAP CROSSHEAD
Traditional design with the benefits of modern technology.

SHOWER HEAD
Set at a fixed angle, the spray cannot be adjusted.

SHOWER SUPPLY
Try to buy all three elements of a fixed shower from the same supplier to ensure that they match.

◁ **TELEPHONE HANDSET**
In general, telephone handset designs fit standard baths where two tap-holes have been punched into the bath rim. However, some traditional handsets are available from specialist bath shops for non-standard baths and for baths that have been recessed into a fixed surround, such as marble.

CERAMIC HANDLE
The "divertor" should move easily but feel secure when located in either the bath or shower position.

SHOWER FITTINGS

A shower must maintain a good flow of water at a constant temperature. Before purchase, check that the controls respond quickly and have built-in safety features to avoid scalding. Always check with the installer that the type of shower you want to purchase is compatible with your water supply.

◁ THERMOSTATIC CONTROL

Thermostatic shower controls are fitted with a shut-off valve to control the water flow and maintain a constant temperature. The heat can be adjusted by mixing different volumes of hot and cold water.

HOSE
The pipe is reinforced to prevent buckling that will restrict water flow.

ELECTRICALLY HEATED ▷
An electric shower is connected to both the mains water and electricity supplies, and only heats water when it is needed, making it very economical.

SELF-CLEAN
By twisting the rim, small filaments push through the spray holes to eject limescale.

△ DIRECTIONAL HEAD

A fixed head is attached to the wall and the pipework is hidden from view. The angle of the shower head can be altered to suit any user, while the spray options range from relaxing pulses to invigorating needle jets.

BAR CONTROL
Hot and cold water inlets deliver a pre-set temperature of water to the shower head.

REMEMBER

■ Single-control thermostatic valves are easy to use by just turning the lever or dial from the off position through cold, warm, and then hot.

■ Dual-control thermostatic valves regulate the water flow and keep the temperature constant. Anti-scald devices are available which cut off over a hot but bearable 38°C/100°F.

■ Try out plumbed-in shower heads and fittings in bathroom showrooms to see how simple they are to operate.

■ When buying antique taps and fittings, check that they will work with your sanitaryware.

BATH FITTINGS

Many bath taps in manufacture have the latest ceramic disc technology, enabling taps to be turned on or off fully with just a quarter turn. Ceramic discs have a hard, polished surface creating a watertight seal and drip-free "off" position. They also work well in hard water areas where limescale can build up around taps, making them difficult to operate.

△ RIM-MOUNTED TAPS

These are fitted to the edge of baths that usually have pre-drilled tap-holes. All have a larger feed and water flow capacity than basin taps.

△ WALL-MOUNTED PILLAR TAPS

A combined tap-head and spout direct the flow of water. The spouts need to be sufficiently long to extend over the rim of the bath.

△ WALL-MOUNTED MIXER TAPS

Two taps and a central spout are wall mounted at the end of the bath or on one side. The plumbing is chanelled into the wall to hide it.

△ WATERFALL SPOUT

A wide band of water cascades into the bath and offers a neat, almost flush finish. Mixer taps keep the water temperature consistent.

WASTE

Dirty water from the bath, shower, bidet, and basin will drain out through the waste where a simple filter catches soap deposits and hair that can then be removed periodically to prevent a blockage in the pipes. Wastes and bath taps are often sold as a package to ensure they match one another.

△ POP-UP WASTE

Modern pop-up wastes are often operated from the tap mounting where a simple lever is lifted or depressed to open or seal the waste outlet. Their smooth surface is unobtrusive and comfortable if touched, and cannot be accidentally pulled out when bathing.

PLUG AND CHAIN
This traditional system is still popular and sold with the waste fitting.

BASIN TYPES

MOST WASHBASINS are supported on a pedestal or fitted within a countertop or washstand. These arrangements work well to conceal the plumbing, but the basin is set at a fixed height which can be a disadvantage if you are taller or shorter than average. A wall-mounted basin, however, can be attached to the wall at a height that suits you.

PEDESTAL BASINS

Available in a huge variety of styles and sizes, pedestal basins usually stand 85–90cm (34 36in) high. If you need even more height, you can raise the pedestal by standing it on a platform. Install the basin before fixing a splashback to the wall behind to ensure that the basin will not interfere in the design.

INTEGRAL STORAGE ▷
The space beneath a basin is a useful place to hide toiletries that are not used on a day-to-day basis and to store bathroom cleaning equipment. As well as boxing in the pipework, a well-designed below-counter unit can become an interesting feature in its own right and contribute to the character of the bathroom. Open storage areas in bathrooms are best kept for attractive bath products and accessories (*see p.137 and pp.142–143*).

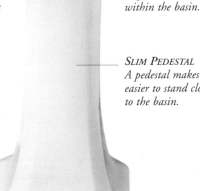

PILLAR TAPS
Crosshead pillar taps with ceramic "hot" and "cold" details complement this period style basin.

OUTER EDGE
A high outside rim keeps the water within the basin.

SWAN-NECK SPOUT
A high spout offers easy access to the washing bowl.

SLIM PEDESTAL
A pedestal makes it easier to stand close to the basin.

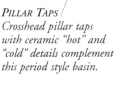

MIXER TAPS
Hot and cold water temperature and flow can be mixed with precision.

△ STANDARD MODEL
Traditional ceramic pedestals are bolted to the floor and sometimes to the bathroom wall for stability. Pedestals provide additional support for the basin and hide any unsightly pipework.

ASYMMETRIC BASIN
The platform for resting a bar of soap adds both an element of interest and practicality to this freestanding design.

REMEMBER

■ Natural wood should be treated regularly with a coat of penetrating wood oil to repel water splashes and to maintain its distinctive graining. Warmth from bathroom radiators and heated towel rails can cause warping, so place wood items away from these elements.

■ Most manufacturers of ceramic sanitaryware offer a choice of pedestal, countertop, or wall-mounted basins, and also smaller or larger than standard basin sizes.

■ Marble countertops can stain so wipe up spills immediately and buff with a soft cloth to avoid permanent damage.

COLOUR DETAIL
A gloss-painted pedestal, a smooth ceramic basin, and a wooden storage unit, make a durable and eye-catching arrangement.

STORAGE SPACE
The maple wood storage unit opens to reveal freshly laundered towels.

TOE SPACE
Feet can be tucked under for closer access.

BASIN SIZE

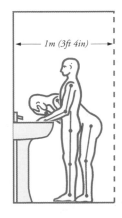

1m (3ft 4in)

Choose a basin that fits the space comfortably and leaves plenty of room to lean over and wash your face or brush your teeth without knocking into the wall behind.

WALL-MOUNTED BASINS

These space-saving basins simply need fixing to a solid wall or upright that can take the weight of the basin when it is full of water. The waste outlet is hidden within a simple syphon cover or a cylindrical "bottle-trap" (*right*). Free space beneath the basin makes the bathroom feel larger, and it can store bathroom weighing scales or a stool.

◁ NEAT FIT
The clever use of space means corner basins can be tucked into the smallest of rooms. Choose taps very carefully; large fittings will take up up too much of the wash area.

GLASS BASIN ▷
A wall-mounted basin is simple to fasten to the wall at your own waist-height for easy use (*see also p.139*).

WASHSTANDS AND DOUBLE BASINS

Traditional and modern washstands offer a range of facilities within one unit: basin, worktop, storage, shelving, and access to plumbing. The basin can be centred within the washstand with a countertop on either side, or placed off-centre to provide a larger uninterrupted worktop for keeping make-up or shaving equipment close at hand.

△ DOUBLE BASINS
Twin basins solve the problem of two people wanting to wash at the same time. A mirror running the length of the wall above the marble countertop and cupboards ensures that users do not get in each other's way.

WOODEN RAIL
Towels can be draped over the rail making a separate towel rail unnecessary.

ACCESS COVER
A removeable plate means that plumbing is easy to reach in an emergency.

△ OPEN STORAGE
Natural wood, frosted glass, stainless steel, and wicker add interest and character to this open-fronted washstand. Simple accessories and white towels keep the look fresh and uncluttered, while semi-opaque drawers mean that stored items are not forgotten but stay dust-free.

SHELF SPACE
An open shelf creates space for large and small items.

△ COVERED STORAGE
Utilitarian items including toilet paper and cleaning materials are kept to hand but are hidden from view. The cupboards are fitted with adjustable shelves for extra flexibility.

BASIN FITTINGS AND MATERIALS

THE CHOICE OF BASIN MATERIAL can add an interesting new dimension to your overall bathroom design, as many basins are now moulded in a variety of exciting shapes from specialist materials. When judging which fittings and surface finish best suit your household needs, take into account your family's washing habits, and how many times the basin is used morning and night.

DECK-MOUNTED TAPS

The ledge or rim of most basins has pre-drilled tap-holes which conform to a standard 3.6cm (1¼in) diameter. Whichever style of basin you choose, there is usually a one tap-hole, two tap-hole, or three tap-hole version to fit any tap combination be it a single-lever tap, a pair of pillar taps, or a three-piece basin mixer. When choosing, remember basin taps are smaller than bath taps.

COLOUR CODED
Blue for cold and red for hot make tap covers easy to interpret.

△ **EASY-ACTION ATTACHMENTS**
Conventional taps often require several turns to operate fully, and can be difficult for the less able and children. Attachments such as these can be gripped and twisted more easily.

▽ **SINGLE LEVER**
Monobloc basin mixer taps fit into a single tap-hole, taking up much less basin space than two- or three-piece taps. The main advantage of this design is the smooth, easy-to-operate lever that controls the flow and temperature of the water from the tap.

LEVER ACTION
A slim, "pen-like" lever is simple to manoeuvre.

CHROME FINISH
A chromium-plated finish reflects other colours in the room.

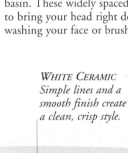

△ **PILLAR TAPS**
Basin pillar taps fit into a pre-drilled two-hole basin. These widely spaced pillar taps allow room to bring your head right down to the basin when washing your face or brushing your teeth.

△ **BASIN MIXER**
Period-style ceramic handles operate the basin mixer to blend hot and cold water. The three-piece mixer set is designed for a three-hole basin.

WHITE CERAMIC
Simple lines and a smooth finish create a clean, crisp style.

MONOBLOC TAP
The monobloc mixer tap delivers water at the desired temperature.

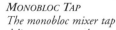

NATURAL FINISH

Wood may seem like an unusual choice of material for a basin but the water-resistant properties of marine plywood make it a good choice if you prefer something a little different. The ply has been cleverly moulded into shape by steam to form a sinuous line, then cut to provide a smooth ledge for storing basin accessories. A back panel protects the wall behind from splashes of water.

◁ SINGLE LEVER
Like other basin mixer taps, this simple design takes the guesswork out of running and mixing water to a comfortable temperature. The pipework is recessed, so that the basin can be set closer to the wall.

▽ DOUBLE LEVERS
The distinctive "pepper mill" style levers have bulbous ends to help you grip and turn them even when wet. The position of the spout is fixed so water falls directly into the basin.

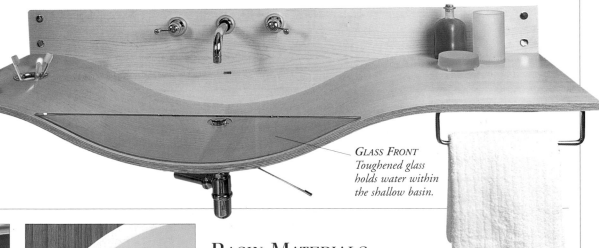

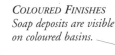

GLASS FRONT
Toughened glass holds water within the shallow basin.

BASIN MATERIALS

Ceramic basins are still the most popular choice, though the use of metal and glass designs are becoming more widespread. Marble, granite, wood, and mineral resin compounds can be custom-made to suit specific requirements but are expensive. It is also worth noting that basins set within a counter or washstand must be well fitted with the basin edge sealed to prevent water and damp from penetrating the surrounding unit. Deep, inward-sloping rather than shallow basin rims will help to protect the countertop area from stray splashes of water.

△ POLISHED BRASS
To prevent discoloration, solid brass is highly polished and the surface coated with a protective finish that resists water and scratching. Non-abrasive cleaners and buffing with a soft cloth maintains the lustre.

△ RECONSTRUCTED MARBLE
Powdered marble is mixed with resin and coloured to create a compound that feels as smooth as marble but is much stronger and stain-resistant. Numerous finishes can be chosen from plain to veined marble effects.

△ TOUGHENED GLASS
Thick safety glass is durable and scratch-resistant. It is shown off to best advantage when fixed on discreet brackets or a block of wood.

△ STAINLESS STEEL
Mirror polished stainless steel looks good with contemporary chrome taps. It wipes clean easily and is hygienic but the mirror finish can scratch so opt for a brushed stainless steel finish for heavily used basins.

COLOURED FINISHES
Soap deposits are visible on coloured basins.

CERAMIC ▷
Hardwearing and very easy to clean, ceramic basins are available in a range of colours to match any other item of sanitaryware.

WCs and Bidets

THE NEED FOR FRESHNESS, cleanliness, and hygiene dictates the most suitable materials for wc and bidet manufacture, though the designs can be as aesthetically pleasing as other items of sanitaryware. The need for water-conservation has been the driving force behind the latest designs, which combine style with environmentally friendly water-saving flush mechanisms.

VISIBLE CISTERNS

Most wcs have a cistern which is both visible and easy to access in emergencies. The cistern is usually placed flat against the wall, either above or directly behind the bowl. Elaborately ornate 19th-century cisterns can be bought independently of the bowl but, on the whole, the cistern is purchased as part of the wc suite, and includes the cistern lever or handle and flush mechanism.

◁ **CLOSE-COUPLED WC**
These wc suites are made with the cistern and bowl attached, giving the most compact of all wc designs. The cistern rests on a ledge or platform at the back of the bowl and is also secured to the bathroom wall with sturdy mountings.

SLIMLINE CISTERN
A narrow cistern allows the wc bowl to be butted up close to the wall, so that it takes up no more space in the bathroom than is absolutely necessary.

SMOOTH EDGES
The seat follows the line of the bowl and does not overlap the edges.

HIGH-LEVEL CISTERNS ▷
If you wish to install this type of wc, check that the room is tall enough; the cistern needs to sit high above the bowl, where it is connected by a long length of pipe, to create enough force for a proper flush. High-level cisterns can be noisy but new technology has produced quieter models.

EMBOSSED PANEL
A decorative panel hides ugly plumbing from view.

PULL CHAIN
Ceramic, wood, and metal handles can be chosen to match other fittings.

FLUSH PIPE
To look their best, chrome, brass, or gold-plated finishes should be mirror-polished.

REMEMBER

■ A high-level cistern requires sturdy mountings to withstand the force applied to the flush, and a strong wall to support the weight of the water in the cistern when it is full.

■ WCs with either high-level cisterns or tall panel-style cisterns will only really fit on an uninterrupted wall space, otherwise the flush pipe or cistern height is likely to obstruct bathroom windows, dado rails, or cornicing.

■ WCs and bidets need to be kept scrupulously clean, so choose models with smooth, curved lines where every area is accessible. Select wc seats with well-spaced hinges so that you can clean between the gaps.

■ The recommended position for using a standard height wc is leaning forward with your feet tucked slightly back to emulate a squatting position.

GOOD POSTURE

Place the wc so that there is sufficient headroom.

The wc bowl should be low enough for your feet to rest flat on the floor when sitting. There should also be headroom for a man to stand upright.

WCs with Hidden Cisterns

Back-to-wall and wall-mounted wcs both use a cistern that can be installed behind a false wall or panelling so that only the flush lever remains visible. The cisterns are usually plastic and set at a minimum height of 80cm (32in).

BACK-TO-WALL WC ▷
With germ-harbouring surfaces hidden away, back-to-wall designs are both hygienic and unobtrusive. Manufactured in brushed stainless steel, the bowl is easy to keep clean, while the adjacent floor and wall area can just be wiped over, making this a good choice for busy family bathrooms.

PRISTINE FINISH
Stainless steel is less likely to stain and take on odours.

◁ WALL-MOUNTED WC
Unlike back-to-wall wcs, wall-mounted designs sit above floor level. The weight of the wc and the person sitting on it has to be borne by the wall and mountings alone. Wall-mounted wcs work well in small bathrooms as they keep the floor area free and easy to clean.

COMFORT FACTOR
With wall-mounted designs, you can have the bowl fixed at a height that suits you.

Personal Hygiene

Bidets are an invaluable aid to personal hygiene. Place them alongside the wc so that they can be used after going to the wc. They should be comfortable to sit on, so take care to choose a bidet with a curved rather than angular rim, and one that is wide enough to support both thighs and bottom.

BIDET MIXER
The directional nozzle also makes rinsing out the bidet much easier.

PEDESTAL BIDET ▷
Bidets mounted on pedestals are also useful for washing feet or the dirty hands and knees of young children. For this reason, it is practical to have towels close at hand and a non-slip floor surface where splashes can be quickly wiped up.

STRONG DETAIL
Select a bidet with a solid pedestal and a chunky outline for classic good looks.

◁ WALL-MOUNTED BIDET
Wall-mounted designs keep the bathroom floor clutter-free so that it can be kept scrupulously clean. The raised rim also prevents water from spilling onto the floor, while the colourful tap-heads introduce a novel element to the functional.

WC Seats

Seats come in many finishes, but standard fittings mean that they can be fastened to most wc bowls. Ideally, the wc seat should have a raised rim at the back so that when you are seated, the body is tilted forward into the squatting position.

△ LESS-ABLED SEAT
This specially designed seat raises the level of the rim so that it is easier to sit down.

◁ POLISHED WOOD SEAT
A wooden seat is often more comfortable than plastic and feels warm. Here, carved out "leg spaces" support the thighs.

JAZZY SEAT ▽
A new range of wc seats made from colourful laminated plastics livens up the wc.

◁ FAMILY SEAT
Smaller members of the family tend to slip through adult-sized wc seats. This flexible adaptor has both a child seat and an adult seat. It helps to make time spent toilet training easier.

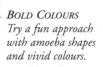

BOLD COLOURS
Try a fun approach with amoeba shapes and vivid colours.

BATHROOM STORAGE

SPACE FOR STORING a range of products is often limited in bathrooms, but if it is well planned you can have shelves and open units to display attractive bottles and jars, plus areas behind closed doors for utilitarian items, such as toilet tissue. Here, medicines can also be hidden from view, and out of reach of small children.

△ OPEN STORAGE TROLLEY
A three-tiered trolley stores towels, toiletries, hair-grooming equipment, and cosmetics where they can be seen. It is easily moved to the activity area where the products are needed. Check that the trolley can glide across the floor and that the drawers do not stick.

FREESTANDING STORAGE

Bathroom cabinets and shelf units that stand alone take up valuable floor space, which can be a problem in small rooms. If this is the case, look for a cabinet that is raised above the floor, so that items can be tucked underneath, or select a unit with glass shelves which will look lighter.

STATIC STORAGE ▷
Take advantage of spaces where sanitaryware will not fit to place a tall storage unit. Towels, soaps, and accessories can be attractively displayed.

COMPARTMENT SPACE
Items kept within closed compartments are less susceptible to dust.

STORAGE HEIGHT

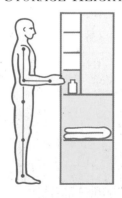

Items taken out frequently, to use morning and night, should be kept at the front of a wall cabinet, somewhere between waist-height and eye-level. Bulkier items, such as towels and cleaning equipment are best kept on lower shelves.

△ CLOSED STORAGE TROLLEY
If you prefer closed storage, a trolley with some covered units may be more useful so that bottles and jars of varying heights will be able to fit within the confines of the sections.

ADJUSTABLE HEIGHT
Shelf heights can be easily adjusted to suit the items you wish to display.

WALL STORAGE

Apart from areas taken up by windows and doors, blank walls in small bathrooms present marvellous storage opportunities. Shelves and wall cabinets leave floor areas clear, and every item can be stored within arm's reach, just above or below eye-level. Try to avoid deep shelves so that items do not become lost or forgotten at the back.

◁ **OPEN SHELVES**
Gradated shelf units – where the lowest shelf is shallowest – will not obstruct the bathroom occupant at shoulder-height. Choose a style that is easy to keep clean and dust-free.

FROSTED GLASS
Less decorative items are hidden behind a semi-opaque door but can be identified.

STREAMLINE SUPPORTS
Glass shelves and slimline brackets do not clutter up the limited wall space.

◁ **CUPBOARD STORAGE**
A mix of everyday items on display will clutter up countertops and look unsightly. Hide them from view by storing them in an attractive cabinet with a child-proof safety lock.

REMEMBER

■ A bathroom can reveal a great deal about its owner. If you share it with others, or visitors are likely to use it, keep your personal products hidden from view to avoid embarrassing yourself or your visitors.

■ Mirrored cupboard fronts often have magnetic catches, making handles unnecessary. This leaves a clear, reflective area that gives the impression of additional light and space.

■ Piles of neatly folded towels look great in a bathroom but they need to be kept fresh and aired or they will become damp and start to deteriorate.

UNDERCOUNTER STORAGE

In compact bathrooms, built-in basins and freestanding washstands with storage space beneath the sink area make good sense. Shelves should be easy to slide in and out so that you can adjust their height at will, as most toiletries, cosmetics, and toilet tissue vary enormously in size. It is also advisable to place very small items in containers so that they do not fall out every time you open the door. Access to plumbing under the basin is vital, a leak in this storage area could ruin items, such as cotton wool.

◁ **UNDERCOUNTER CUPBOARDS**
Melamine-faced units are easy to clean and can withstand knocks in bathrooms subject to heavy traffic. Use plastic containers to keep delicate items, such as cotton-wool, dust-free.

BOTTLE SAFETY
A rail holds bottles in place and prevents them from falling out when the door is opened or closed.

PEDESTAL STORAGE ▷
A contemporary freestanding basin balances both aesthetic and practical needs. The conical-shaped pedestal tapers to the ground so that it occupies less floor space, and is fitted with storage shelves.

TAP FEATURE
A pop-up waste mechanism is fitted under the basin.

BASIN DESIGN
A shallow basin sits neatly on top of the conical pedestal.

HEATING AND VENTILATION

NOTHING DESTROYS THE PLEASURE of a warming bath or shower more than having to step back into a cold room or dry yourself with damp towels. Wet skin is particularly sensitive to a drop in temperature, so heating and ventilation are important considerations when designing the room to make time spent in the bathroom, particularly during the colder winter months, an enjoyable part of your daily routine.

FREESTANDING HEATING

Radiators are the easiest and most widely used method of heating a bathroom because they are virtually maintenance-free. Other freestanding options – which look fabulous in traditional bathrooms – include coal-burning stoves and gas-fired fuel-effect designs. Both of these need adequate ventilation to prevent condensation.

BALL JOINTS
For a classic touch, choose high-polished finishes and ball joints.

△ HEATED TOWEL RAIL
Useful for drying out and warming up towels, most heated rails should not be relied upon to heat the bathroom too. Install a wall radiator as well for this purpose.

REMEMBER

■ Floor-mounted radiators and towel rails can take up valuable space and restrict your movements. You should be able to bend down and dry your feet without your body coming into contact with the rail.

■ Electrically heated towel rails can be operated from outside the bathroom on a timer device. Pre-set the timer to warm towels when they are likely to be needed.

■ Cold bathroom walls can absorb heat and reduce the effectiveness of the radiator. Try fixing an aluminium pad to the wall behind the radiator to reflect heat back into the bathroom.

■ If the radiator is situated under a window on an outside wall, choose curtains or blinds that finish just above it. This will prevent heat from the radiator from going to waste by becoming trapped between the window and the fabric.

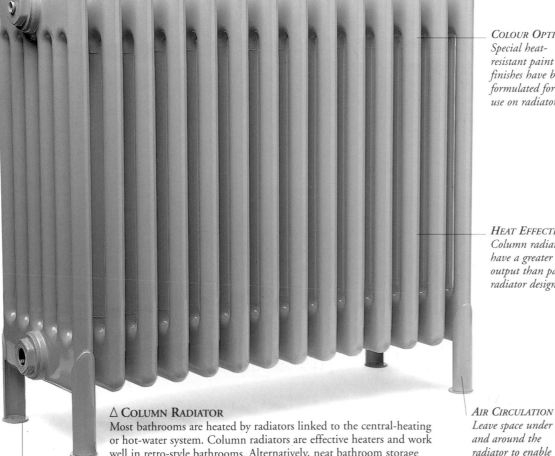

COLOUR OPTIONS
Special heat-resistant paint finishes have been formulated for use on radiators.

HEAT EFFECTIVE
Column radiators have a greater output than panel radiator designs.

△ COLUMN RADIATOR
Most bathrooms are heated by radiators linked to the central-heating or hot-water system. Column radiators are effective heaters and work well in retro-style bathrooms. Alternatively, neat bathroom storage heaters can be installed to work on cheap-rate electricity.

AIR CIRCULATION
Leave space under and around the radiator to enable warm air to circulate.

METALLIC FINISHES
The rail is available in brass, chrome, and nickel finishes to match existing bathroom fittings.

△ RADIATOR TOWEL RAIL
If you only have space for one heater, choose a combination radiator that works in conjunction with your heating system and also has a rail for warming towels. Place the radiator so towels can be in easy reach of the bath or shower.

Space-saving Heating

It is surprising how much wall space a radiator or heated towel rail occupies – space that could well be used for an additional item of sanitaryware or storage. Several discreet, dual-purpose heaters are now on the market that will fit into the smallest of spaces. Some can be incorporated into the bath panel while others fit into the kickspace under a storage unit.

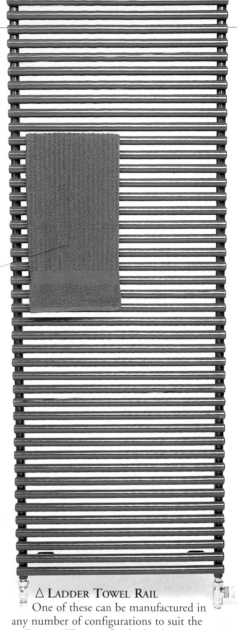

△ Wall Heater
A fan heater will provide warmth within moments of being switched on. Look for additional features, such as a choice of speed and heat settings, and a shaver socket.

Towel Space
Make sure that the spaces between the rails can hold the largest of your towels.

◁ Heated Panel
Panelling around baths is purely cosmetic, but some manufacturers produce a low surface temperature panel that will also keep bath water warmer for a longer period.

◁ Plinth Heater
Take advantage of "dead" space under bathroom units by installing a plinth radiator. The slim panel design is connected to the existing hot-water central-heating system, and also works as a fan during the summer months. Booster settings will rapidly take the chill off a bathroom as the hot air rises from ground level to warm the room.

△ Heated Shelf
Towels placed on the shelf are kept warm and aired with a heater element. Placed directly below a bathroom mirror, the heater element will also reduce misting and condensation.

△ Ladder Towel Rail
One of these can be manufactured in any number of configurations to suit the wall space. They are finished in heat-resistant metallic or plain colours. Towels can be hung at a height that is practical for the user.

Ventilation Systems

Good ventilation is required in bathrooms because insulation and double-glazing are so effective in modern homes that moisture-laden air does not disperse after a hot, steamy bath or shower. Instead, the moisture condenses on the walls causing damp and mould growth, as well as fabrics to rot and wallpaper to peel.

◁ Light Extractor
A build-up of steam in a shower cubicle tends to block out the light. To overcome this problem, install a low-voltage ceiling light in the shower unit. Choose a system that has a built-in extractor fan to suck away the steam.

△ Heat Recovery
A heat exchanger saves 80 per cent of heat that is expelled into the air with moisture; it transfers heat from warm out-going air to cold incoming air.

Airflow in a Bathroom

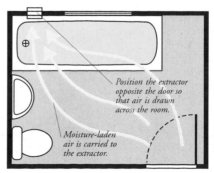

Position the extractor opposite the door so that air is drawn across the room.

Moisture-laden air is carried to the extractor.

Fitting an extractor fan to the outside wall is a simple way to expel air quickly from the room and reduce steam and condensation; ducting is a more complicated alternative.

FITTED BATHROOM PLAN

ALL BATHROOMS BENEFIT from good planning, as key items of sanitaryware have to be fitted into a limited area without the user feeling cramped. A fitted design capitalizes on every available space from floor to ceiling. All pipework and ducting is boxed in, and slim storage units are shoe-horned into narrow spaces. Mosaic and melamine offer durable finishes in bold colours and present simple, clutter-free surfaces in both wet and dry areas.

SLIM UNIT
A fitted cupboard, set between the windows at eye-level, stores soaps, shower gels, and shampoos close to the bath.

Fitted bath   Wall-mounted wc   Mosaic counter

INTERNAL ROOM DIMENSIONS:
2.4m (7ft 8in) wide
2.7m (8ft 8in) long

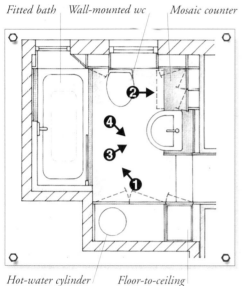

Hot-water cylinder   Floor-to-ceiling shelves

△ BIRD'S EYE VIEW
Windows above the bath and wc filter daylight into the room. The wc is against the outside wall for access to the soil pipe. Other items are built in so as not to obstruct movement in the room.

OPTICAL ILLUSION
A wide, sloping sill balances the small window frame with the larger one next to it.

SANITARYWARE
A white bath, wc, and basin look clean and simple within this bold colour scheme.

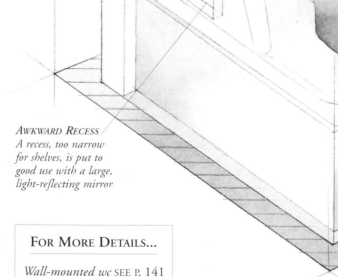

AWKWARD RECESS
A recess, too narrow for shelves, is put to good use with a large, light-reflecting mirror.

△ ❶ BATH SURROUND
The back wall is just long enough for a full-sized bath to be fitted against it. Dazzling blue mosaic tiles provide a hardwearing, waterproof surface for the back wall and bath edge, while a mirror fitted into the recess reflects light from the window keeping the area bright and open.

FOR MORE DETAILS...

Wall-mounted wc SEE P. 141

Wall storage SEE P. 143

Opaque glass SEE P. 289

Mosaic tiles SEE P. 297

BATH SURROUND
Mosaic provides a waterproof ledge on which to place washing items.

❷ SMALL DIVISIONS ▷
Most bathroom products are
packaged in small containers and
tubes, so individual cupboards
divided up by shelves keep them
tidy, easy to find, and less likely
to become lost or forgotten.

DISCREET CUPBOARDS
Personal items and medicines
are hidden behind push-open
panels without handles.

BASIN HEIGHT
A semi-countertop
basin is sunk into
the surface so that
the basin sits at a
suitable height.

FLOOR-TO-CEILING
STORAGE
A slim unit with
adjustable shelf
heights stores
bathroom towels
and toilet tissue.

△ ❸ SPACE SOLUTIONS
The basin is off-set to the right of the fitted units to
provide a large area of mosaic worktop to the left on
which to place items in use. The orange panelling beneath
the basin neatly conceals the plumbing and has space for
storing essential bathroom cleaning materials. To the left
of the basin, a large wooden linen box slides open to
collect dirty laundry. Like the rest of the cupboards, there
is no handle on the linen box to interrupt the simple,
fitted look; instead it opens by placing your finger into
the cut out "finger-hole". The mirror magnifies the room
making it appear much larger than it actually is.

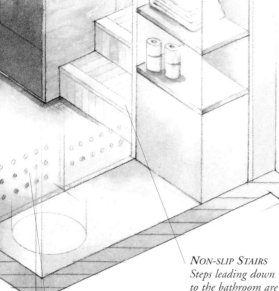

NON-SLIP STAIRS
Steps leading down
to the bathroom are
trimmed with a
non-slip edge to
prevent accidents.

AIRING CUPBOARD
Decorative holes in the
plywood doors allow air
to circulate around the
hot water cylinder inside.

DESIGN POINTS

■ Strong blocks of colour work
best where there is plenty of
natural daylight to maintain
a fresh, spacious environment.

■ Marine plywood can be used
throughout bathrooms as it is
water-resistant. Alternatively,
use standard plywood and coat
the natural wood finish in
yacht varnish; this will protect
it from water splashes and
humidity which can cause the
wood to warp.

■ Back-to-wall wcs and bidets
require panelling to hide away
the pipework and plumbing
mechanics of each item. This
often creates storage space
within the area boxed in, and a
top edge that serves as a useful
shelf for accessories.

△ ❹ PRACTICAL MATERIALS
All the surfaces have been constructed out of materials
that suit bathroom conditions, are inexpensive, and
are readily available; water-resistant paint finishes for
the front of the units and window surrounds, plywood
for the airing cupboard, and mosaic. The result is an
interesting and original fully fitted bathroom.

FITTED BATHROOM IDEAS

△ WALL-TO-WALL VENEER
A rich veneer clads the walls, cupboards, and drawers to produce a uniform effect which ensures the back-to-wall wc panel and varying height units blend unobtrusively. Sets of drawers contain toiletries and accessories, leaving surfaces clear for decorative items. Areas that could become wet or marked are finished in marble, which is both practical and attractive.

△ FITTED HEATING
Primrose-yellow panelling is chosen throughout the bathroom to make it appear brighter and larger. Fitted units and open shelves make good use of space below the basin, and a panel heater in the "kickspace" makes a wall radiator unnecessary.

◁ LESS IS MORE
Simple chrome fittings ensure that the beauty of the natural wood and marble can be fully appreciated. The two basin recesses, cut out of a marble worktop, echo the straight lines and symmetry of the wall cupboards. Diffused lighting reflects in the wall-to-wall mirror.

MARBLE SIMPLICITY ▷
A single sheet of pale grey marble is fitted along the length of the left wall with a basin set to one end to maximize the countertop area. The same finish is applied to the end wall and the bath surround, creating continuity as well as an attractive hardwearing surface; spillages must be wiped up or marble may stain.

UNFITTED BATHROOM PLAN

UNLIKE FITTED BATHROOMS, where cabinets fill every space from floor to ceiling, the unfitted plan takes a more relaxed approach. Here, furnishing the bathroom like a boudoir with a comfortable armchair and other pieces of furniture, not usually associated with bathroom design, is encouraged. With a large bath as the focus, this room becomes a special place in which to unwind.

WINDOW TREATMENT
A plain roller blind softened by drapes provides warmth, style, and privacy.

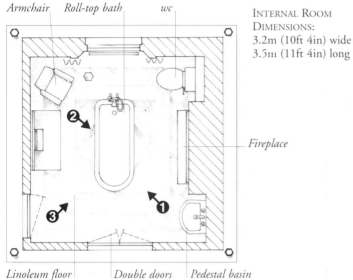

Armchair   Roll-top bath   wc

INTERNAL ROOM
DIMENSIONS:
3.2m (10ft 4in) wide
3.5m (11ft 4in) long

Fireplace

Linoleum floor   Double doors   Pedestal basin

△ BIRD'S EYE VIEW
The bath sits in the middle of the room in front of a traditional cast-iron fireplace. An alcove to the left of the fireplace houses a close-coupled wc; the alcove on the right has a pedestal basin.

△ ❶ ROLL-TOP BATH
A beautiful piece of furniture in its own right, an antique roll-top bath can be placed at any angle in the room because the plumbing is concealed within metal shrouds that rise up from the floor. This bath has been positioned in front of the fireplace and makes a wonderfully bold focal point.

ARMCHAIR
A big comfortable chair provides a place to relax following a luxurious bath.

CHEST OF DRAWERS
Towels and toiletries are stored in deep drawers, while cosmetics, brushes, and a mirror sit on top.

FIREPLACE
The coal-burning fire creates a cosy, intimate atmosphere when lit.

ANTIQUE DETAIL
A mahogany wall shelf adds to the "furnished" look of the room.

DESIGN POINTS

■ Unfitted bathroom designs also work with contemporary sanitaryware and furniture.

■ Exploit architectural features, such as alcoves and fireplaces to add extra character to the room.

■ Details, such as pictures, fresh flowers, and candles, contribute to the "furnished" look.

■ Polish wooden furniture to protect it from bathroom humidity and water splashes which cause wood to warp.

SHELF UNIT
A brass gallery shelf displays a selection of bottles and jars.

△ ❷ PERIOD STYLE
The alcove to the right of the fireplace is large enough to accommodate a full-sized pedestal basin with "elbow room" and wall space above for a shelf and cabinet. Brass taps and other fittings have been chosen to reinforce the period theme. The deep ochre painted walls create a warm backdrop for the white sanitaryware and pale fireplace surround, and also show off the mahogany furniture to best advantage.

FOR MORE DETAILS...

Freestanding bath SEE P. 128

Pedestal basin SEE P. 136

Linoleum flooring SEE P. 293

FLOOR DETAIL
Cut to resemble a period tiled floor, linoleum provides warmth underfoot.

△ ❸ BATHING ATMOSPHERE
The importance of lighting for setting the atmosphere in a room is often under-estimated. Here, the roll-top bath and other pieces of furniture are lit by the warm glow of the candlelight and firelight which creates a soothing environment for bathing. For some, candlelight may seem an impractical choice. Low-voltage halogen downlights operated from a dimmer switch (outside of the room) may offer a more practical solution; halogen downlights are both neat and unobtrusive, and will cast a bright light for everyday tasks.

UNFITTED BATHROOM IDEAS

△ CLEAN LINES

Diagonally placed sanitaryware offers an interesting alternative layout. The bath's position contrasts with the horizontal lines of the windows and doors in the adjacent room, while the monochromatic colour scheme creates a strong visual link, and gives a sharp, clean-cut look to this stylish bathroom.

△ SET PIECE

A large limed oak linen press with panelled doors and raised cornice is the focal point of this traditional bathroom. The press is placed on a wall opposite the bath, so that the fresh towels and toiletries are only a few steps away. The freestanding clothes horse, washstand, and large oval mirror create an air of elegance.

◁ CLASSIC COMFORT

Dark wood and antique furniture turn this bathroom into an informal, comfortable room that blends easily with the classic sanitaryware and flooring. A weeping fig tree in the corner has architectural proportions and creates a natural screen between the bathroom and the bedroom, when the adjoining doors are open.

FUN AND FUNCTION ▷

Acres of space in this warehouse flat allows an adventurous bathroom layout. There are no hard partitions or walled-in areas to inhibit one's movement. When privacy is needed, an area can be divided off with a striped screen. Two stainless steel washstands and a clever division of space mean that more than one person can use the room at once.

IMPROVISED BATHROOM PLAN

EVEN WITH LIMITED FUNDS, it is possible to apply the ergonomic principles of bathroom design and produce excellent results. Rather than pulling out your existing sanitaryware and starting from scratch, assess what you like and dislike about the bathroom. Perhaps by just changing the lighting or bath and basin fittings you can create a space that is a pleasure to use.

Low-level wc   Fitted bath

OPAQUE GLASS
Inexpensive to fit, opaque glass offers privacy and a modern finish.

◁ **BIRD'S EYE VIEW**
This narrow bathroom contains a rectangular bath, pedestal basin, and wc, with enough space between each item to use them comfortably. It benefits from a large window on the end wall that lets in natural light.

Basin

Linen basket

INTERNAL ROOM DIMENSIONS:
1.5m (4ft 9in) wide
3.1m (10ft 1in) long

△ **❶ WORKING SPACE**
If existing sanitaryware is in good condition, there is no need to change it. Replacing small details, such as the seal around the bath and renewing or whitening tile grouting can make all the difference, giving a room a new lease of life.

LOW-LEVEL WC
The original low-level wc remains against the exterior wall. The pipes have been repainted to give them a fresher look.

FOR MORE DETAILS...

Basin fittings SEE P. 138

Lighting SEE PP. 288–291

Linoleum SEE P. 293

Tiles SEE P. 297

LINOLEUM TILES
New buff-coloured tiles are laid on a hardboard base; they must be glued down well or water may cause them to lift.

PAINT FINISH
Specially formulated bathroom paint is inexpensive and reduces the chance of condensation and mildew forming.

MIRRORED CABINET
A cabinet that doubles up as a mirror offers a budget solution to storing products used on a daily basis.

WALL TILES
Half-tiled walls provide a durable waterproof surface where needed.

DESIGN POINTS

■ Unless the layout of the bathroom needs improving, leave the sanitaryware in place, as removing it could cause unnecessary expense.

■ Updating the bath and basin fittings alone can transform the look of sanitaryware at a fraction of the price of a complete refit.

■ New white grouting can improve the look of old tiles.

■ New blinds and curtains divert attention from a dull view.

△ ❷ NEW TECHNOLOGY
Old taps and fittings lose their mirror brightness over time and limescale builds up on the surface making them look permanently dirty. Tap-holes are pre-drilled to a standard size, so it is simple to replace old bath and basin taps with new ones that have the latest technology (*see p.135*). Plugs and wastes can also be changed.

LINEN BOX
A wooden linen box adds style and can also double up as a bathroom stool.

△ ❸ IDEAS IN ACTION
A central ceiling light has been removed to make way for chrome halogen downlights which are low-voltage and operated by a pull-cord, so safe to use in bathrooms. Arranged in pairs, the lights accentuate areas over the bath, wc, basin, and doorway. A mirror-fronted cabinet and long mirror on the opposite wall also help bounce light around the room. As an inexpensive alternative to a combined radiator towel rail (*see p.144*), a chrome rail has been fixed over the panel radiator so that towels can be warmed while the room is being heated.

IMPROVISED BATHROOM IDEAS

△ BRIGHT DESIGN
Plain white tiles are inexpensive and widely available. When teamed up with brightly coloured ceramics, paint, and towels, the finished effect is fun and upbeat. Here, old cabinet doors have been replaced with fabric to match the ceramics.

STENCILLED STARS ▷
If it is not within your budget to change the design of your bathroom to suit your needs, transform its appearance by stencilling the walls, floor, and ceiling. On a larger budget, clever wood panelling and lighting can make a huge difference.

◁ MEDITERRANEAN UPDATE
Painting the bathroom is one of the least expensive ways to instantly improve its appearance. Here, deep blue and sea foam colours make a focal point of the white bath, while a beachcomber's hoard of stones and pebbles, arranged under the bath, create an artistic finishing touch.

▽ FRESH APPROACH
Keep existing sanitaryware but clad the bathroom walls in tongue and groove panelling, painted white for a fresh look. A budget wallcovering, it helps to conceal uneven walls and ceilings. A new wc seat and taps help update old sanitaryware.

△ OLD FASHIONED FITTINGS
One way to improve a large bathroom on a restricted budget is to buy sanitaryware and fittings from an architectural salvage yard. Although supplies are not guaranteed, a hand-decorated wc, roll-top bath, and fittings can be bought for less than the cost of modern reproductions.

DUAL-PURPOSE BATHROOM PLAN

A LARGE, LUXURIOUS BATHROOM where space is given over to activities other than bathing can make good planning sense. Obvious partnerships include a bathroom-cum-dressing room where you can wash, dress, and groom yourself in privacy, or a bathroom and fitness room where you can shower after exercising, or taking a sauna.

Roll-top bath   Wardrobes   Dressing table   Shelves

Towel rail   Double basin   Bidet   wc

△ BIRD'S EYE VIEW
The bath sits in the centre of the room well away from the fitted wardrobes, shelves, washbasins, dressing table, wc and bidet. All the facilities are well spaced around the large room so that a sense of order prevails.

INTERNAL ROOM
DIMENSIONS:
3.5m (11ft 4in) wide
3.6m (11ft 7in) long

HANGING SPACE
Clothes are hung up while hats and shoes are stacked on shelves above and below.

PANELLED DOORS
The lower section of the doors are panelled to match the other walls.

METAL SHROUDS
Chrome-plated cylinders cover the pipework.

◁ ❶ SURFACE DETAIL
All the surfaces – wall panelling, door fronts, and floorboards – are painted in the same low-sheen paint finish so that they are both durable and waterproof. The wardrobe doors are panelled to look like the walls and are fitted with self-closing magnetic catches, so that they are unobtrusive when closed.

STORAGE
Shelves beneath the double basin store toiletries and cosmetics.

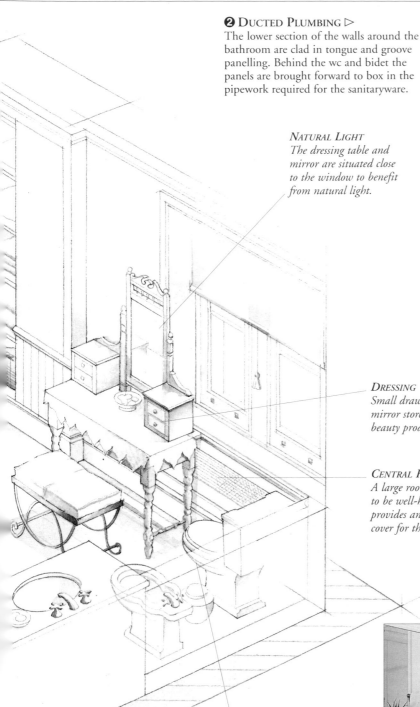

❷ DUCTED PLUMBING ▷
The lower section of the walls around the bathroom are clad in tongue and groove panelling. Behind the wc and bidet the panels are brought forward to box in the pipework required for the sanitaryware.

NATURAL LIGHT
The dressing table and mirror are situated close to the window to benefit from natural light.

DRESSING TABLE
Small drawers next to the mirror store cosmetics and beauty products close to hand.

CENTRAL HEATING
A large room such as this needs to be well-heated. A grille provides an attractive and safe cover for the large radiator.

WALL SPACE
Lining up a low-level wc, bidet, and basin unit, leaves wall space above for a mirror and painting.

FOR MORE DETAILS...

Roll-top bath SEE P. 128

WCs and bidets
SEE PP. 140–141

Heating and ventilation
SEE PP. 144–145

DESIGN POINTS

■ Leave access points in the panelling where pipework can be easily reached for any essential maintenance.

■ Painted floors can be slippery when wet so choose a suitable low-sheen finish, and provide cotton mats with non-slip backings to absorb splashes.

■ When a bath sits in the middle of a room, supply a bath rack for soap and sponge.

❸ LIGHT AND SPACE ▷
Every activity area is carefully placed so that it is just a few steps from the main activity – bathing. From the bath you can reach out and take a towel from the heated towel rail, and step out of the bath on either side to dry yourself in comfort. From here, it is just a few steps to the basin to continue your routine before getting dressed.

DUAL-PURPOSE BATHROOM IDEAS

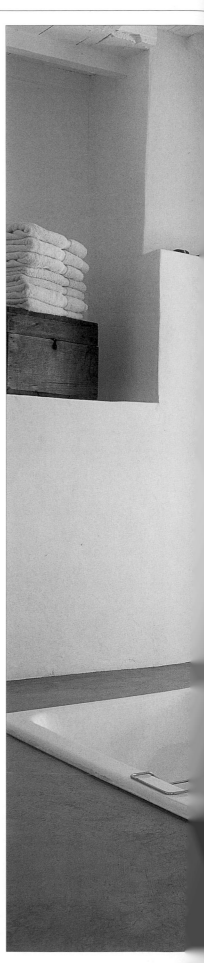

△ BATHROOM-CUM-SITTING-ROOM
Space beneath the window has been fitted with a sofa and plenty of cushions, to create a comfortable, quiet place in which to relax and read a book or magazine. It also enables other family members to sit in and catch up on the day's events with the bath's occupant.

▽ BATHING UNDER THE EAVES
This converted attic space remains open plan so that the pitched ceiling and beams can be fully appreciated. Separate zones have been allocated for a breakfast and dressing table, while the bath occupies centre stage.

△ CLOTHES-WASHING IN STYLE
Partitioning off a section of the bathroom to install a washing machine makes good use of the existing plumbing. For the laundry area to blend with the adjacent bathroom fittings, the machine alcove, like the other walls, are painted a pale colour.

SIMPLE RELAXATION ▷
Two floor levels in one room present the opportunity to create a special bedroom-cum-bathroom. The close proximity of the bath to the bed makes it easy to slip effortlessly from one to the other, which is particularly enticing when you are tired or simply want to relax.

CHILDREN'S BATHROOM PLAN

CREATING A BATHROOM for young children which is both fun and safe to use is simple as long as you are aware of a few basic principles when planning and fitting the room. For example, fit child-proof locks to cupboards, ensure there are no sharp edges around the bath and basin area, choose a non-slip flooring, and have plenty of water toys to keep the users happy.

Standard bath   *Storage*   *Part-enclosed wc*   *Wall shelf*

Tiled surround   *Steps*   *Recessed basin*

△ BIRD'S EYE VIEW
The bath and basin sit flush against the walls so that no element juts out which may be knocked. The wc area is screened off but accessible, and steps help children reach the basin.

INTERNAL ROOM DIMENSIONS:
3.2m (10ft 4in) long
2.5m (8ft 1in) wide

△ ❶ PRIVATE CORNER
The partitioned-off wc area offers a degree of privacy for young children but because there is no door, they cannot accidentally lock themselves in. Intended for children learning to use a grown-up wc independently, this allows adults to easily help if the child needs it.

FOR MORE DETAILS...

WC seats SEE P. 141

Storage SEE PP. 142–143

Heating and ventilation SEE PP. 144–145

Rubber flooring SEE P. 293

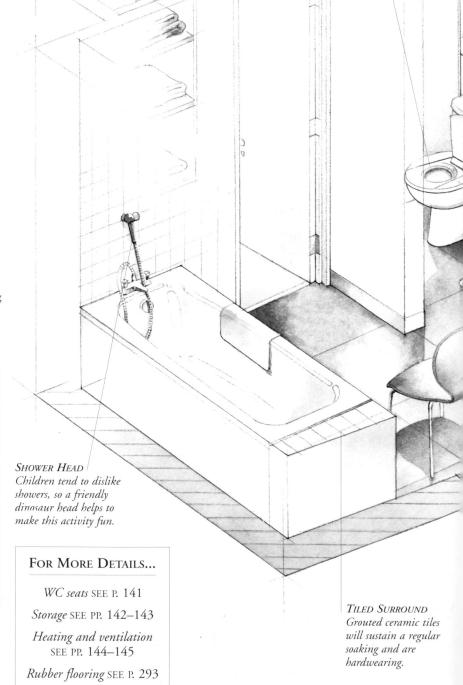

CHILD'S SEAT
Bolted on to a standard size wc, the small seat can be replaced when the child is older.

SHOWER HEAD
Children tend to dislike showers, so a friendly dinosaur head helps to make this activity fun.

TILED SURROUND
Grouted ceramic tiles will sustain a regular soaking and are hardwearing.

❷ USING THE BASIN ▷
Brushing teeth or washing hands can be difficult when taps are hard to reach. A step that will not topple over and can be moved around as required will encourage children to perform their morning and bedtime routine independently.

WALL CUPBOARDS
Choose a unit that locks to keep toiletries and medicines out of children's reach.

COUNTERTOP
Rounded edges and an easy-clean finish are essential.

LAUNDRY BIN
A brightly coloured fabric laundry bin can be tucked under the countertop, out of harm's way.

WOODEN STEPS
Choose a sturdy but light design that children can move into place.

CHAIR
Install a chair for adults supervising bathtime and for towel-drying children sitting on their lap.

DESIGN POINTS

■ Provide a laundry bin to encourage children to deal with their dirty clothes rather than leaving them strewn all over the bathroom floor.

■ A cold bathroom will make children grumble and resist baths; warmth, fresh towels, and water toys will go a long way to overcoming their dread.

■ Flooring should be chosen for its resistance to accidental spills and splashes, and should be soft and warm enough for children to walk on barefoot.

❸ BATH SAFETY ▷
To make bathtime as safe as possible for young children, choose a bath with a curved edge so that little hands can get a grip when climbing in and out of the bath. Fit a brightly coloured grab rail for children to hold on to when standing up in the bath, and place a rubber mat on the enamelled bath bottom to make it less slippery.

CHILDREN'S BATHROOM IDEAS

△ DEVELOPING SKILLS

With the help of your children, paint murals on ceramic bath tiles to make bathtime fun. Use cold ceramic paints that are easy to apply and durable once fully dry.

◁ FUR EFFECT

Add a touch of humour by painting a cow print or tiger print on the side of the bath. Alternatively, a mix of bright colours, spots, and squiggles will make it fun to use.

△ CUT-OUT CREATIONS

Cut-out superheroes and TV characters bring instant colour to bare walls, while red rubber flooring and red wc seat, blind, and pipework appeal to children. Colour-coded plastic jars keep soaps and sponges tidily.

3-D DESIGN ▷

Clever ideas transform this colourful bathroom into an underwater kingdom children will treasure. All the decorative surfaces are varnished so that they are waterproof and can be wiped clean when necessary.

SHARED BATHROOM PLAN

COMMUNAL BATHROOMS with a shower, a bath, and a double basin unit need not be very large but they must be well planned. There should be space around the sanitaryware so that the user does not feel too cramped, and a plentiful supply of hot water to feed the shower, bath, and basins so that they can be enjoyed by different members of the family at the same time. An efficient heating and ventilation system to heat the room and extract steam is also essential.

◁**❶ CORNER DETAIL**
This discreet area, tucked around the side of the shower, is practically planned; the bottom shelves keep toilet tissue next to the wc, while a wall radiator warms towels which are easy to reach when you step out of the bath.

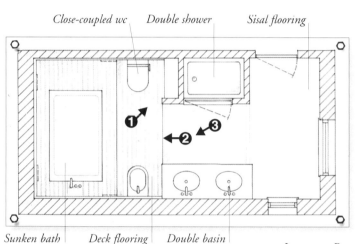

Close-coupled wc   *Double shower*   *Sisal flooring*

Sunken bath   *Deck flooring*   *Double basin*

△ **BIRD'S EYE VIEW**
In this large room, two runs of sanitaryware sit opposite one another along the walls; the double basin and bidet are placed opposite the shower and wc. The sunken bath, set within a cedarwood platform, at the far end of the bathroom, creates an inviting focal point.

INTERNAL ROOM DIMENSIONS:
2.7m (8ft 8in) wide
5.5m (17ft 9in) long

GLASS SHELVING
Space left at the side of the shower is fitted with glass storage shelves.

WALL LIGHTS
Sealed lights are waterproof and shatterproof, making them an ideal choice for this setting next to the bath.

LIFT-UP SECTIONS
A tiled surface below the decking means that the wood planks can be lifted out and the area beneath cleaned.

◁**❷ EFFECTIVE LIGHTING**
The simplicity of this two to four person sunken bath benefits from its bright position beneath a clear glass skylight which can be opened wide on bright days. At night, a far more subtle lighting effect is achieved by recessed wall lights; these cast a soft glow for relaxing, intimate evenings.

SCENTED WOOD
When splashed with water, the cedarwood releases a fabulous woody aroma.

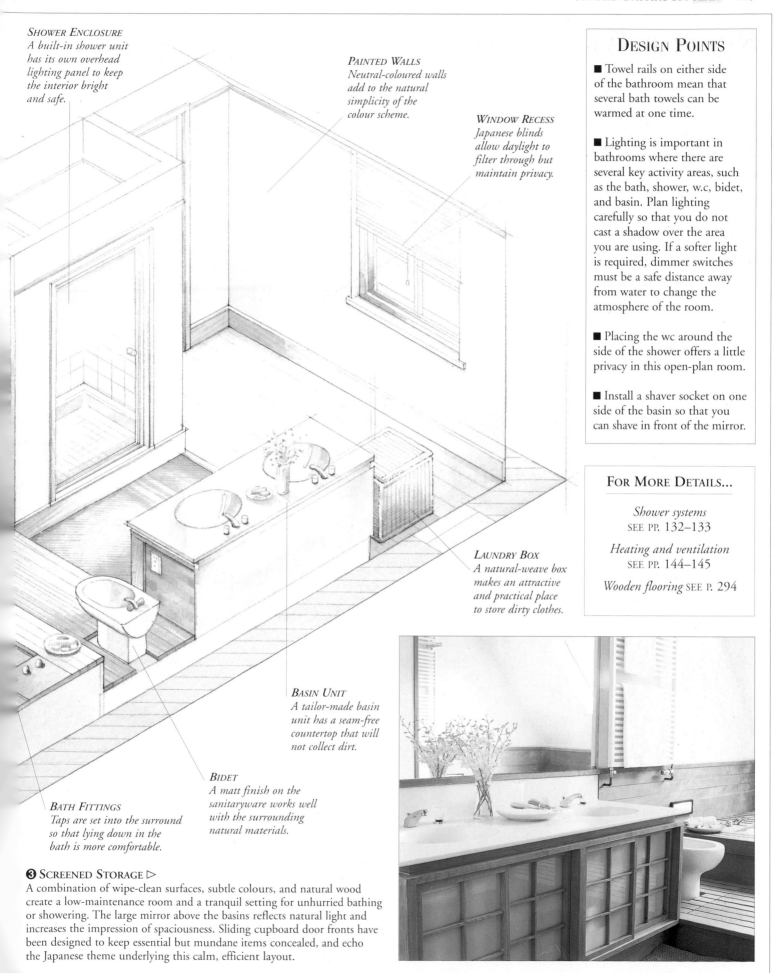

SHOWER ENCLOSURE
A built-in shower unit has its own overhead lighting panel to keep the interior bright and safe.

PAINTED WALLS
Neutral-coloured walls add to the natural simplicity of the colour scheme.

WINDOW RECESS
Japanese blinds allow daylight to filter through but maintain privacy.

LAUNDRY BOX
A natural-weave box makes an attractive and practical place to store dirty clothes.

BASIN UNIT
A tailor-made basin unit has a seam-free countertop that will not collect dirt.

BIDET
A matt finish on the sanitaryware works well with the surrounding natural materials.

BATH FITTINGS
Taps are set into the surround so that lying down in the bath is more comfortable.

DESIGN POINTS

■ Towel rails on either side of the bathroom mean that several bath towels can be warmed at one time.

■ Lighting is important in bathrooms where there are several key activity areas, such as the bath, shower, w.c, bidet, and basin. Plan lighting carefully so that you do not cast a shadow over the area you are using. If a softer light is required, dimmer switches must be a safe distance away from water to change the atmosphere of the room.

■ Placing the wc around the side of the shower offers a little privacy in this open-plan room.

■ Install a shaver socket on one side of the basin so that you can shave in front of the mirror.

FOR MORE DETAILS...

Shower systems
SEE PP. 132–133

Heating and ventilation
SEE PP. 144–145

Wooden flooring SEE P. 294

❸ **SCREENED STORAGE** ▷
A combination of wipe-clean surfaces, subtle colours, and natural wood create a low-maintenance room and a tranquil setting for unhurried bathing or showering. The large mirror above the basins reflects natural light and increases the impression of spaciousness. Sliding cupboard door fronts have been designed to keep essential but mundane items concealed, and echo the Japanese theme underlying this calm, efficient layout.

SHARED BATHROOM IDEAS

△ OPPOSITE CORNERS
Placing the bath and the shower opposite one another ensures that conversations can continue when both are in use. Planned space for bathrobes and essentials has been designed for each user to keep their belongings within easy reach.

△ ANGLED LAYOUT
A corner bath and shower butted up against one another make full use of the space, allowing two people to use the room in comfort. Basins placed side by side with storage below keep the area clutter-free.

△ DOUBLE SHOWER
A large double shower unit, rather than a single shower and bath, may be more suited to your lifestyle. It can save on water consumption and speed up time spent in the bathroom. It can be shared with a partner or muddy children can be piled in to wash. Choose hardwearing ceramic tiles for the interior, especially if the shower is frequently used.

SPACE TO MOVE ▷
Although it is possible for two people to share a standard-sized bathroom, it may be cramped. Here a spare bedroom is converted into a luxuriously large shared bathroom. Space out the items of sanitaryware so that each piece is easy to access. Plan the space to allow for a large freestanding bath, shower, and a chair for towels and clothes.

UNUSUAL SHAPE BATHROOM PLAN

THE INCREASING demands of homeowners for ensuite bathrooms often means that in a house the largest bedroom is divided up, or a bathroom is squeezed in under the eaves. Both of these solutions can leave you with an irregular-shaped room with little natural light. Imaginative planning, however, can ensure that the sanitaryware is well situated, and that irregular walls and odd angles are an asset, not a drawback.

ROOF SKYLIGHT
Light filters through a roof panel in each partition, making the bathroom brighter.

MOSAIC TILES
Lining the shower area, mosaic protects the walls from damp.

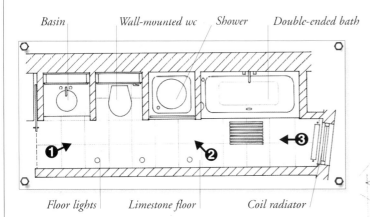

Basin   *Wall-mounted wc*   *Shower*   *Double-ended bath*

Floor lights   *Limestone floor*   *Coil radiator*

△ BIRD'S EYE VIEW
A long, narrow space under the gabled roof has been cleverly divided to create a galley-style bathroom. All the sanitaryware sits in a row along one wall for an uncomplicated plumbing run, while a corridor along the length of the room connects the different activity zones.

INTERNAL ROOM
DIMENSIONS:
1.6m (5ft 2in) wide
4.9m (15ft 9in) long

△ ❶ ALL ON ONE SIDE
Placing the basin, wc, shower, and bath along the left-hand side of the room, while keeping the right-hand side of the bathroom free to walk between each item, is inspirational planning. Partitions create identities for each activity zone without the need for doors, so the room feels light and spacious.

SLIDING DOOR
A space-saving sliding door opens and closes without interrupting the basin area.

PARTITION
The wall offers privacy while allowing air to flow freely.

FLOOR LIGHTS
Sealed halogen units are safe for bathroom use as they are low voltage and water-resistant.

❷ SHOWER INTERIOR ▷
The shower cubicle stands in the middle of the roof area – where the ceiling is highest – so that there is ample room for showering. The cubicle is subjected to a regular soaking so the walls are clad in mosaic tiles for a hardwearing, waterproof finish, which combined with quality door seals prevents water seepage.

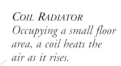

ROLLER BLINDS
Blinds take up little space and allow diffused light to pass into the room.

SLOPING CEILING
A bath under the eaves makes good use of space; you sit up without hitting your head.

COIL RADIATOR
Occupying a small floor area, a coil heats the air as it rises.

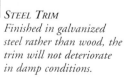

STEEL TRIM
Finished in galvanized steel rather than wood, the trim will not deteriorate in damp conditions.

FOR MORE DETAILS...

Shower and bath fittings
SEE PP. 134–135

Limestone flooring
SEE P. 295

Mosaic wallcovering
SEE P. 297

---

❸ DESIGN DETAIL ▽
Stone flooring is water-resistant and is ideally suited to heavy-wear areas such as the narrow passage between each item of sanitaryware. Sealed floor lights sunk into the limestone tiles are shatterproof, and produce a soft diffused light that illuminates the length of the walkway and adds character.

DESIGN POINTS

■ Showers fit into most small and awkward areas but make sure they are well lit or they can be hazardous.

■ Good ventilation is essential – even more so when space is limited and air-flow restricted. Plan the position of the extractor fan opposite the door where it will draw fresh air in.

■ Keep colours and patterns simple in a small bathroom, and avoid fussy fittings.

UNUSUAL SHAPE BATHROOM IDEAS

△ CORNER SOLUTION
If you do not have the wall space to fit a standard bath, a corner bath may solve the problem. A shower rose and curtain rail suspended over the bath mean that it can double up as a shower cubicle; the curtain can be pulled to one side to let light in.

▽ MEZZANINE FLOOR
A good architect will pay dividends when faced with a studio conversion. Here, a high-ceilinged room is divided up to create a spectacular ensuite bathroom on the upper level. A tensile steel structure offers a strong platform for the fittings.

△ DEEP TUB
A deep bath tub makes the best use of space in a small room. A bath and shower mixer tap offers a sit-down shower option. Shelves and a towel rail make use of the wall space, and an offset basin leaves room for the door to open.

△ IRREGULAR LEVELS
The floor of this bathroom drops deeply into a small recess, making the perfect place to sink a bath. Once lying down in the bath, the windows are no threat to privacy. Clear glass roof panels allow light to flood into this small room.

SUNKEN BATH ▷
Recessing a bath into the floor is an imaginative way to create the illusion of space. The underside of the bath is cushioned for protection, and the weight of the marble walls and tiles are taken by the solid floor. Glass blocks replace the window, filtering the light.

HOME OFFICE

INTRODUCTION

OUTDOOR OFFICE △ ▽
For George Bernard Shaw, the Irish dramatist, this simple summer house served as a secluded home office where he was freed from distraction and able to make the most of fresh air and fine weather.

ORKING FROM HOME is not a new phenomenon: it is, of course, the original work environment, having evolved from the artist's studio, the man of letter's study, the scholar's library, and the writer's den. Looking at some famous examples of historical home offices may provide inspiration for your own. One of my favourites is Vita Sackville West's library/writing room in a tower at her home in Sissinghurst, Kent, with fine views of her famous garden, pale walls, kelim-strewn floors, and books everywhere in handy reach of her chair. A simpler, less-cluttered favourite is Ernest Hemingway's retreat in Cuba

– a separate writing tower next to his villa in San Francisco de Paula, Cuba – where he could climb up to work in a single room containing only a wooden chair, desk, telescope, mug of pencils, and a few hunting trophies. The Irish dramatist George Bernard Shaw's summer house (*see left*) is also simple, apart from an ingenious rotating mechanism under the floor, which allowed the writer to enjoy all-day sunshine.

But working from home is no longer just a dream that can be realized only by the talented few. A combination of new technology and rationalization of working practices, along with demands for a better quality of life, means that more and more people work from home; recent estimates suggest that worldwide, the figure is around 40 million and growing.

CHANGING WORK PRACTICES

As the nature of work changes, the nine-to-five "battery chicken" approach to working in commercial offices has, for many, become outmoded. In any case "jobs for life" are no longer guaranteed, nor even desired; short-term contracts are commonplace, and many people expect to have a number of jobs over their working life. Many companies now contract out their services, employing consultants instead of full-time staff to provide specialist skills. These consultancies are often one-person set-ups that can be operated successfully from home. A growing number of companies, inspired by the increasing sophistication of computer and communication systems, have come to realize the value of teleworking, allowing staff to work

◁ INDIVIDUAL STYLE
Colour, pattern, personal objects, and domestic-style furniture combine to create an informal and stimulating work environment that is far removed from the standard commercial office.

ABOUT YOU

Consider these basic questions relating to your personality to help you create a successful method of home working and a suitable home office environment.

☐ Are you used to a sociable office? Do you find other people's input stimulating? If so, when working at home, would you enjoy sharing your office?

☐ Are you a tidy worker? Do you clear your desk when you stop work? Or, do you need to screen off your office area after work?

☐ Are you easily distracted by other people, household chores, or phone conversations with friends? If so, would working in total privacy, away from intrusive phonecalls, be helpful?

☐ Do you plan to set formal hours for working, such as 9am to 5pm, or would you prefer more flexible hours? Do you have the self-discipline to work irregular hours?

either full or part time at home, and to keep in touch with the parent company by computer and telephone links. Organizations now exist to give advice on teleworking.

Working at home is not merely a business decision but an important lifestyle choice. It can radically transform the way you work, the way you spend your leisure time, and how you view your home. For large numbers of workers who have to combine work with bringing up children, it provides a flexible and manageable solution to childminding problems.

Current research shows that for some people, work is no longer the be-all and end-all of life. There has been a change in priorities for many of today's workers, who believe there is little

point in working twelve hours a day, six days a week if you are too tired or have no spare time to enjoy spending the money you earn. Home working, however, can fit in with other areas of your life, such as family commitments and entertaining friends, allowing you greater flexibility and the freedom to work from 6pm to 6am, or in your pyjamas, if that is how and when you are most productive.

The increase in severe cases of stress, repetitive strain injury, and so-called "sick-building syndrome" – all modern afflictions associated with unhealthy office environments – have resulted in the health-conscious worker demanding a work environment that respects the user and is as pleasant and stress-free as possible.

△ MODULAR STORAGE
Work files and storage need not be dull and messy. The availability of colourful folders and box files, and of stylish, modular storage units like these, ensures that filing can be kept both neat and attractive.

And the conditions people are demanding in the office can often be most easily satisfied at home.

A well-designed home office is the ultimate expression of personal choice, embodying the power to create an environment that is specially designed to meet your individual needs, idiosyncracies, and tastes. It can provide all the facilities of a commercial office plus the many advantages of being at home, such as choice of decor and colour scheme, good natural light, comfort, and personal control.

THE ROLE OF ERGONOMICS

Your home office should be designed with practicality as well as comfort in mind. The perfect environment to aid creativity and productivity requires careful planning and analysis – in other words it needs to be designed ergonomically. Ergonomics is the study of the relationship between workers and their environment, particularly the equipment they use. In practice, it means choosing the right desk and chair and positioning furniture and equipment to maximize efficiency and minimize physical effort and discomfort.

By considering your work patterns and requirements before making any decisions, you will not only save yourself needless time and expense but, more importantly, you will avoid strain and injury from using badly designed or incorrectly positioned products. Think about how you work, how long you spend at your desk, how often you go out, and what items you need around you. Think, too, about how long you will spend working at home. What are your

SHELF STORAGE ▽
The desk is kept clear by placing accessories and task lamp on a wall unit, which includes a noticeboard below the storage sections.

priorities in terms of furniture and equipment, and what can you afford to spend? Look at other offices and notice what you like and dislike about them. Borrow ideas and inspiration from others, look in magazines and catalogues to see what is new, and, just as importantly, examine your home carefully to see whether any existing items of furniture can be adapted for office use.

WHERE IN THE HOME?

Choosing the right space to convert into your home office is important. If you plan to work full time at home, then most of your day will be spent there, so choose a space that can be made attractive and welcoming, not some dank, dark area that is inadequate for any other function. The space you choose may be dictated by your work needs: for example, illustrators and designers prefer good, even light, so a loft space or rear extension with ample natural light would be ideal. On the other hand, if your work

MOBILE STORAGE ▷
Look for functional products that retain a domestic scale and finish, such as this blue plastic trolley with four storage drawers.

requires supplies of heavy materials that have to be carried back and forth, then lofts and upper floor offices would be ruled out as potential locations. Position your office on the quieter side of the house if possible, away from utility areas such as laundry rooms, particularly if you need peace and quiet to concentrate. If you are considering converting a basement, remember that areas without good sources of natural light and ventilation can be depressing, tiring, and unhealthy to work in. Views can be either inspiring or distracting: looking out onto a busy street scene may make concentration difficult and turn you into a nosey neighbour.

Employing others at home can bring additional problems. Check local regulations about the number of people who can work in your home before health and safety regulations come into force. Think, too, about whether you would find it irksome to have colleagues traipsing through

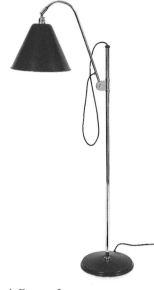

△ FLOOR LAMP
An adjustable floor lamp provides a good source of task lighting without taking up valuable desk space. It must have a heavy base to ensure stability.

WHAT DO YOU WANT FROM YOUR OFFICE?

Before committing yourself to expensive furniture and equipment, analyze your work patterns and lifestyle and how you intend to use your new office. To help you decide what will work best for you, consider the benefits of the work spaces shown below.

❶ Light and views

❷ Warmth and domesticity

❸ Simplicity

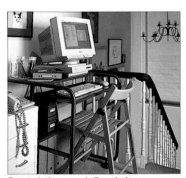

❹ Mobility and flexibility

❺ Ability to conceal

❻ Order and efficiency

△ ADAPTABLE STORAGE
Fibreboard storage boxes, such as these, provide a flexible, hardwearing, yet inexpensive storage system for your home office. The boxes, in a range of sizes, can be bought individually and stacked to allow for expanding needs.

your home, and bear this in mind when deciding where to set up your office. Remember, too, that if co-workers want to get into work early, you will probably want to be up and dressed – a constraint that may detract from the freedom of working from home.

HOME-WORKING PSYCHOLOGY

Creating the correct environment is essential, but so too is developing the right attitude towards working at home. For those who have gone from working five days a week in a frenetic open-plan office, surrounded by colleagues, suddenly being on one's own can come as a shock. Most home workers admit to finding the lack of social interaction difficult, and cite this as the main drawback to working at home. Many break up their day by visiting clients, shopping, or playing sports, which bring them into contact with other people. Some have even set up networks with other home workers whom they can meet regularly during the daytime.

Although the telephone or e-mail is not always an adequate substitute for direct human contact, most home workers spend more time on the phone than other workers, partly through the need to talk to someone. Friends, who wouldn't dream of disturbing you if you were at work in a commercial office, feel that they can call you at anytime when they know you work at home, thereby creating distractions and loss of concentration. A separate business telephone line can help, as can urging your friends to leave you in peace during office hours.

Starting work each day can be the hardest part. A friend of mine can begin working in his home office only if he dresses in formal office clothes, leaves the house at a regular time, walks round to the back door, and then heads for his home office. An extreme example perhaps, but getting into the right frame of mind and being disciplined is vital when you work at home.

Keeping your home office sacrosanct can help, for example by banning family members and demanding pets during office hours. There are endless distractions at home so, if you know that you lack self discipline, make sure that you keep possible temptations out of sight.

THE RIGHT CHAIR ▷
Ergonomic consideration is vital in both your choice of task chair and in ensuring that it is positioned correctly to support your lumbar region and prevent backache. The chair should move with you as you move, whether you are leaning forwards over your desk, or leaning back to stretch tired limbs.

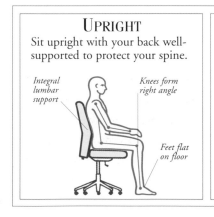

UPRIGHT
Sit upright with your back well-supported to protect your spine.

Integral lumbar support

Knees form right angle

Feet flat on floor

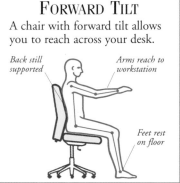

FORWARD TILT
A chair with forward tilt allows you to reach across your desk.

Back still supported

Arms reach to workstation

Feet rest on floor

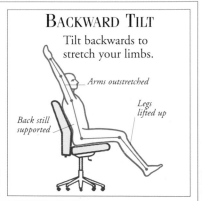

BACKWARD TILT
Tilt backwards to stretch your limbs.

Arms outstretched

Back still supported

Legs lifted up

◁ **STABLE CONVERSION**
A former stable has been transformed into a delightful, light and airy studio space. The original tethering post has been retained, adding to the studio's character.

The temptation to keep working, when time is money, can be overwhelming. But being able to work anytime should not mean that you work all the time. Learning to switch off can be difficult, especially if your carefully designed home office is such a wonderful space that you don't want to leave it. Some home workers set themselves a maximum number of working hours per day. Some stop when a partner who works elsewhere returns home. Don't become a slave to your home office, it should help you to work more efficiently, creating more time for other activities. If one of your reasons for setting up a home office is to spend more time with your family, remember not to equate working at home with being at home. Avoid arranging meetings in the evenings, and anything else that will interfere with your home life routine. It is very important to know when to switch off.

Everybody has their own way of working and only you can decide what your needs are and what works best for you. The French novelist, Marcel Proust, used to work in a room with the shutters closed and the curtains drawn – but not everyone has to go to such lengths to work effectively at home. This chapter concentrates on the practical factors that you need to consider when setting up a home office, and suggests general pointers that might help you to work more efficiently, happily, and safely.

CHOOSING YOUR OFFICE STYLE

Part of the fun is deciding how you want your office to look, especially as there is no need to recreate the look of a commercial workplace. Consider carefully the style and type of furniture you need, and plan where everything is to go before indulging in a spending spree. If your budget is limited, check around your home for little-used items that can be recycled into your office, such as kitchen chairs for meeting chairs, bedside lamps for ambient lighting, or a music-

△ **STACKING STOOLS**
Spare seating taken from elsewhere in your home, such as these stacking stools, can double as temporary seating when clients or colleagues visit your office.

TUB CHAIR ▷
Compact and comfortable,
this tub chair, upholstered in
bright red leather, provides
ideal seating for a relaxed
business meeting.

INTEGRATED OFFICE ▽
A modern, open-plan flat
offers the opportunity to
create a home office that is
integrated into the main
living space, while still
providing partial visual
separation and privacy.

centre as a printer or fax stand. Visit local junk shops and second-hand office furniture suppliers: respraying or reupholstering will transform your bargains. Select your colour scheme, integrating items such as files, furniture, and accessories to create a coordinated office. Invest in extra files of the same type to maintain the look of your office in case they are discontinued. And remember: home working is a positive lifestyle choice, offering freedom to control your working environment and flexibility in how you work.

Appreciate planning a tailormade home office that reflects your style and personality, and caters for your specific work needs as well as fitting in with your other commitments. Pamper yourself with a luxury item, be it a leather chair or espresso machine. And don't rush decisions, you may be working with the results for a long time. Enjoy the process, it is an exciting challenge.

SARAH GAVENTA

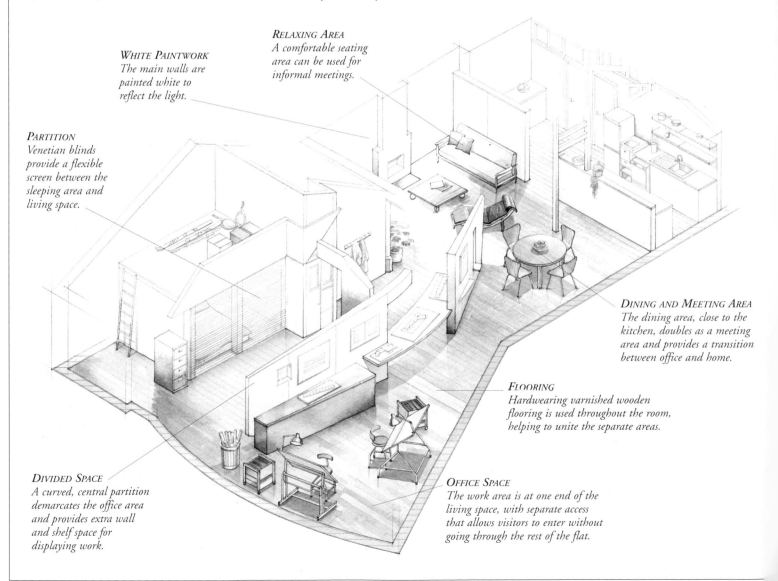

RELAXING AREA
A comfortable seating
area can be used for
informal meetings.

WHITE PAINTWORK
The main walls are
painted white to
reflect the light.

PARTITION
Venetian blinds
provide a flexible
screen between the
sleeping area and
living space.

DINING AND MEETING AREA
The dining area, close to the
kitchen, doubles as a meeting
area and provides a transition
between office and home.

FLOORING
Hardwearing varnished wooden
flooring is used throughout the room,
helping to unite the separate areas.

DIVIDED SPACE
A curved, central partition
demarcates the office area
and provides extra wall
and shelf space for
displaying work.

OFFICE SPACE
The work area is at one end of the
living space, with separate access
that allows visitors to enter without
going through the rest of the flat.

PLAN OF ACTION

If you plan to convert part of your home into an office, you will have to coordinate the work of architects, builders, and electricians. Before starting on alterations, use this checklist to ensure you have not overlooked important requirements.

☐ Have you received permission from the relevant authorities for structural alterations?

☐ Will you need professional help to convert your office?

☐ Have you estimated costs correctly and checked that delivery dates will allow you to have a fully functional office from the start?

☐ If your budget is tight, could you build a desk rather than buy a ready-made one?

☐ Is your office design flexible enough to allow for your work to adapt and grow?

☐ Will your alterations detract from the value of your property?

☐ While building is in progress can you work elsewhere in the home?

◁ **TRADITIONAL STYLE**
If you do not require a lot of equipment, a traditional study area may be sufficient. In this comfortable space, books and files are concealed behind simple drapes.

ASSESS YOUR NEEDS

THE FOLLOWING QUESTIONS will help you to focus on the major issues affecting where you place your home office, how you furnish it, what equipment you require, and the type of office environment that best suits you and your lifestyle.

FURNITURE

Investing in well-designed office furniture is vital for a safe and comfortable working environment. Your starting point should be the choice of task chair – the most important tool in your office.

■ SEATING

☐ Do you spend more than two hours every day seated at your desk? If so, have you budgeted for an ergonomic chair?
☐ If you intend to employ people to work in your home office, have you checked office seating regulations?
☐ Do you suffer from backache? If you do, have you considered a chair with specialist back support?
☐ Do you require extra seating for clients and meetings, or could you use your dining-room or kitchen chairs?
☐ Will you need to seat clients or guests for long periods of time, or will stacking chairs or stools be adequate?
☐ Do you need to store away your chair after work? If so, is it sufficiently mobile to be easily moved?
☐ Have you investigated which type of task chair castor will best suit the flooring in your office?

■ WORKSTATIONS

☐ Do you have a special routine or method of working that requires expansive worksurfaces for planning, organization, reference, and layout?
☐ Can you use or adapt an existing piece of furniture, such as a dining-room table for your desk, or do your require a specially designed worksurface?
☐ Do you require constant access to storage and reference material from your workstation? If so, do you want your worktop linked to storage facilities?
☐ Would you prefer a fitted workstation or do you want the flexibility of a freestanding desk?

☐ If you want to easily conceal your workstation, would you prefer a complete, closeable office unit or to section off your work area behind a screen?
☐ If your home office is situated in a living area, would a mobile desk be useful?
☐ If you need a large work area, would an L-shaped desk with a return be helpful?
☐ If you use a laptop, do you actually need a fixed workstation?

■ SURFACES AND FINISHES

☐ Does your type of work require a particularly hardwearing worksurface?
☐ Is the existing floor covering suitable for office furniture? If the room is carpeted, is the pile too thick for castors to work properly?
☐ Does the floor covering provide a measure of acoustic control?
☐ If you are working with electrical equipment, have you considered a non-static floor covering?
☐ Do you want all your surface finishes to coordinate, for example, to match wooden floors with a wooden desk?

MEETING AREAS

Think about the type of meeting area you require: formal or informal, permanent or temporary, large or small. How frequently will you receive visiting clients or colleagues? Will you regularly be meeting more than one person at a time?

☐ Have you considered the type of impression you want to make on clients or visitors, for example, informal and creative or business-like?
☐ How many people will be working in your office or visiting on a regular basis? If you are going to have frequent visitors, have you considered what facilities you would like to offer?
☐ Is it important to you that your meetings do not intrude on your home life and vice versa?
☐ Do you have the space for a dedicated meeting area, or do you need to adapt other rooms in the house, such as the kitchen or dining room?
☐ Do you want easy access to amenities, such as coffee- or tea-making facilities or the telephone, during meetings?
☐ Would it be useful to create a waiting area for visitors?
☐ Do you require additional space and specialist equipment for displays and presentations?

STORAGE

Think about your present storage requirements, and how much material you will accumulate over six months, then over a year. Work out which items you use frequently, which you use only occasionally, and which you can place in archive storage.

☐ Are there files and equipment that you use every day that need to be close to your workstation? Are there any heavy or large items that you can successfully store out of reach?
☐ Would you prefer your stored items to be visible or concealed?
☐ Do you require secure storage for valuable goods or cash?
☐ Does your regular work involve storing over-sized items, such as plans?
☐ Do you work with many documents that need long-term storage? Have you planned for archive storage space?
☐ Do you require secure archive storage or would wooden or cardboard boxes be sufficient for your needs?
☐ Have you specific paper size requirements which would affect your choice of storage systems?
☐ Do you need fireproof storage for precious files?
☐ Are there some items you would prefer to hide behind closed doors?

LIGHTING

Correct levels of lighting while you work help to reduce eyestrain, headaches, and fatigue. Your lighting requirements vary according to the type of work involved, and the quality and quantity of natural light the office receives. Office outlook will also have a bearing on how the room is best lit.

☐ When making your choice of work area, have you thought about whether you prefer natural or artificial lighting?
☐ Is the quality of natural light in the room good, or should you consider adding a window? Would a new window raise the level of natural light without taking away valuable wall space?
☐ Can you position your desk to take advantage of natural light while avoiding glare on your computer screen?
☐ Is it important that your work area is well-lit with task lamps?
☐ Would your environment be improved by atmospheric lighting?
☐ Are you short of floor space? Have you considered desk and wall lamps?
☐ Do you need to simulate daylight for your work?
☐ Have you considered using low-energy lamps to save energy?
☐ Could painting the room in a light colour make more of the available natural light?
☐ Would blinds help you to control sunlight shining in your eyes?

TECHNOLOGY

Although it it advisable to consult a specialist about your information technology requirements, consider beforehand some basic questions about space availability, electricity supply, ventilation, and safety.

☐ What office equipment will you need? Will your requirements change?
☐ Do you have the space for large office machines, such as photocopiers?
☐ Before you place your furniture, have you considered your cabling needs?
☐ Have you positioned regularly used equipment close to your workstation?
☐ Does noise bother you? Is there space to house noisy equipment away from your workstation?
☐ Would it be helpful to combine information technology, such as a joint fax and photocopier, to save space?
☐ Have you considered the heat build up from your equipment and planned to install proper ventilation?

PERSONALIZING YOUR SPACE

Working at home gives you the opportunity to personalize your space in a way that working in a commercial office does not allow. Make a list of the luxuries you would like to have around you at work. But take into account how this environment will affect your attitude to work.

☐ Do you want to bring your home into your office or do you want to create a distinct office environment?
☐ Would you like your office to reflect your personality or to remain neutral?
☐ Do you prefer working in an informal or formal atmosphere?
☐ Do you feel at home with a particular style of decor and furniture?
☐ If your office is part of a shared living area, do you want the office decor to match the style?
☐ Have you considered which colours you find relaxing and calming, and which you find stimulating?
☐ If you have children, would you enjoy being able to see or hear them while you are working?
☐ If you have pets, do you want them around you while you work?

SPACE AND ACCESS

When choosing a room or area for your office, assess its accessibility to the exterior for receiving letters, goods, and visitors, and the level of security. Access to and from your office to the rest of the house, the kitchen, and the garden is also crucial. Estimate how much space you need to fulfil your basic requirements.

☐ Is the total space big enough for your needs? Have you chosen an area that can be extended?
☐ Is there a particular part of your home to which you would like your office to be linked, such as the kitchen, garden, or living room?
☐ Is there easy access to the front door for clients and to receive deliveries?
☐ If space is limited, can you remove architectural features, such as fireplaces, to create more room?
☐ Do you plan to install expensive equipment? If so, have you worked out security precautions?
☐ Will clients have to walk through the house to reach the office? If so, is this a problem in terms of domestic privacy?
☐ Do you value quiet while you work? Is this more important than having easy access to other areas of the house?

WHERE IN THE HOME?

Your office can be successfully situated in most rooms or areas of your home; it can occupy part of a living area, have its own room, or be situated in an outbuilding. If you answer yes to several or all the questions in a particular group below, the space described may be the most appropriate one for your working needs.

■ **DEDICATED ROOM**
☐ Do you require privacy from other household members?
☐ Do you use noisy equipment?
☐ Will you be holding regular meetings or frequently using the telephone?
☐ Do you require extensive storage space for files and equipment?

■ **SHARED LIVING AND OFFICE SPACE**
☐ Is your work part-time?
☐ Do you enjoy working in the company of other family members?
☐ Do you have the house to yourself during the day?
☐ Do you have limited equipment and storage needs?

■ **DUAL-PURPOSE ROOM**
☐ Do you have a room that you use only occasionally, such as a guest bedroom or a formal dining room?
☐ Is your need for office space only occasional?

■ **OUTBUILDING**
☐ Would you enjoy complete privacy while you work?
☐ Does your work involve using noisy equipment?
☐ Have you considered the cost and possible problems involved in installing heating, and power and telephone points?
☐ Have you thought about how to make the outbuilding secure?

WHICH ROOM?

Decide on the type of office or work space that best suits your needs, such as a dedicated room or shared living and office space. Then weigh up the advantages and disadvantages of each area, bearing in mind considerations such as the amount of natural light, privacy, and ease of access.

LOFT WINDOW
If you need to install new windows in your attic conversion, make sure they can be opened to give good ventilation.

1ST-FLOOR ROOM
Good for security, this room also provides a degree of isolation from day-to-day household activities. Clients may have to walk through the house to reach the office.

GARAGE
An isolated space which is suitable for loud equipment, a garage is easily adapted for office use, although new windows may be required.

GARDEN SHED
You can enjoy privacy and quiet, but it may feel isolated. Power points and a telephone line may need to be installed.

GARAGE DOOR
If there is no door to the garage from the house, you may need to install a new garage door for easy access.

ATTIC CONVERSION
A loft has the benefit of light and good views, but temperature control, ventilation, and access may be a problem. It may need extensive work before it is suitable as an office.

BACK ROOM
Access to the garden, good light, and ventilation are bonuses. Working here is less secure but more private than the front room.

BASEMENT
A useful, often underused space which offers privacy, but may be damp, dark, poorly ventilated, and lack headroom.

FRONT ROOM
Working in the front room gives you good access to deliveries and visitors, but provides little privacy from other household members and passers by.

FRONT ROOM WINDOW
Working next to a window in a front room can pose a security problem if equipment is visible from the outside.

LONG-TERM SEATING

YOUR WORK OR TASK CHAIR is, in many ways, the most important piece of equipment in your home office. Prolonged use of an inadequate chair can result in backache, fatigue, and stress injury. Investment in a good-quality, ergonomically designed chair is essential for your health and productivity.

TASK CHAIRS

The strain on your back from sitting with a curved spine is approximately three times greater than that from standing. To minimize this, choose a chair with a back that inclines inwards to support your lumbar area, and that moves as you stretch or lean back and forwards. Ideally, the chair back should be high and wide enough to support your back and shoulders, with arm rests to take the weight off your neck and shoulders.

BACK SUPPORT
A chair with an adjustable back provides proper support for the user, whatever their height.

PRACTICAL FABRICS
Choose a chair with a hard-wearing wool or polyester fabric cover. A removable cover is easily cleaned or replaced to fit a new colour scheme.

◁ **TOTAL ADJUSTABILITY**
This chair has much to recommend it as a task chair: it is height-adjustable, it tilts backwards and forwards, and it has a wide supportive back, padded seat, integral lumbar support, and stable five-star base.

PADDED SEAT
A rounded, padded seat edge helps to relieve pressure on your legs.

DIVERSITY
Ergonomic office chairs are now available in a wide range of colours and fabrics.

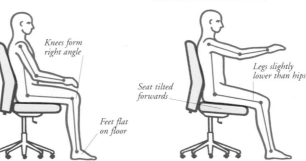

STABILITY
Maximum stability is provided by the five-star base, which allows you to move around freely without fear of the chair tipping over.

MOBILITY
A heavy chair is easier to manoeuvre if fitted with castors.

REMEMBER

■ Make sure that your task chair complies with national regulations, especially if you employ someone at home.

■ Allow about 1m (39in) of floor space between the desk and another piece of furniture or wall, so that you can get in and out of your chair easily.

■ Think long-term and choose seating that is likely to stay in production. Otherwise, if your business develops and you have to expand your office, you may end up with odd chairs.

CHAIR ADJUSTABILITY

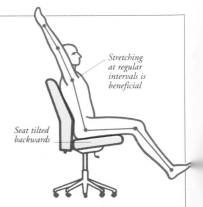

Knees form right angle

Feet flat on floor

Seat tilted forwards

Legs slightly lower than hips

Stretching at regular intervals is beneficial

Seat tilted backwards

UPRIGHT POSITION
Place your feet flat on the floor or on a footrest, so that your legs form a right angle. Allow enough space for a fist between the seat edge and your knees.

FORWARD TILT
A chair with forward tilt allows you to reach across your desk without tipping up the chair. It also lets you occasionally sit with your legs lower than your hips.

BACKWARD TILT
With an adjustment allowing backward tilt, you can stretch tired limbs and reach objects at the side of the desk without tipping the chair over.

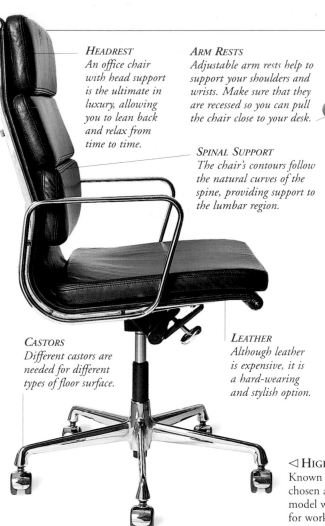

HEADREST
An office chair with head support is the ultimate in luxury, allowing you to lean back and relax from time to time.

ARM RESTS
Adjustable arm rests help to support your shoulders and wrists. Make sure that they are recessed so you can pull the chair close to your desk.

SPINAL SUPPORT
The chair's contours follow the natural curves of the spine, providing support to the lumbar region.

CASTORS
Different castors are needed for different types of floor surface.

LEATHER
Although leather is expensive, it is a hard-wearing and stylish option.

STATE-OF-THE-ART FABRIC △
Upholstered in a fabric that allows air circulation, good support, and even weight distribution, this chair is designed to adjust to the user's range of movements, providing proper support at all times.

◁ **HIGH-BACK CHAIR**
Known as an executive chair, and often chosen as a status symbol, this high-backed model with head support is a good option for workers who spend much of the day on the telephone or talking to people.

ACCESSORIES

For workers using an ergonomic task chair, accessories are unnecessary. However, if you use a household chair, or already suffer from back problems, adding a wedge cushion or lumbar roll can give extra comfort and help to prevent back strain.

△ **BACK SUPPORT**
A lumbar roll gives extra support to the small of the back, and helps to prevent slouching. Most attach to the chair by straps and come in removable covers for easy washing.

△ **WEDGE CUSHION**
A wedge-shaped cushion, placed on a hard seat, gives padding and comfort. Its tapered design helps to correct poor posture, in the same way as a forward-tilt mechanism.

△ **FOOTREST**
A footrest can help to relieve pressure on the thighs. It also enables you, if you are short, to keep your knees at right angles to the floor and still be at the correct height for your desk.

△ **DRAFTING CHAIR**
Higher than a normal task chair, a drafting chair enables the user to work at an angled drawing board. A well-designed drafting chair is height-adjustable, with an upholstered seat for comfort, a circular foot support, and castors for mobility.

LUMBAR SUPPORT
This drafting chair has an integral lumbar support for long-term seating comfort.

FOOT BAR
A circular bar supports the feet, helping to ensure correct posture when seated.

OCCASIONAL SEATING

ADDITIONAL SEATING, to cater for visiting colleagues and clients, meetings, and for relaxation, must be comfortable and stable. If space is at a premium, do not overlook stacking or folding chairs, which can be stored when not in use, or chairs that can be used in other parts of your home.

OFFICE-STYLE CHAIR

If you do not spend more than a couple of hours a day at your desk, a traditional office-style chair will probably be adequate. Such chairs have some ergonomic features, such as height adjustability, but will not give you full support. Avoid using kitchen or dining-room chairs for office work, as most provide no back support and will not be the correct height.

ANTIQUE ALTERNATIVE △
This upholstered nineteenth-century office chair is adjustable and has a pivoting base.

HARD SEAT
If used for long, a wooden seat can put pressure on your legs, leading to poor circulation.

WOODEN DESK CHAIR △
Natural wood is an attractive option for a modern-style office, as well as being hardwearing and easy to clean.

TYPIST'S CHAIR ▽
A traditional typist's chair, although height-adjustable, is adequate only for short-term use as the separate back section does not provide full support to the lumbar region.

FLEXIBILITY
The back section can be adjusted in height and moved in and out from the seat.

EASY TO ADJUST
The chair height is adjusted by pressing the gas lift lever.

SOFT COVER
Personalize your chair by covering it with a fabric of your choice.

CASTORS
Even a fairly light chair is easier to move on castors.

SPACE-SAVING SEATING

There is no shortage of options for space-saving seating; your choice will depend on your budget and the likely frequency of use. Well-designed, colourful, stacking and folding furniture doesn't take up valuable storage space when not in use; stacked up or hung on the wall, it can provide an attractive feature in the office.

STACKING STOOLS ▷
Stools are an excellent space-saving option as they can be stacked or stored under a table. However, they are not suitable for prolonged sitting as they provide no back support.

STABILITY
It is worth investing in good quality, heavy stools for improved stability.

STACKING LIMIT
Stack no more than five chairs at a time to ensure stability.

STACKING CHAIRS △
Good quality, colourful seating helps to brighten up a room. You may find a trolley useful when moving around a stack of chairs.

△ **FOLDING CHAIRS**
Though folding chairs are often a cheaper option, they are less sturdy and comfortable than stacking chairs. However, to save space they can be hung on the wall where they provide a decorative feature.

SOFT SEATING

One of the advantages of working at home is that you can tailor the surroundings to your own comfort. There is no reason why you shouldn't sit in an easy chair while you are reading, or thinking, or even taking a tea break. The easy chair can double as a welcoming reception-area chair for visitors to your home office.

TUB CHAIR ▽
Small yet comfortable seating such as the tub chair is often seen in commercial office reception areas, where its compact shape saves space. A tub chair is equally suitable in a home office, providing ideal seating for a relaxed business meeting, or in a waiting area.

STYLE AND COMFORT
A reclining chair with a separate foot rest provides a superb place to read, relax, and think.

COMPACT AND COLOURFUL
Upholstered in bright red leather, this chair brings warmth to an office environment.

△ RECLINING CHAIR
Although a comfortable chair for reading and relaxation may seem like an unnecessary luxury in the office, research shows that short breaks from work, spent resting, can enhance productivity.

CUSHIONS AND COVERS
Introduce colour, warmth, and individuality into your home office with cushions, chair covers, and throws. Some suppliers will cover chairs in a fabric supplied by the customer.

INSTANT COVER
A throw provides an instant and inexpensive colour change for chairs and sofas.

SOFA BED ▷
If you are using a spare bedroom as your home office, a sofa bed can provide soft seating for visitors during the day, and a comfortable bed for overnight guests. It can also be easily reincorporated into your home if you have to change your office back into a bedroom at some point in the future.

WORKSTATIONS

CHOICE OF WORKSTATION depends primarily on the type of work you do. The needs of a laptop user, for example, will be different from those of a worker with a large array of equipment. If you work full time, you may need a large, fitted desk, whereas a part-time worker may prefer a workstation that can be concealed when not in use. Style is another consideration, especially if your office is part of a living area.

FITTED DESKS

If you want a permanent home office and need a large workstation, a fitted desk is a good choice. It can be built along an entire wall, round a corner, and be adapted to fit awkward and narrow spaces. If it has to support heavy equipment, ensure that it is fitted with strong brackets and supports.

△ ERGONOMIC CURVES
The soft lines of a curved worktop not only create a pleasing, organic look, but also make it easier to reach every part of the desk. For a cheaper version, make your own from medium-density fibreboard (MDF).

◁ FITTED L-SHAPED DESK
Ideal for computer work, this desk fits neatly into the corner of a room and makes good use of natural light. There is plenty of room for the task chair to be moved around the work area, as well as integral storage for a computer hard drive and filing.

AREA OF REACH

Sit at your desk and stretch out your arms

75cm (29½in)

Make sure that frequently used equipment, such as the telephone, keyboard, and current files, are within easy reach. For most people this will be about 75cm (29½in) from their body when seated.

DESK EDGES

The choice of desk edges is important, not just because of the way they look, but also because sharp or uneven edges can cause injuries to you, your clothing, and to your equipment. Most desk manufacturers offer a choice of at least three desk-edge options – usually straight, bullnose, and waterfall.

△ STRAIGHT
Although still a very common option, a sharp, straight edge can cause injury and split rubber cables.

△ BULLNOSE
A more rounded edge, known as a bullnose, is less likely to dig into your arms, or to chip.

△ WATERFALL
A tapered edge, such as the waterfall, helps protect against injury, but it chips more easily than a bullnose.

FREESTANDING DESKS

Unlike the fitted desks most commonly associated with commercial offices, traditional desks, such as secretaires (with an upper cabinet) and kneehole desks, have an established place in the home. They are available in a range of styles, from hi-tech to traditional, and in a variety of materials, from glass and steel to different types of wood.

DRAWERS
Shallow drawers are useful for storing stationery and writing equipment.

ROLL-TOP COVER
Simply pull down the roll-top cover to conceal evidence of the day's work.

STORAGE COMPARTMENTS
Small cubbyholes provide easily accessed storage space for work materials.

PULL-OUT DESK
A convenient pull-out worksurface slides smoothly out and in as required.

△ ROLL-TOP DESK
Known as a roll-top because of the slatted wooden cover that rolls down to conceal work equipment and files, this compact desk is suitable for workers who need only a limited workstation. With its simple, elegant lines and warm, wooden finish this desk will look equally at home in a study or living room.

△ KNEEHOLE DESK
Solid desks such as these can be expensive and difficult to move because of their weight, but generous storage space is provided by drawers in the two pedestals and under the worktop. Beware of using antique desks for heavy computer equipment.

ELEGANT LINES
The elegantly tapering legs continue the unbroken line from the curves holding the roll-top cover.

REMEMBER

■ As a guideline, standard measurements for desks are 73–75cm (28½–29½in) for height, and 140–180cm (4½–6ft) for length. A height-adjustable task chair will fit under most desks.

■ When choosing a desk, make sure that its surface is suitable for your work. If you need a hardwearing surface, select one that is heat- and stain-resistant, and that can be replaced or revarnished if necessary.

■ If you opt for a fitted desk, measure and list your desk-top equipment to make sure that it will all fit onto the worksurface. Drill holes in the desktop to allow power cables to feed through to sockets. Check that storage pedestals will fit underneath.

WORK TABLES

Providing the simplest and least expensive form of workstation, a table can be used for a wide range of work from computer-based to craft activities, and will probably offer you more working surface than a desk. A kitchen or dining table is suitable, but bear in mind that heavy equipment may mark polished or softer wooden surfaces.

TRESTLE TABLE ▷
If space or your budget are limited, a trestle table can provide an inexpensive workstation that is easily stored. However, trestle legs may be a little unsteady.

WORKSURFACE
The melamine surface is hardwearing, durable, and easily cleaned. It will not be marked by heavy equipment.

TRESTLE LEGS
Although they are easily stored when the desk is not required, trestle legs leave little room for under-desk storage.

COMPUTER DESKS

TODAY'S FURNITURE designers are acutely aware of the needs of computer users, and they have created desks that are not only practical but also look good. The desks come in a variety of styles, from the hi-tech to the traditional, with good cabling systems and spacious worksurfaces for equipment. Shop around – you'll find that computer desks can be more than just functional.

CONTEMPORARY DESKS

Instead of the traditional L-shaped desk, consisting of a worksurface and return for work equipment, contemporary desks have a more pleasing, organic shape, with soft curves substituted for sharp corners and unfriendly edges, and pastel shades and patterned laminates instead of grey melamine. Most also have cable management facilities, so work out your requirements and select a desk that is appropriate for your system.

BACK VIEW
The panel hides the back of the computer, unattractive cabling, and any clutter on the floor beneath the desk.

CABLE SCREEN
Power cables run through ducting in the screen to floor sockets.

GLARE PREVENTION
A non-reflective worksurface prevents glare on the computer screen.

△ DISCREET COMPUTER DESK
If most of your work is computer based, a small desk may be adequate. This model will look at home in a contemporary-style room, and has a panel to conceal cables so that the rear view is uncluttered.

MOBILE SHELF
A filing tray slots into holes in the screen. Additional trays can be added if required.

DESK SURFACE
Plastic laminate offers a hardwearing, easily cleaned worksurface.

CURVED END
A rounded, extended end provides a useful small meeting area around the desk.

PARTIAL SCREEN
The half-height screening panel offers a degree of privacy, which is useful if you work in a living area.

LEGS
Power cables from the computer are channelled through the legs of the desk.

△ ROUND-ENDED DESK
A modern version of the L-shaped desk, or desk with return, this model is large enough for computer- and paper-based work and provides discreet cable control as well as a rounded end for meetings. The matching, mobile storage pedestal can be easily moved around to suit the user's needs.

PEDESTAL
The under-desk pedestal stores computer disks and hanging files. When tucked in the corner, it leaves plenty of leg room.

MOBILE DESK

Compact, mobile computer workstations are perfect for temporary or part-time work. When not in use, they can be wheeled into a cupboard or another room. Be sure to choose a stable model that will take all your equipment, and won't topple over when it is moved. Strong castors are vital if you intend to move the desk when it is loaded with equipment.

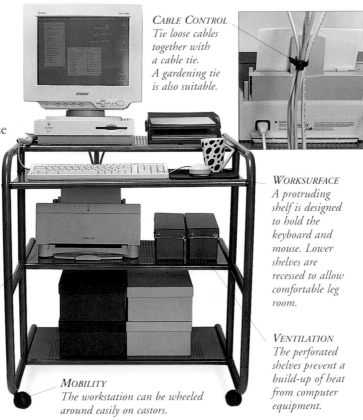

CABLE CONTROL
Tie loose cables together with a cable tie. A gardening tie is also suitable.

SHELVES
Deep shelves provide storage for a printer or fax machine.

THREE-TIER SYSTEM ▷
This cleverly designed, three-shelved work trolley holds a surprising amount of computer equipment and storage, but it has no worksurface for writing or paper-based work.

WORKSURFACE
A protruding shelf is designed to hold the keyboard and mouse. Lower shelves are recessed to allow comfortable leg room.

MOBILITY
The workstation can be wheeled around easily on castors.

VENTILATION
The perforated shelves prevent a build-up of heat from computer equipment.

CONCEALED COMPUTER DESK

If you prefer not to have your work equipment permanently on view, or if your office shares space with a living area, a concealed or disguised computer desk is the ideal option. When not in use, most of your work equipment can be stored in drawers and cupboards built into the desk. Concealing a monitor presents a problem; if you want a completely clean desk top, consider a laptop.

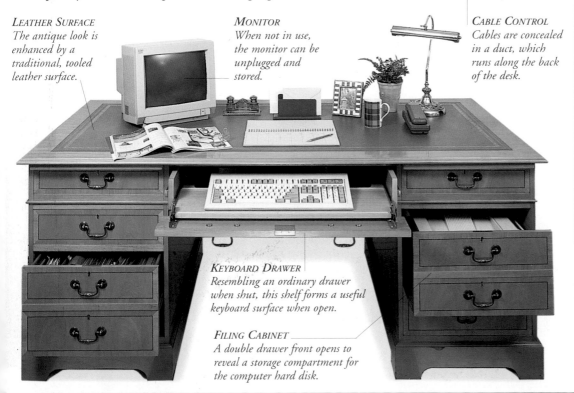

LEATHER SURFACE
The antique look is enhanced by a traditional, tooled leather surface.

MONITOR
When not in use, the monitor can be unplugged and stored.

CABLE CONTROL
Cables are concealed in a duct, which runs along the back of the desk.

KEYBOARD DRAWER
Resembling an ordinary drawer when shut, this shelf forms a useful keyboard surface when open.

FILING CABINET
A double drawer front opens to reveal a storage compartment for the computer hard disk.

COMPUTER SAFETY

Sit upright and keep your lower back supported at all times.

Tilt screen to eye level or just below, about 45cm (18in) from your face.

When working at a computer for long periods, minimize the risk of strain by holding your fingers, wrists, and lower arms in a straight line from your elbow to the keyboard.

REMEMBER

■ Establish your requirements before choosing a desk as these will affect the size of the worksurface. For example, do you need a computer with a separate hard drive, or is a laptop sufficient?

■ Do you need equipment other than a computer on your desk, such as a scanner or printer? A desk with a return or a rounded meeting end provides additional surface area for equipment.

■ Consider whether you require extra cabling facilities on your desk for your telephone and task light.

■ Some manufacturers design desks with built-in sockets hidden under a flip-up panel. These offer a neater solution than wires running across the floor to wall sockets.

◁ **ANTIQUE-STYLE DESK**
A range of desks specifically designed for computer work now offer cable management and other related facilities, disguised within a reproduction, traditional-style piece of furniture. These are available in a variety of wooden finishes from mahogany to beech.

OFFICE UNITS

SPACE EFFICIENT and increasingly popular as an alternative to the standard office set-up, office units combine a worksurface with a built-in storage facility. They are particularly useful if you have to work in the living room or bedroom and prefer to keep your work area separate from your domestic arrangements. Assess your needs first, as some units are expensive and not all are suitable for computer-based work.

MOBILE UNITS

Ranging from a complete office-on-wheels to a simple pedestal, mobile units can be closed up to conceal work equipment and moved out of the way when not in use. Smaller units are unsuitable if you have extensive computer and cabling needs, but are ideal for laptop users, workers with limited space, and part-time workers.

REMEMBER

■ Consider your cabling requirements, as most units have limited integral cable management facilities.

■ Office units are not suitable if your work demands easy access to large quantities of files, books, other reference materials, and equipment.

■ If you are considering buying a unit, make sure that it suits your needs and that it will not become redundant if your business expands. Some units, especially mobile or disguised models, are costly.

■ Remember the storage of your task chair. If your office is concealed during out-of-work hours, choose one that matches the decor or one on castors that can be wheeled out of sight when not in use.

WORKSURFACE
The small, pull-out worksurface forms the top of the unit when it is closed.

CLOSED UNIT
When closed, the unit is small enough to be stored in a cupboard or pushed under a table. Light in weight, the unit has handles and castors to provide easy mobility.

STORAGE SPACE
A drawer beneath the pull-out worksurface allows storage space for accessories and files.

△ **PEDESTAL UNIT**
Handles add to the mobility of this light unit, which combines a small worksurface with storage provision consisting of a drawer and space for hanging files.

FOLD-OUT UNIT ▽
A complete home office folds out from the trunk of this cleverly designed mobile unit. It provides ample worktop space, including a pull-out shelf for a computer keyboard or laptop, a useful privacy screen, and an extended worksurface.

CLOSED UNIT
The entire office unit, with equipment stored inside, closes into a box on wheels. The worksurface legs fold up to double as handles.

MARKER BOARD
A useful feature is the wipe-clean marker board and pen-rest.

PINBOARD
Conveniently situated above the worksurface, a pinboard holds personal and work notices.

SLIDING SHELF
A pull-out shelf provides space for a computer.

LOCKABLE WHEELS
The castors can be locked.

DISGUISED UNITS

The office-in-a-cupboard is a modern version of the traditional secretaire. When closed, it resembles a piece of domestic furniture, but inside, a compact yet comprehensive office is stored. A disguised unit is particularly useful in a dual-purpose space (*see pp.208–211*), allowing you to conceal files and work equipment within a unit or cupboard that suits different domestic environments.

EASY TO CONCEAL
Close the doors when you finish work for the day.

SLIDING SHELF
The keyboard remains in place when the shelf is pushed in and the cupboard closed.

CLOSED UNIT
When closed, the unit resembles a kitchen cupboard, giving no hint of the office that is contained within.

DEEP SHELVING
The large, deep shelf is suitable for storing books, files, and reference material.

TIDY DESK
Shallow drawers are useful for storing small items such as computer disks, stationery, pens, and accessories.

CUBBY HOLE
A large, deep recess provides convenient space for heavy and bulky items such as computer equipment.

◁ **OFFICE-IN-A-CUPBOARD**
This wooden cupboard is specifically designed as a complete home office, but would not look out of place in a kitchen. It is cable-managed to power points behind, making it ideal for computer-based work.

OPEN UNITS

If you are a neat, well-organized worker, an open unit can provide a simple and satisfactory home office. A variety of ready-made units are available, but you could make your own from medium-density fibreboard (MDF) – an inexpensive material that can be painted or varnished to blend with surrounding decor. Units can be wall-mounted or freestanding, but make sure that they are strong enough and securely fixed to bear the weight of work equipment.

DESIGNED FOR COMFORT
A deep worksurface allows plenty of leg room as well as space for file storage.

BOX COMPARTMENTS
Neat, box-shaped storage compartments help to keep files and books in order.

ON DISPLAY ▷
This open unit, made from medium-density fibreboard (MDF), is attached to the wall. The spacious desktop is unsupported at the front so can hold only light equipment.

MEETING AREAS

MOST HOME workers require a place to hold meetings with clients and colleagues. Give careful thought to how much room is needed and how private the space should be. Access is an issue too: you may want to avoid having clients wandering through your home to reach the meeting. A dedicated room is not always necessary as you can section off a space in your living room or office with room dividers, such as freestanding screens. If possible, locate your meeting area near to drinks facilities, an especially important point if you receive large groups of visitors.

FORMAL MEETING AREAS

If your work requires regular meetings in which uninterrupted quiet is necessary, a formal meeting area may be the solution. Choose furniture that is comfortable, but not homely, indicating that this area is for work, not relaxation. Opt for a space where there will be no through traffic, and where you can shut the door to block out domestic noise.

PENDANT LIGHT
An overhead light that illuminates the whole table surface is ideal for a meeting area.

VENETIAN BLINDS
Blinds control the sunlight that floods in through the large window.

△ SHARED DINING AND MEETING ROOM
In many homes, the dining room offers the best meeting space but it often requires additional ambient lighting so that the room does not appear gloomy. If the meeting table is near a window, make sure you can control the natural light with blinds or curtains.

MEETING TABLE
A circular table is often the most successful option for meetings; it is considered democratic as no one sits at the head and dominates.

INFORMAL MEETING AREAS

A conventional meeting space may not be necessary if your meetings take the form of informal discussions or creative brain stormings. To create a relaxed meeting area, atmosphere and comfort are a priority, but so too is practicality. For example, although sofas and easy chairs are fine for general discussions, they are inconvenient if you need to refer to papers. Indeed, some people feel uneasy without the presence of a table to denote work. If this is the case, a quiet area in the corner of the office, or sitting round the kitchen table might be a better option. In fine weather, hold meetings in the garden or on a terrace to take advantage of the fresh air. Bear in mind likely distractions though.

ROOM DIVIDERS

Use a screen to separate your office from your meeting area or your meeting area from the living area. A screen can provide a helpful visual break that prevents the eye from being distracted by office clutter or by others working in the room. If your office is part of your living space, a screen creates a physical division between work and leisure at the end of a working day. For a more permanent separation, consider room dividers which pull out from the wall and offer better acoustic control than screens.

△ FREESTANDING SCREENS
Choose a screen that is stable and heavy, but not too weighty to move. You can buy semi-transluscent screens that let through light or fully opaque screens to provide a total block.

▽ BLIND DIVIDER
Venetian blinds make inexpensive room dividers. Good quality, heavy blinds made of wood or metal are most effective as they do not buckle or damage easily.

PINE TABLE
An antique pine table strikes an informal note and provides plenty of space for paper work.

△ KITCHEN MEETINGS
For informal meetings, the kitchen offers a relaxed, friendly, and welcoming environment at the heart of your home, with the added advantage of access to food and drinks. If other people are at home during the day, it may not be suitable for regular long sessions, as you could find yourself at the centre of domestic activity and noise.

REMEMBER

■ Choose an area that is light and airy, conducive to inspiring thoughts and productive meetings. No-one wants to meet in a gloomy environment.

■ If your meeting space is limited, consider a fold-down table with stackable stools or chairs.

■ A meeting table can double up as a spare desk but it will need to be cleared before meetings.

SOFT SEATING
The living area is ideal for hosting comfortable informal meetings. The adjacent workstation is disguised behind a blind.

ADAPTABLE BLINDS
There are several advantages to using a venetian blind as a space divider: closed it blocks out light, open it lets light in, and, when not needed, it can be drawn up.

WORKSTATION STORAGE

Good organization of frequently used items close to your desk is vital to working efficiently. Begin by considering which items you use regularly. Then decide whether you need to store these on your desk (the most immediate storage area), on nearby shelves, or in under-desk pedestals. If workstation storage is well planned, you should be able to grasp items easily by reaching up, across, or swivelling round in your chair.

EASY-REACH STORAGE

Store often-used files, papers, and books on shelves within reach of your desk and at mid-height, so that you don't have to stand up to grasp them. Avoid storing regularly used material in cupboards, as repeatedly opening doors wastes time. Thick shelves are best for office use, with strong supports to prevent bowing, instability, and an untidy appearance.

FIXED STORAGE ▷
Even if your shelves are built into the wall, aim to have a couple of adjustable shelves for flexibility. Use shelf dividers, so that when you remove a file, others do not fall over.

FIXED BUT FLEXIBLE
Here, whitewashed bricks form a strong support for the shelves.

BOX FILE UNIT ▷
This unit holds open box files for storing a variety of items, such as loose papers and smaller files. When needed, a box file is placed on the desk and acts as a mini-storage unit.

FITTED FILES
Made-to-measure box files fit neatly into the compartments, creating a tidy appearance.

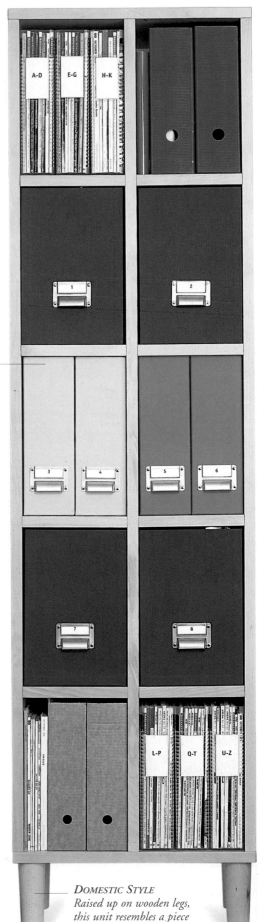

DOMESTIC STYLE
Raised up on wooden legs, this unit resembles a piece of domestic furniture.

REMEMBER

■ A shelf's strength depends on the material used, its thickness, and the length between supports. Check the load-bearing capacity of the wall before hanging shelves.

■ When planning your shelves, allow plenty of extra space to accommodate the inevitable expansion over several years.

■ Store frequently used items at waist height and above. Less used articles that are light should be kept on high shelves. Heavy items that are also used less frequently should be stored low down where they can be reached safely.

STORAGE SYSTEMS

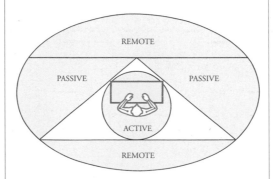

Storage areas in the work space can be divided into three zones: **active** denotes frequently used material; **passive** denotes occasionally used items; **remote** denotes rarely used articles, such as reference books. Archive storage space for old material should be kept elsewhere.

DESKTOP STORAGE

Try to store as little as possible on your desk surface, leaving it clear for current work, your task lamp, computer, and telephone. Keep items such as pens and stationery in a desk drawer or on nearby shelves. If you have to store objects on your desk, it is neater and more efficient to keep them in containers. Use domestic objects, such as pots and mugs, as alternatives to commercial office boxes and trays.

MODULAR DESK STORAGE ▽
An upright storage system fitted to your desk allows you to clear the worksurface of everything except equipment. Wall units like this can be purchased separately or as an optional extra with shop-bought desks.

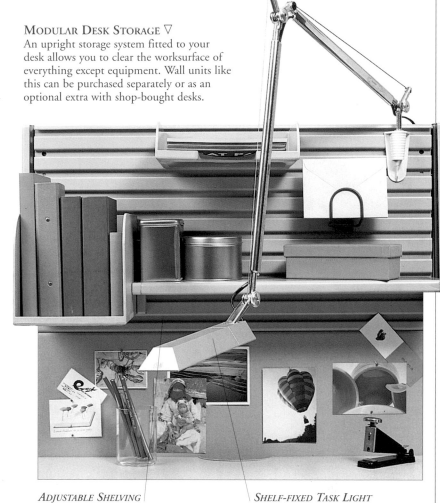

ADJUSTABLE SHELVING
Slotted into the grooves, these shelves can be moved around to suit changing needs.

SHELF-FIXED TASK LIGHT
Create more surface space by fixing your task lamp to the wall or shelf.

DISK STORAGE
A drawer or box protects computer disks from dust and moisture.

BOOK ENDS
Order books on your desk in a neat row between a pair of traditional book ends.

△ VISIBLE ACCESSORIES
Your worksurface can quickly become unmanageable and messy if you cover it with too many loose items. Store pens, papers, and disks tidily in transparent or colourful containers.

△ FIXED PEDESTALS AND SHELVES
The expansive under-desk storage space created by this double-width desk is taken up with tambour-fronted pedestals and open shelves to hold magazines and loose papers. This is a useful system if you do not have adequate wall space for shelving.

LOW/UNDER-DESK STORAGE

Floor-level storage is ideal for keeping essential items close by but out of sight. The most common form of under-desk storage is in pedestals, which can be either freestanding and mobile or built into the desk. Usually pedestals consist of a drawer and lateral space for filing, but they are also available as multiple drawer space. Unlike shelving or desk-top storage, they offer a degree of security as most pedestals are lockable.

DRAWERS ON WHEELS ▷
This trolley can be placed under or alongside a desk to provide extra drawer space. Made of durable light plastic, it can be wheeled easily between users and also serves as a central store.

CONTEMPORARY STYLE
Made from coloured plastic, this trolley offers a modern alternative to conventional office storage units.

REMOTE OFFICE STORAGE

MUCH OFFICE MATERIAL is used only occasionally but must still be accessible when required. The storage system you choose – for example fixed shelves or freestanding cabinets – and the space and position you allocate depends on the material involved. Begin by making a detailed and realistic calculation of how much remote storage space you need.

DISCREET STORAGE

Most storage systems are bulky, and it is important that they fit visually into your home. Specialized units that disguise office storage as household furniture, such as dressers, sideboards, or wardrobes, are one option. Alternatively, you can integrate conventional office storage, such as a filing cabinet, into your home by giving it a finish to match your domestic furniture.

ROLL-DOWN FLAP
Simply roll down the canvas cover to hide office equipment when not in use.

CANVAS-COVERED STORAGE ▷
Concealing shelving within a fabric cover is an inexpensive way of storing office material. Units come in a range of covers that can be coordinated to match your home.

IN DISGUISE ▷
This sideboard, which includes a drawer for hanging files, would look at home in a dining or living room. It cleverly combines open display spaces for personal items with concealed storage space for work materials.

STANDARD SHELVES
The shelves concealed behind the cupboard doors are designed to accommodate standard A4 box files and folders.

CLOSED UNIT
When the cupboard doors and drawers are closed, all evidence of files and other office material is concealed, leaving only decorative items on display.

VISUAL APPEAL
The overall domestic look of this item is enhanced by the warm tones of the wood finish.

DISPLAY SPACE
Decorative objects, such as flowers and ornaments, remain displayed on the open shelves.

SIDE STORAGE
A bank of narrow, deep drawers on either side of the sideboard holds smaller items, such as pens and computer disks.

LATERAL FILING
The spacious lower drawer has been specifically designed to hold hanging files.

OPEN SHELVES

Shelving is a cheap and flexible form of storage. Fill the full height of the room with shelving, using higher levels for rarely used materials, and the lower shelves for more frequently used items. For easy access, allow 90cm (36in) clearance in front of a row of shelves.

STRENGTH
A shelf must be thick enough to prevent sagging, and this depends on the span between supports, the material, and load. A minimum thickness of 19mm (¾in) is recommended.

STABILITY
For maximum stability, shelving supported only by brackets should not overhang the brackets by more than one sixth of the shelf width. Adjustable brackets give greater flexibility for storage.

△ NATURAL LOOK
Wooden shelving creates a softer, more homely look than metal or laminates. Fit it on a strong, wall-mounted aluminium shelving system with adjustable brackets for stability and flexibility.

◁ INDUSTRIAL STRENGTH
If your books, files, and other work materials are particularly heavy, you may require an industrial-style steel storage system, which provides shelving strong enough to hold the weightiest items.

△ OVERSIZE PAPERS
A traditional plan chest holds oversize documents, such as plans, maps, and artwork. Choose a chest with an anti-curling device to keep plans flat, and check that the drawers open smoothly, even when full. An alternative is to roll up large papers and store them in a dustbin or similar container.

FILING AND ARCHIVING

Don't be put off by the grey steel image of filing cabinets. Today's models come in a range of attractive colours and still provide the best system for storing files and papers. To archive materials that you no longer use but don't want to throw out, store them in steel, wood, or cardboard boxes and place them somewhere cool and dry. Keep valuable documents in a fireproof safe.

DUAL-PURPOSE BOX ▷
Designed for the storage of hanging files, this neat box is fitted with castors for easy mobility. When the lid is closed, the box can be used as a small occasional table.

REMEMBER

■ Place filing cabinets on an even floor surface so that the drawers glide open smoothly.

■ If you require substantial filing space, consider a lateral cabinet, which holds more material by volume than a traditional vertical unit.

■ Store files and papers in a basement only if it is dry.

■ For comfort and safety, allow 1m (3ft 3in) clearance in front of a filing cabinet.

■ Store valuable papers in acid-free boxes to prevent them from yellowing.

DEDICATED OFFICE PLAN

A ROOM DEVOTED solely to home working has many advantages. Whether a luxurious spacious attic or a small spare room, a dedicated room gives you total privacy and the freedom to organize your space to match your working needs. This option is most suitable for people who work full time from home, who employ other workers, or who plan on expansion.

◁ ❷ SPACE FILLERS
Spaces in and around the chimney flues have been converted into deep shelves to hold large books and files. The larger bottom shelf houses storage boxes.

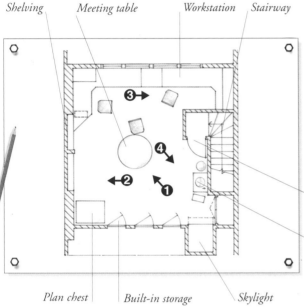

Shelving   Meeting table   Workstation   Stairway

VENETIAN BLINDS
Made-to-measure blinds regulate the natural light.

INTERNAL ROOM DIMENSIONS:
5.3m (17ft 4in) WIDE
6.2m (20ft 2in) LONG

Access to office

Sink

Plan chest   Built-in storage   Skylight

△ BIRD'S EYE VIEW
A large, square room, such as this, is one of the easiest to plan as it has no awkward spaces. Desks adjoin the wall of windows to take full advantage of the light.

CORNER DESK
A wall-fixed corner desk allows the computer monitor to be positioned at a right angle to the window to avoid glare.

FLOORING
Maple strip floor lightens the room and gives a contemporary look.

◁ ❶ CENTRAL TABLE
A round table breaks up the otherwise empty central area. It can be used for meetings and as an additional worksurface. Its proximity to shelving holding reference material makes it an ideal place for reading and research.

FOR MORE DETAILS...

Fitted desks SEE PP. 192

Round tables SEE PP. 198–199

Venetian blinds SEE P. 289

Shelving SEE P. 298–299

❸ BUILT-IN DESK AND SHELVING ▷

The white laminated fitted desk is an integral part of the built-in shelf unit, giving overall continuity of style and line. Shelves, designed to fit under the eaves, are tailor-made to hold specific pieces of equipment.

PORTHOLES
Unusual circular windows were specifically installed to shed light on a previously dark staircase.

WATER SUPPLY
The sink is situated well away from the work area and computer equipment in case of spillages.

CATERING TROLLEY
A neat trolley stores mugs, crockery, and other utensils useful for making drinks and snacks.

DESIGN POINTS

■ The first step when planning a dedicated office is to work out your power and cabling requirements. Most people considerably underestimate, so calculate how many power points you think you will need, then add a third more.

■ If the office is large, do not attempt to fill up all the space by spreading out your work and storage areas. Estimate your requirements and place the elements according to convenience and accessibility.

■ Decide whether you need a dedicated office water supply. This will depend on ease of access to the kitchen.

SKYLIGHT
An additional window lights up a gloomy area and provides ventilation.

REMOTE STORAGE
Cupboards built into the lowest part of the eaves provide storage for archive material.

PLAN CHEST
Ideal for storing oversize papers, this plan chest doubles as a worksurface.

❹ CATERING POINT ▷

A sink has been installed so that tea and coffee can be prepared in the office. A rack holds kitchen equipment, and a covered bin limits food or drink odours.

DEDICATED OFFICE IDEAS

△ ORDERED ACTIVITY
An open-plan office gives a feeling of space and light. In this room, clutter is restricted to the rear wall, forming an impression of hectic activity, but leaving space elsewhere. A drawing board is positioned to take advantage of the natural light, which is reflected throughout by the white walls.

△ FUNCTIONAL
Keep your office simple if your work activities are limited. Here, only a large worksurface is needed for laying out materials; specialist, built-in shelving holds portfolios, and a trolley provides mobile storage.

REFLECTED SPACE ▷
Reacting against the charmlessness of many commercial offices, the owner of this traditional-style mirrored study has created a more personal space, displaying family photographs and art, and filling shelves with ornaments alongside reference books.

◁ WORK AND PLAY
Bright primary colours give this home office an informal, domestic look, suggestive of both work and play. Generous built-in storage space allows files and office accessories to be completely concealed.

DUAL-PURPOSE OFFICE PLAN

IF YOU DO NOT HAVE a whole room to spare for your home office, consider a dual-purpose space, such as this office/dining room, which functions as an office in the daytime but by careful design becomes a dining room in the evening. This option requires careful planning and cleverly adaptable furniture. Firstly, decide the primary function of the room and then design the space around this decision.

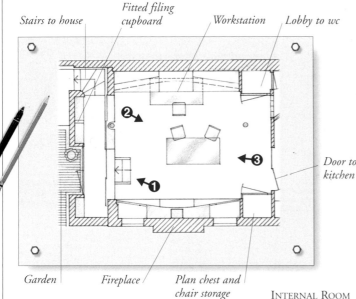

Stairs to house · Fitted filing cupboard · Workstation · Lobby to wc

Garden · Fireplace · Plan chest and chair storage · Door to kitchen

△ BIRD'S EYE VIEW
The desks and storage areas are placed around the perimeter, leaving a central space for meetings or a dining area.

INTERNAL ROOM DIMENSIONS:
5m (16ft) WIDE
6m (19ft 6in) LONG

DESIGN POINTS

■ Choose furniture that is suitable for work but does not look out of place in the home. Take advantage of multi-functional furniture.

■ Design the room around its primary function. For example, as this room is firstly an office and only used occasionally as a dining room, crockery and other items are not stored here, but in the adjacent kitchen.

■ Hide all cabling and power points behind panelling.

■ Design the storage space so that it can be easily concealed behind cupboard doors.

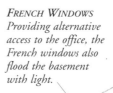

STORAGE CUPBOARD
Filing can be exposed or hidden behind attractive tambour-fronted units.

FRENCH WINDOWS
Providing alternative access to the office, the French windows also flood the basement with light.

MOVEABLE STEPS
Leading to the raised level and garden, these steps can be removed at night when the sliding glass doors are closed.

FIREPLACE
A relaxed working and cosy home atmosphere is created by the fireplace.

◁ ❶ OUTSIDE ACCESS
The mezzanine provides access to the garden, a separate office entrance, and further filing space. It allows as much natural light and ventilation as possible into the basement.

GLASS DOORS
Sliding glass screens help to divide the space from the stairs and doors, and reduce draughts in winter.

LOW-LEVEL STORAGE
Lateral hanging files are stored at low level for easy access.

DUAL-PURPOSE DESK
A glass table doubles as a desk and as a dining table.

FOR MORE DETAILS...

Occasional seating SEE PP. 190–191

Roll-top desk SEE P. 193

Plan chest SEE P. 203

Concealment SEE PP. 302–303

OFFICE EQUIPMENT
A roll-top wooden cupboard opens to hold a computer and printer.

△ ❷ MEETING AREA
Most of the office equipment is ranged along one wall, which is the focus of the office. An extra table in the centre can be used as a second desk or as a meeting table.

PERFORATED CUPBOARDS
The door folds back to reveal office equipment. When closed, the perforations ensure electrical equipment does not overheat.

DOOR TO KITCHEN
Direct access to the kitchen is useful for preparing drinks and meals.

PLAN CHEST AND STORAGE
A built-in plan chest holds oversize material. Space above and below stores the dining-room chairs.

ADDITIONAL TABLE
A second table can be moved around to be used as a desk, or as a meeting or dining table.

△ ❸ DINING ROOM
When work is over all evidence of the office can be closed away behind cupboard doors. The two glass-topped tables are pushed together to form a large dining table. Dining-room chairs replace the task chairs.

DUAL-PURPOSE OFFICE IDEAS

△ **UNDER-BED OFFICE**
Many manufacturers produce raised-bed kits with a study area below, offering a workstation and storage space. Although these don't allow for expansion, they provide a simple part-time office solution.

△ **DEFINED WORK AREA**
Guest bedrooms often double as home offices. Denote the boundary between work and sleep with a raised platform, below which useful storage space is created. A sofa, used as additional office seating, becomes a bed when guests come to stay.

△ **DESK/DRESSING TABLE**
A simple office space for occasional use has been created in an alcove in this spare bedroom, with a work-surface doubling as a dressing table. Pastel colours and soft furnishings help to retain a bedroom ambience.

△ **STORE-AWAY BED**
The office is permanent and the bedroom occasional in this dual-purpose room. A desk, fitted with castors, can be pushed back to the window to make room for the bed, which is stored in a cupboard.

AMPLE STORAGE ▷
In this spacious bedroom, the attractive drapes screen off the substantial office storage space, while the light, mobile workstation can be wheeled away and stored when work is finished.

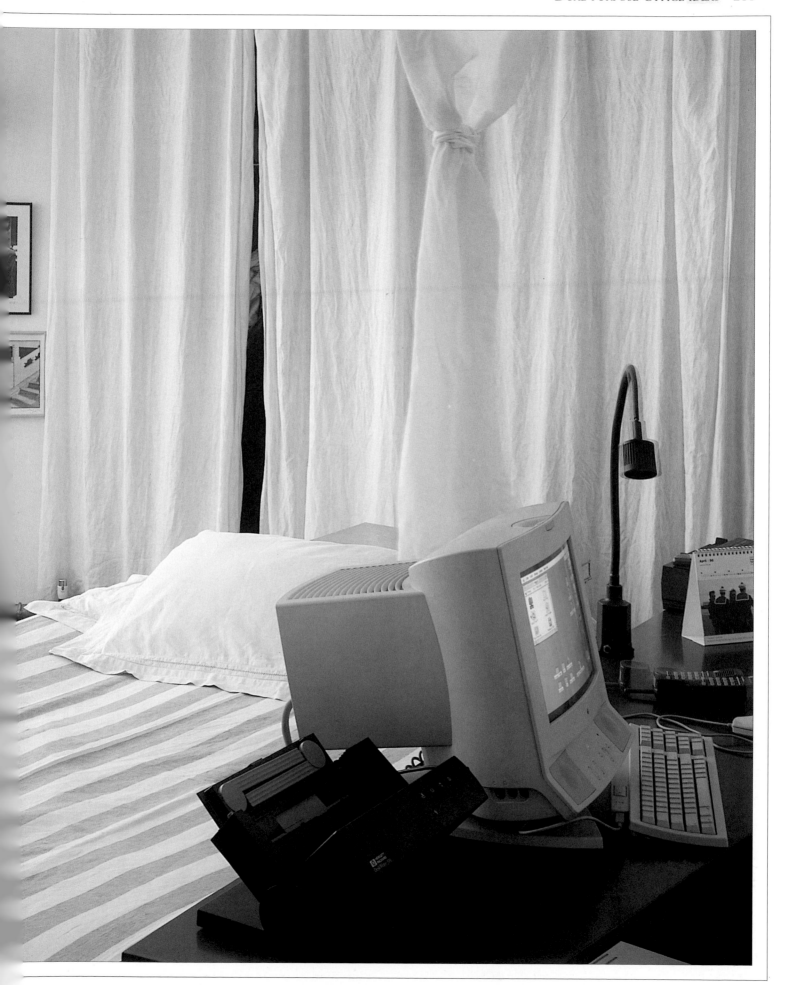

INTEGRATED OFFICE PLAN

THE CHALLENGE OF CREATING an office in a living area is to find a way of combining the two functions without compromising privacy, or creating two small, disparate sections. Although an office that shares space with a living area is more suited to part-time work, careful and imaginative planning can produce an office suitable for full-time use. One solution is to separate work and domestic areas with a flexible partition.

DOMESTIC FOCUS
A working fireplace provides a focus for the living area.

Sleeping and storage area   Main entrance   Coffee table

INTERNAL ROOM DIMENSIONS:
7.5m (24ft 5in) WIDE
15m (48ft 11in) LONG

Sofa

Access to rest of flat

Kitchen sink

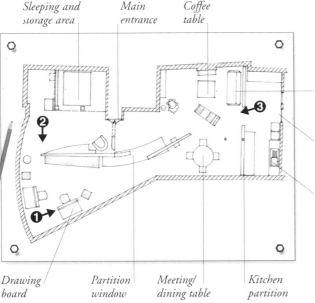

Drawing board   Partition window   Meeting/dining table   Kitchen partition

SEPARATE ENTRANCE
The partition doorway allows direct access to the office, without having to walk through the living area.

△ BIRD'S EYE VIEW
Distinct areas have been created for sleeping, living, and working in this irregularly shaped room. A freestanding, curved, central partition demarcates the office area.

△ ❶ OPEN PLAN
The office is situated in one corner of the room, but has views through to the dining area, which doubles as a meeting area, and to the living area, which is situated in the opposite corner.

HIDDEN STORE
A discreet storage space has been created above the sleeping area by building a false ceiling.

BEDROOM PRIVACY
Venetian blinds screen the sleeping area from clients and co-workers.

IMPROVISED PLAN CHEST
A galvanized steel dustbin provides convenient storage for architectural plans.

CONTINUOUS FLOORING
Wooden flooring runs throughout, integrating the separate areas.

SOFT SEATING
A sofa by the fire provides a place for relaxation, but can also be used for informal business meetings.

WHITE WALLS
The brick walls are painted white to make the most of the limited natural light.

PREPARATION AREA
Cooking clutter is hidden from the work area by a raised upstand on the main kitchen worksurface.

△ ❷ **PARTIAL SEPARATION**
The main work area is situated directly beneath the skylight, the room's main source of natural light. The partition is designed to allow this light to filter through to the other parts of the room.

KITCHEN PARTITION
A half-height wall separates the kitchen from the dining area.

DINING/MEETING TABLE
Placed close to the kitchen, a round dining table doubles as a meeting table.

FOR MORE DETAILS...

Drafting chair SEE P. 189

Circular tables SEE P. 198

Mobile storage units SEE P. 201

Light control SEE PP. 290–291

Concealment SEE PP. 302–303

DESIGN POINTS

■ If possible, create a separate entrance to the work area so that clients can enter the office without having to go through the living area first.

■ Store filing and equipment in cupboards rather than on shelves as this helps to leave the work area looking tidier at the end of the day.

■ Install dimmer switches for lights as it is usually preferable to have lower light levels in the evening than for work.

■ Instead of installing a fixed partition between your work and living space, consider the flexibility of venetian blinds or freestanding screens.

MOBILE STORAGE
Files and work tools are stored in multi-purpose mobile units.

TASK LIGHTING
Adjustable task lights are clipped to the drawing boards, leaving adjacent floor space free.

△ ❸ **DISPLAY AND PRESENTATION AREA**
The large window in the partition has a deep windowsill that acts as a surface for displaying work or household artefacts. The partition itself also provides a presentation area for work designs on the office side, and for a personal choice of pictures and prints on the other.

INTEGRATED OFFICE IDEAS

△ DISCREET OFFICE

When working and living in the same room, one design option is to keep the office discreet. This work area fits neatly between the shelving and has a mobile filing cabinet and stool that can be pushed under the desk when not in use.

LIMITED SPACE ▷

In a small, dual-purpose room, a tidy desk and generous storage space are essential. Here, the desk with pedestals, and the large storage unit keep the area uncluttered. Domestic and work furniture is co-ordinated in colour and materials.

△ OFFICE AND HOME IN HARMONY

In a home office that is a visible and permanent part of a living space, choose office furniture and accessories that blend in with the decor of the room. Here, the chrome task chair and task light echo the chrome of the living-room chair, candlestick, and clock.

△ ROOM DIVIDER

Venetian blinds make good space dividers and are especially useful when creating an office within a living area. If there is only one natural light source, they allow light to filter into both areas.

△ SPACE-SAVING DESK

The corner of a living room is often a good site for an office. Here, the task chair can be neatly pulled into the curve of the desk, which provides a spacious workstation without imposing on the rest of the room.

CONVERSION PLAN

Converting a room such as a loft or garage, or utilizing an extension provides a blank canvas on which to create your ideal home office, and often offers the opportunity to incorporate character and unusual features into the room. Before embarking on major conversion work, consult an architect or builder and work out a plan in full.

Hallway to house *Fitted shelves line the wall* *Printer and stationery store* *Fitted desk behind window*

Photocopier and fax *Window in front of wall-length fitted desk*

△ BIRD'S EYE VIEW
By placing the extensive fitted desks and shelves against opposite walls, and leaving the central area empty, this narrow extension has enough room for up to three home workers.

INTERNAL ROOM DIMENSIONS:
2.2m (7ft 2½in) WIDE
9.3m (30ft 3½in) LONG

FITTED TABLE
A small fitted table creates an extra surface for sorting papers and occasional work.

REMOTE STORAGE
Infrequently required inactive storage is housed in the service area, away from the workstation.

SERVICE AREA
The lobby provides a separate service area for the main office.

PARTITION WINDOW
Natural light floods into the service area through a window in the partition.

PEDESTALS
The fitted worksurface is supported by pedestals which store regularly used filing.

SECURE FILING
Metal filing cabinets provide a secure place for precious files.

DOMESTIC TOUCH
A fitted carpet helps this room maintain a warm, domestic atmosphere.

DESIGN POINTS

■ Start by assessing the room's structure and essential requirements, such as thermal insulation or damp-proofing.

■ If you require additional windows, invest in quality ones with security locks. Make sure they are draught-proofed.

■ Position all plugs and power points away from windows to prevent water seeping in and damaging them.

■ An outhouse may require extra security. If it is situated some way from the house and is accessible from the street, consider investing in a burglar alarm or secure locks.

△ ❶ USING NATURAL LIGHT
Despite its narrow shape, this light-filled room looks surprisingly spacious. This impression is achieved by a combination of the extensive windows and the bright yellow walls and white ceiling, which help to reflect the ample natural light.

❷ FROM THE OUTSIDE ▷
As a security measure, there is no door leading
directly from the garden to the office. The entrance
is either through the house, or through the service
area, which has a lockable door into the main office.

WALL OF SHELVES
Tailor-made shelves,
fitted to cover a whole
wall, hold all the office
equipment and files.

AMBIENT/TASK LIGHT
This anglepoise provides
background light and
doubles as a task light for
the printer station.

PRINTER AND
STATIONERY
Storage for the
printer and stationery
are conveniently
placed together within
easy reach of the
workstation.

REMOTE STORAGE
Rarely used loose papers are
stored high up in box and
ring files.

WORKSURFACE
Low-cost varnished
plywood is used for
the extensive fitted
worksurface.

TASK CHAIRS
All the task chairs match,
which helps to give the office
a sense of stylistic unity.

L-SHAPED DESK
The fitted desk turns the
corner, providing an
additional workspace.

TABLE LAMP
A small table lamp
provides soft, diffused
lighting.

FOR MORE DETAILS...

Fitted desks SEE P. 192

Workstation storage
SEE PP. 200–201

Shelving SEE PP. 202–203

Natural light control
SEE PP. 288–289

△ **❸ SERVICE AREA**
A partition separates the workstation from noisy
equipment in the lobby. The glass window lets in
light but not noise, and allows workers to check
incoming faxes from the main office area.

CONVERSION IDEAS

LOFT SKYLIGHT ▷
A skylight solves the double problem of lack of natural light and inadequate ventilation, common in loft conversions. For the best results, install the window with a blind directly above your working area.

▽ **BEAMED CEILING**
Converting an outhouse with original features does not mean that you have to continue the period look throughout the office. Here, exposed beamwork sits happily with modern office furniture.

△ **ROOM WITH A VIEW**
If you value an attractive outlook, install a picture window (one with no panes) to provide uninterrupted visual access to the outdoors.

◁ **STUDY ROOM**
An outhouse offers a peaceful place for work. This simply furnished room is painted in calming white, creating an almost monastic feel.

RURAL STUDIO ▷
The furniture in this converted stable enhances the rustic setting. The wooden floor matches the chest and chairs and the iron table legs complement the tethering post.

UNUSUAL SPACE OFFICE PLAN

CONSIDER UTILIZING DEAD SPACE in the house, such as a hallway or landing, if you cannot devote a room or part of a room to home-working. Here, a double-height kitchen offers the perfect opportunity for adding a mezzanine level for a small, open-plan office.

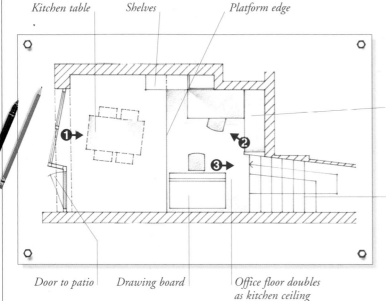

Kitchen table   *Shelves*   *Platform edge*

INTERNAL ROOM DIMENSIONS:
3m (9ft 10in) WIDE
4.3m (14ft) LONG

L-shaped worksurface

Half staircase to front door and rest of flat

Door to patio   *Drawing board*   *Office floor doubles as kitchen ceiling*

△ BIRD'S EYE PLAN
The mezzanine level projects out less than halfway across the kitchen area, allowing the dining area to enjoy the spaciousness of a double-height ceiling.

STURDY BASE
A metal beam is used to strengthen the plasterboard and timber platform.

EXTENDED SPACE
Strong shelving extends beyond the platform to make the office space appear larger.

HEATING
A custom-made vertical radiator heats both floors.

DISCREET KITCHEN
Kitchen units are situated under the platform, which means that kitchen mess is invisible from the office.

WALL-TO-WALL WINDOWS
The double-height wall of windows and patio doors gives the office space excellent light and ample ventilation.

◁ ❶ ILLUSION OF SPACE
Although the office floor area is limited, the open design gives the room a feeling of space. The lack of a barrier at the edge of the office allows the eye to travel uninterrupted to its back.

FOR MORE DETAILS...

Drafting chair SEE P. 189

Workstation storage SEE PP. 200–201

Natural light control SEE PP. 288–289

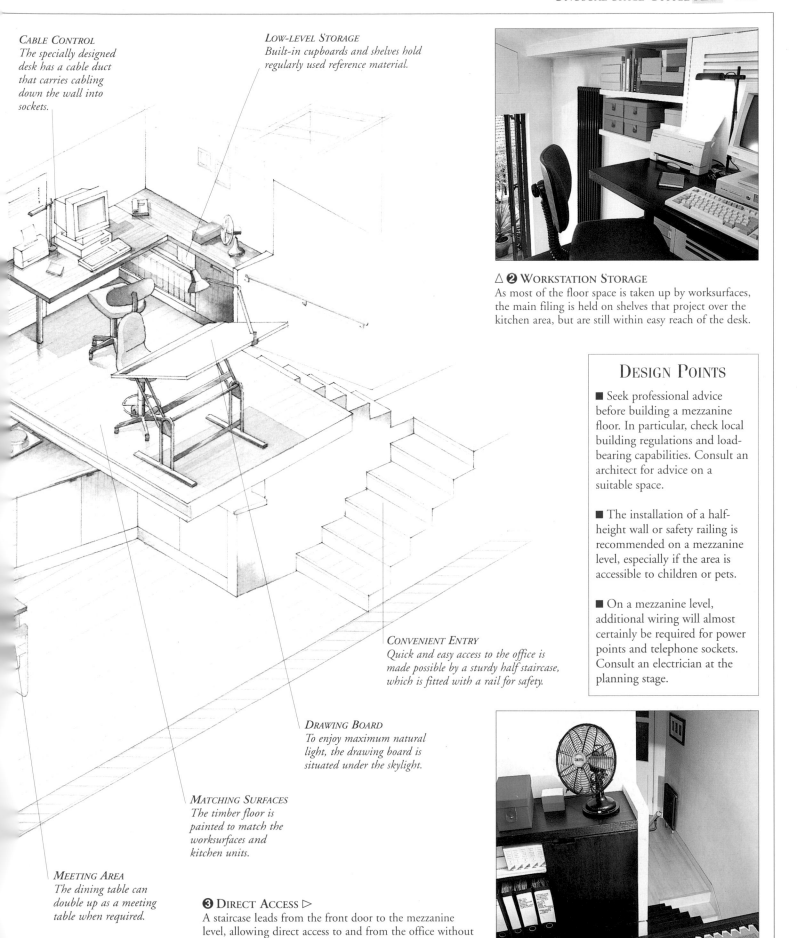

CABLE CONTROL
The specially designed desk has a cable duct that carries cabling down the wall into sockets.

LOW-LEVEL STORAGE
Built-in cupboards and shelves hold regularly used reference material.

△ ❷ **WORKSTATION STORAGE**
As most of the floor space is taken up by worksurfaces, the main filing is held on shelves that project over the kitchen area, but are still within easy reach of the desk.

DESIGN POINTS

■ Seek professional advice before building a mezzanine floor. In particular, check local building regulations and load-bearing capabilities. Consult an architect for advice on a suitable space.

■ The installation of a half-height wall or safety railing is recommended on a mezzanine level, especially if the area is accessible to children or pets.

■ On a mezzanine level, additional wiring will almost certainly be required for power points and telephone sockets. Consult an electrician at the planning stage.

CONVENIENT ENTRY
Quick and easy access to the office is made possible by a sturdy half staircase, which is fitted with a rail for safety.

DRAWING BOARD
To enjoy maximum natural light, the drawing board is situated under the skylight.

MATCHING SURFACES
The timber floor is painted to match the worksurfaces and kitchen units.

MEETING AREA
The dining table can double up as a meeting table when required.

❸ **DIRECT ACCESS** ▷
A staircase leads from the front door to the mezzanine level, allowing direct access to and from the office without entering the living space. Cabling is kept away from the stairs to prevent accidents.

UNUSUAL SPACE OFFICE IDEAS

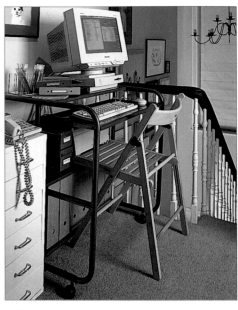

△ **TEMPORARY OFFICE**
A stair landing is a suitable site for occasional work, although access to the staircase must always be kept clear for use as a fire escape. Here, the mobile desk and folding chair are easily removed if necessary. Remember, a landing can be noisy if other people are in the house.

◁ **END OF HALLWAY**
Dead space, often found at the end of a hallway, can be transformed into a compact office. The window makes this area a particularly attractive office. Such space may not be suitable if considerable storage facilities are required.

△ **UNDERSTAIRS ALCOVE**
Utilize the area under the staircase as an office for occasional work. Here, a freestanding table is used as a desk, though a fitted desk would work as well. Good artificial lighting is needed to compensate for the lack of natural light.

△ **GALLERY SPACE**
This large landing provides ample desk space and an area for meetings. A fitted desk with integral storage facilities takes little room, and the balcony allows in natural light. This is only a viable option in quiet houses.

IN SUSPENSION ▷
Dead air space in a stairwell is occupied here by an imaginatively designed suspended office. The wall, worksurface, and floor are constructed from toughened glass, allowing natural light to filter into the living space beneath.

EXECUTIVE OFFICE PLAN

IF RECEIVING AND IMPRESSING CLIENTS forms an important part of your work, you may require a formal, executive-type office. A spacious room is always impressive, though a small office can create the right ambience if it is well organized and equipped with stylish furniture and finishes. A crucial element is the provision of a desk or table for meetings with clients, which helps to set the businesslike tone of the office.

Entrance to flat

Sliding doors

Workstation

Fitted cupboards

Living room and meeting area

Workstation

Shelving

SOLID SCREEN
Solid-timber sliding doors provide good acoustic control between office and living area. The doors are top-hung, so the sliding mechanism is concealed when the doors are open.

MEETING CHAIRS
Leather chairs in the meeting/living area provide seating for both domestic living and informal meetings.

TASK CHAIR
A high-backed, leather task chair signifies executive status.

Fireplace

Window

△ **BIRD'S EYE VIEW**
Opening into the living room, which doubles as a meeting area, this large room comfortably contains two workstations.

INTERNAL ROOM DIMENSIONS:
5.5m (17ft 11in) WIDE
6.0m (19ft 6in) LONG

FITTED SHELVING
Adjustable shelves, made of medium-density fibreboard (MDF), hold books and files.

FLOORING
Pre-sealed oak laminate provides attractive, hard-wearing flooring.

COMFORT ZONE
The fireside rug helps to create the impression of a self-contained reading and rest area.

DESIGN POINTS

■ To prevent office noise penetrating to the floors above, or noises from above disturbing your work, insulate the ceiling with 100mm (4in) mineral fibre insulation.

■ The stylish look of an office can be ruined by power cables trailing across the floor. Avoid this by installing floor sockets directly under the workstation.

■ Lacquered finishes look luxurious but they chip easily, so avoid using them on areas of heavy use in your office.

◁ ❶ **EXECUTIVE DESK**
Providing a spacious workstation, this stylish large square desk, made of black lacquered wood with steel legs, has two pedestals that can be moved to make room for meetings of up to four people.

DISPLAY SPACE
An entire wall has
been allocated for
displaying wall charts
and notice boards.

❷ READING AREA ▷
A comfortable, leather easy chair and ottoman on a rug
by the fire create a cosy and relaxing reading area. The
space is well lit by a floorstanding downlighter and
natural light from the window, which is fitted with
electronically operated blinds.

WORKSTATION
A second desk is situated near
filing cupboards and office
equipment, giving easy access
to frequently used material.

STORAGE SURFACE
The top surface of the cupboards
holds office equipment such as the
fax machine and printer.

CUPBOARDS
Ample storage for files is provided by
the run of white-painted cupboards,
which match the book shelves.

WINDOW
Sandblasted,
industrial
glass blocks
are used for
the windows.

FOR MORE DETAILS...

Executive high-back chair
SEE P. 189

Workstations SEE PP. 192–193

Meeting areas SEE PP. 198–199

Shelving SEE P. 298–299

FOCAL POINT
A gas fire with realistic
flame effect warms the
entire space, both
visually and physically.

FLEXIBLE FURNITURE
A stacking stool doubles
as an occasional table or
plant stand.

❸ ACCESS FROM THE LIVING AREA ▷
Two flush, sliding doors screen off the office from the
main living area. When the doors are open, the living
room becomes an extension of the office, providing a
large meeting area and letting light flow through from
the adjacent windows.

EXECUTIVE OFFICE IDEAS

△ IMPOSING A STYLE
Think about your professional image, and how you would like to convey this to your clients. Here, the owner's idiosyncratic personality is reflected in the unusual and flamboyant furnishings and decor. The luxurious soft seating communicates to clients that their comfort is considered important.

△ GRAND BUT INFORMAL
The strikingly high ceiling and floor-to-ceiling windows make the most of natural light in this space. The focus of the office is the desk, which projects into the room and creates the impression that it is a centre of activity.

△ MAKING A STATEMENT
If you live in a building with traditional features, but you want a modern style for your office, don't be afraid of placing contemporary furnishings within a conventional setting. Here, the glass worksurface, table lamp, leather chairs, and unusual wall display look at ease with the wood panelling.

CREATING FORMALITY ▷
One way to achieve a formal look is to use a traditional desk, which indicates the status of the owner and defines the relationship between the visitor and user. Remember that a large desk, while impressive, can also be intimidating.

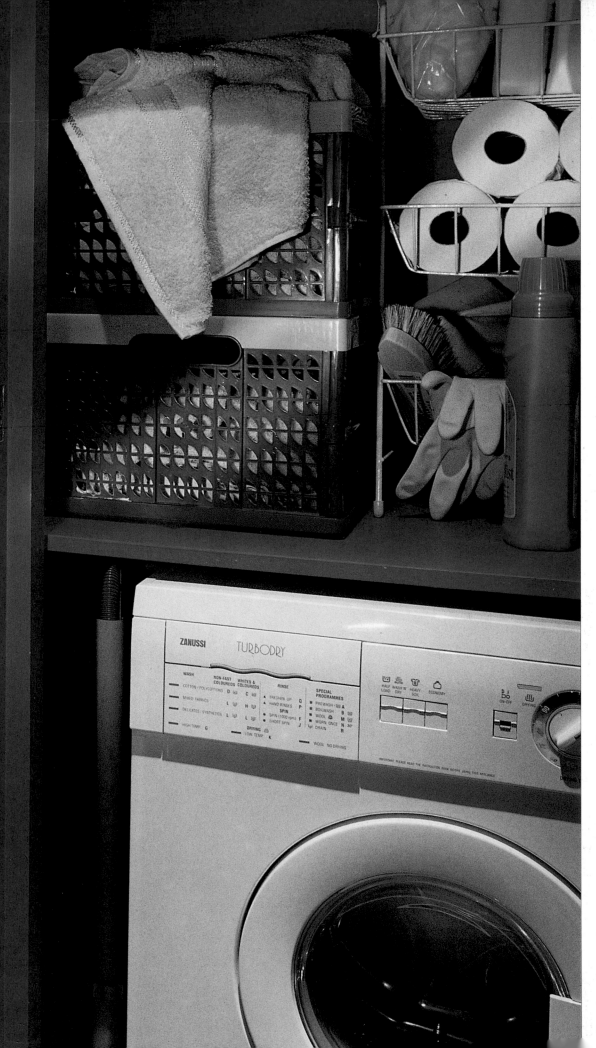

INTRODUCTION

H ALLS, STAIRCASES, lofts, and utility rooms are probably the most under-valued spaces in the house, even though they provide essential support so that the rest of the home can function properly. If at present your loft space does nothing but supply overflow storage, the hallway is used as simply a passage from kitchen to living room, and the understairs cupboard is a space where sports equipment is stashed haphazardly, these small areas have potential for improvement. Take a fresh look at these spaces and ask yourself how they can be altered to create additional storage or living areas that everyone can use.

Ancillary, or secondary, spaces are often awkwardly shaped, badly lit, unheated, and do not benefit from large windows or a good view. In most cases these difficulties can be overcome, but all too often the usefulness of these areas is underestimated and most receive a fraction of the time and money spent on other rooms in the house. There is no reason why dead space cannot

△ EASY ACCESS
It is vital that access to lofts and cellars is safe. Low-profile rungs secured to the wall are easy for all family members to use and do not clutter areas in regular use.

WELCOMING HALLWAY ▷
Pale colours and abundant daylight contribute to the fresh calm atmosphere of this hallway. Comfortable chairs, pictures, and a table make a welcoming entrance.

be transformed into a valuable asset that is easy and safe to use by installing efficient lighting, adaptable storage, and practical flooring.

CHANGING USES

Many older properties include original scullery and pantry facilities and occasionally cellars too. The cool, steady temperatures of these areas were designed to store perishables, fine wines, and even coal. Nowadays, refrigerators, freezers, and efficient heating systems have made these rooms largely redundant for their original purposes, but they can make ideal areas for conversion.

Cellars and lofts may have restricted headroom, but they still offer good space for storage. As long as they are dry, warm, well lit, and safe, cellars and lofts are ideal for children to play in, and are invaluable for keeping toys and games out of spaces in more frequent use. The inherent sound-proofing in cellars makes them the obvious place to install noisy laundry equipment, tools, and other machinery.

IMPROVING THOROUGHFARES

Halls, stairs, and landings are in continual use as they form the essential link between the outside world and all the rooms inside. The hallway should make returning home a pleasure, as well as providing an important first impression of what lies within for visitors. Space-saving ideas, good lighting, and controlled heating will create a calm and relaxed environment, even in narrow halls and passages. Whether your chosen style fits the original period of the house or is the essence of modernity, clever planning and use of colour

▽ **ABUNDANT NATURAL LIGHT**
To maximize an impression of space and light, the stairwell wall has been designed to give a sculptural effect rather than divide the hall, stairs, and landing into separate areas. Light from the windows on both levels easily filters through.

SUZANNE ARDLEY

HOW CAN THIS SPACE WORK FOR YOU?

When planning to convert or improve an ancillary area, first assess whether the space is habitable or whether it would be better used for storage purposes.
☐ Would converting the space under the stairs provide further living space, a study, or even a small bathroom?
☐ Could additional storage be incorporated into the landing or hall? Take into account that fixed stairs and grip rails take up floor space underneath but will improve access to lofts and cellars.
☐ Macerator units for w.c.s and compact basins can enable a bathroom to be fitted in an unused space to provide extra washing facilities with minimal disruption.
☐ Custom-built shelving will increase storage options in awkward ancillary areas.

will breathe life into these areas and make them a valued part of the home. If there is insufficient space for a table, chair, or cupboard, opt for wall-mounted fittings and shelves that will not use floor space or restrict ease of movement.

FORM AND STYLE

Observe how the hall or landing opens out into each room; strong contrasts in colour and design will lead to a disjointed overall effect, while using similar flooring throughout creates an impression of spaciousness and light. Remember that halls, stairs, and landings are subject to heavy wear and tear, so make sure that wallcoverings are durable and the flooring is designed to withstand the constant passage of feet and frequent cleaning.

AWKWARD LOFT ▽
A small loft hatch can restrict normal access and the size of item that can pass easily in and out. Plan your furniture and storage accordingly.

WHAT DO YOU WANT FROM YOUR SPACE?

Before embarking on expensive alterations and fittings, analyze your lifestyle and the needs of the family to ensure the changes planned will satisfy your requirements. To help you find the best solution, consider the benefits of the facilities shown below.

❶ Space – to extend the living or dining area.

❷ Organization – to provide additional specific storage.

❸ New appliances – finding room for labour-saving goods.

ASSESS YOUR NEEDS

ADAPTING OR IMPROVING the facilities in a loft, cellar, hallway, or utility room can offer a number of exciting possibilities and options. The following questions will help you identify your specific requirements and compile a list of elements and designs that suit you best.

HALLS, STAIRS, AND LANDINGS

The size and shape of your hallway, stairs, and landings, and the amount of wear and tear they receive will govern the options available to you when planning to improve their use.

☐ Do you like to be able to sit down and carry on a private telephone conversation without being interrupted by television, children, or other noise from the living area or kitchen?
☐ Do you find boots, coats, umbrellas, and bags are regularly discarded by the front door or on the stairs, causing an obstruction that hinders access?
☐ How important is it that passers-by do not intrude upon your privacy when you open the front door to greet visitors, bring in post, or unload the car?
☐ If any members of the household are less able and have special needs, would they benefit from the installation of a stair lift or from ramp access to the house or to rooms from the hallway?
☐ Can you easily reach the electricity and gas meters to take readings, and the consumer unit to change a fuse?
☐ Do your hallway, stairs, and landings need to be purely practical with bright lighting, and hard-wearing surfaces and finishes, or would you prefer a softer, more comfortable or welcoming space fitted with accent lighting, carpeting, and soft furnishings.
☐ Do you need to use the space under the stairs to store cleaning equipment or coats, and shoes, or could these items be stored elsewhere and the space converted to give better use?
☐ Do you find there is sufficient natural light in your hall, and on stairs and landings, to see clearly during the day, or would additional lighting improve your use of these areas?

☐ Is it difficult to move past free-standing furniture in the hall or on landings? If so, could you make use of wall-space for wall-mounted fixtures?
☐ Do you need space to store or unload items of sportswear or work equipment just inside the front or back door?

LOFTS AND CELLARS

How you organize activities in your home and how much space you need for them will determine whether you would benefit from extending the habitable areas of the house into the cellar or loft.

☐ Are you likely to get optimum use from converting a loft or cellar into a habitable area, or is it likely that the extra space will end up as storage for clutter which would be better thrown away?
☐ Do you need plenty of natural light for the activity or work you intend to pursue in your loft or cellar?
☐ Is it easy and safe, particularly for children, to access the loft or cellar and move around freely?
☐ If your loft or cellar is large, would it be practical to divide the space to give both an extra room and storage space?

☐ Do you need to store or use books, stationery, fabric, or antiques that might be damaged by damp, humidity, or erratic changes in temperature?
☐ Are the items you want to install simple to dismantle and assemble, to allow bulky, heavy, or awkward pieces to be moved easily to their final position?
☐ If you convert your loft area, would the noise of overhead footsteps, equipment, or talking be disruptive, especially if children's bedrooms are located directly below?
☐ Is there sufficient headroom to comply with building regulations for the tallest household member to move about freely without stooping or knocking their head?

UTILITY ROOMS

The availability of a utility room is a great advantage, providing the space has been well planned and caters for the diverse needs of a family.

☐ Do you need space for a tumble drier, or do you prefer to hang clothes outdoors to dry naturally?
☐ Do you need storage space for pet foods and grooming equipment?
☐ Are there sufficient electrical sockets to run the appliances you use regularly?
☐ Is it important to have access to another sink other than the one in the kitchen for soaking clothes, refreshing flowers and pot plants, or rinsing out paint brushes?
☐ Could the area under the stairs be converted into a utility space to house the washing machine and tumble drier?
☐ Do you like to keep recyclable materials in separate containers or bins until you can take them to the recycling centre?

HALL, STAIRS, AND LANDINGS

BRIDGING PUBLIC SPACE and domestic privacy, the hall is an important place of first impressions. As a main thoroughfare, it must be designed to take a considerable amount of traffic and to provide for people discarding coats, keys, and various other items. Stairs and landings are primarily circulation spaces, but they may also offer extra storage opportunities.

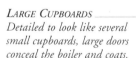

◁ HAT STAND
A freestanding hat stand, though more space-consuming than wall hooks, is better for wet outdoor clothing as it allows air circulation.

STAIR CUPBOARDS ▷
Here, spectacular use has been made of "dead" space under the stairs by fitting pull-out shelving units, thus exploiting the potential of even the tightest corner.

TOP LEVEL
High cupboards house "dead" storage, such as suitcases.

LARGE CUPBOARDS
Detailed to look like several small cupboards, large doors conceal the boiler and coats.

SMALL CUPBOARD
Household maintenance items and tools are stored in a small, lockable cupboard.

ALCOVE
An alcove for display also provides an essential surface near the front door for keys and post.

SPATIAL ILLUSION ▷
In a narrow entrance hall, a formal row of concealed cupboards can give the impression of the space being more generous than it actually is. The eye is caught by the detailing on the doors, which distracts from the real scale of the area.

HIDDEN DOORS ▷

Every house or apartment has its share of unsightly elements to conceal, whether it is the boiler or the gas meter. The owner of this house commissioned an artist to paint the staircase walls leading to the basement, making a feature of the meter cupboard.

CONCEALMENT
Curtains screen off the landing to form a private ante-chamber with hidden seating.

PADDED SEAT
The seat lifts up to provide extra storage beneath for bulky items, such as blankets.

◁ WINDOW SEAT

Landings are usually the most redundant spaces in a house. This one, however, was spacious enough to create a curtained seating area beneath the window. A window seat acts as a strong focal point on a landing, and provides useful storage in an otherwise "dead" space.

REMEMBER

■ Storage on stairs is restricted by fire prevention regulations: cupboards must be fire rated to the appropriate codes.

■ Halls accumulate a lot of clutter. You need somewhere near the front door, such as a shelf or bench, to store post and keys. Coats, hats, shoes, and umbrellas must be tidied away, but remain accessible.

■ A set of hooks at a low level encourages children to hang up their own coats. Consider boot racks for muddy wellingtons.

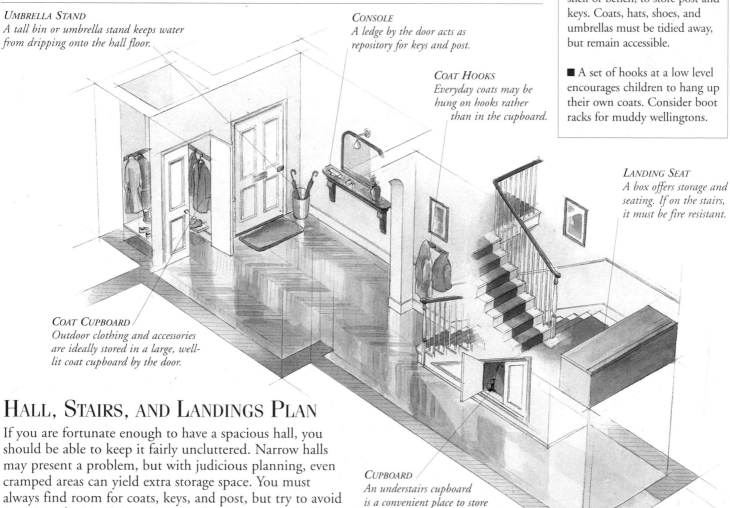

UMBRELLA STAND
A tall bin or umbrella stand keeps water from dripping onto the hall floor.

CONSOLE
A ledge by the door acts as repository for keys and post.

COAT HOOKS
Everyday coats may be hung on hooks rather than in the cupboard.

LANDING SEAT
A box offers storage and seating. If on the stairs, it must be fire resistant.

COAT CUPBOARD
Outdoor clothing and accessories are ideally stored in a large, well-lit coat cupboard by the door.

HALL, STAIRS, AND LANDINGS PLAN

If you are fortunate enough to have a spacious hall, you should be able to keep it fairly uncluttered. Narrow halls may present a problem, but with judicious planning, even cramped areas can yield extra storage space. You must always find room for coats, keys, and post, but try to avoid too many freestanding solutions, which may impede flow.

CUPBOARD
An understairs cupboard is a convenient place to store bulky items, such as a vacuum cleaner.

LOFT AND CELLAR

THESE TWO SPACES at the extremes of the house are often inefficiently used. Instead of providing organized storage for infrequently used items, they tend to be filled with junk that should have been disposed of long ago. Insulating the loft and damp-proofing the cellar will improve storage conditions and household efficiency. Add built-in cupboards and shelves to maximize the storage opportunities. Improving accessibility will also help: good lighting, strong flooring, and safe access are essential.

▽ CELLAR STORE
A cool cellar can serve as a pantry for tins, jars, and bottles, saving space in kitchen cupboards. Simple shelves ensure that everyday items can be found quickly and easily. Large or infrequently used items are stored at ceiling height to keep the walkway clear and improve access.

▽ **UNDERGROUND WINE STORE**
A pre-fabricated concrete wine cellar can be fitted in houses without a cellar, provided there is space to excavate a couple of metres deep. The bottles are stored on their sides in individual honeycomb modules, which keep the wine in optimum condition.

BASKETS
Irregularly shaped items can be kept in order using baskets and boxes.

△ **LOFT STORAGE**
Hidden from view, a loft does not need to have sophisticated storage. However, order is essential if it is not to degenerate into a jumble, and to make best use of space. Here, tea chests stacked on their sides create a cheap, but effective, rudimentary modular storage system.

SPIRAL STAIRWAY
Needing less room than straight steps, spiral stairs are ideal for cellars and other small spaces.

TRAP DOOR
Entrance to the wine cellar is provided by an ingenious trap-door inserted in the wooden floor.

LOFT PLAN

Fitting out your attic to take an overspill of household storage is often more useful – and certainly less expensive – than converting it to provide an extra room. The space under the roof is ideal for long-term storage, but it can get very dusty. Protect stored items with boxes or plastic, and reduce dust by sealing the floorboards with varnish or paint.

CHEST OF DRAWERS
Furniture no longer deemed suitable to grace living areas provides useful storage for small items.

CUPBOARDS
Deep cupboards containing fixed shelving provide ample space for large boxes.

FITTED DOORS
Flush doors neatly conceal deep shelving, and keep stored items free from dust.

CLOTHES PROTECTORS
Lightweight hanging wardrobes protect out-of-season clothes from dust; moth repellent is essential.

SHELVING
Capitalize on wasted space under the eaves by fitting it with simple, sturdy shelving.

UTILITY AREA

A ROOM DEVOTED to the practicalities of living – laundry, household maintenance, and tools – is a great luxury, as it frees up storage space and prevents clutter in the rest of the house. If you do not have a utility room, you will need to create storage space elsewhere, perhaps in a kitchen cupboard or under stairs. Clever fittings can help you store cleaning equipment and appliances so that they remain tidy and accessible.

STORING EQUIPMENT

Solutions to storing cleaning equipment range from simple, imaginative ideas to integrated appliances. Industrial systems such as pull-out larder units, which were formerly found only in warehouses and factories, are now being appropriated by the domestic market because they are so practical and use a minimum of materials.

WIRE RACK STORAGE SYSTEMS ▷

In restricted areas, wire rack and basket systems provide an invaluable and flexible method of storage. They can be fitted into virtually any space, whether under the stairs or on the backs of cupboard doors. They do not gather dust and everything that is stored is immediately visible and accessible. Hooks and small containers can be added to extend their storage possibilities.

NO CLUTTER
Use wall brackets and clips to hold vacuum cleaners, extension tubes, and tools neatly in place.

SPACE SAVERS
Wire racks, of stainless steel or plastic-coated wire, are widely available in a range of designs.

LARGE ITEMS
Ensure that there is room for large items such as a vacuum cleaner ironing board, and buckets.

REMEMBER
■ Reduce clutter by fitting racks and baskets, hooks, and hanging pockets on the backs of cupboard doors and inside any useful concealed space.
■ Make the best use of hard-to-reach corner spaces under worktops by installing carousel storage trays.
■ Store dusters and shoe-cleaning equipment in bags hung inside cupboards.
■ Good ventilation is vital for cupboards where cleaning equipment is stored.
■ Marine-grade plywood, being impervious to moisture and steam, is an ideal material to use in badly ventilated small kitchens and washing areas.

◁ SIMPLE SOLUTIONS
One cheap and cheerful solution to storage of cloths and cleaning items is a simple fabric "shoebag" that can be hung up wherever there is space. Other inexpensive ideas include plastic baskets and stacking boxes.

▽ **BELOW-STAIRS UTILITY ROOM**
Despite its location under the stairs, this utility room –
which houses a washer-dryer as well as other essential
household equipment – appears spacious. The bright
colour scheme and the full-width mirror in the adjacent
washing area not only help to create an airy feeling, but
also seem to double the size of this internal room.

LAUNDRY FACILITIES

The requirements of people living alone or in small spaces has resulted
in a new generation of compact washing and drying machines. When
teamed with retractable ironing boards and high-level clothes-drying
rails, these basic services take up very little space and may even be
concealed entirely from view.

TRADITIONAL PULLEY ▷
A simple rise-and-fall
"pulley", made of plastic-
coated steel or natural wood,
provides one of the most
space-saving methods of
drying and airing laundry.

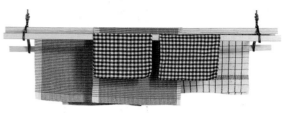

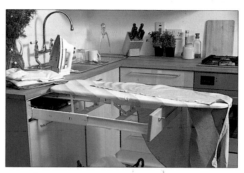

◁ **FOLD-AWAY IRONING BOARD**
Stored behind a false drawer front
in a sink unit, this pull-out, folding
ironing board takes up limited
storage space, but includes an extra
extension for ironing sleeves. The
telescopic supporting brackets are
part of an extensive range of
mechanisms designed to allow fold-
away appliances to be integrated
and concealed in your own choice
of cupboard or drawer units.

UTILITY ROOM PLAN

A well-planned utility room minimizes the drudgery of household tasks.
As aesthetics are not a prime concern here, channel your resources into
fitting out the room for maximum efficiency. If you are planning from
scratch, remember that utility areas can act as a useful transition zone to
the outside world – a place to keep muddy boots or sports equipment.

RECYCLING BINS
Stackable recycling bins are
practical for sorting waste,
such as bottles and tins.

CUPBOARD
This purpose-made cupboard
is fitted with a pull-out for
cleaning materials.

CLOTHES AIRER
Operated by a pulley
system and sited over the
sink, an airer enables
clothes to drip-dry.

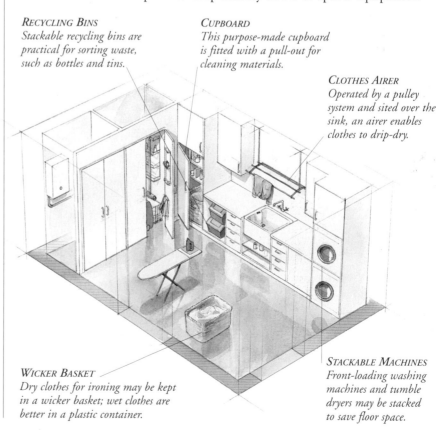

WICKER BASKET
Dry clothes for ironing may be kept
in a wicker basket; wet clothes are
better in a plastic container.

STACKABLE MACHINES
Front-loading washing
machines and tumble
dryers may be stacked
to save floor space.

ANCILLARY SPACE IDEAS

△ **HALLWAY STORAGE**
Open cubby hole spaces beneath a coat rack provide handy storage for organizing the family's shoes. The far corner is fitted with cupboards and a well-lit mirror.

GLASS AND BEECH ▷
Stairways and landings are often neglected compared to the rooms they lead on to. Here, beech and frosted glass floor panels make a striking feature of the floor.

△ **BUILT-IN SHELVING**
The wall panelling on this stairway has been replaced with recessed shelving to house a large collection of books and household files.

RECESSED STAIR LIGHTING ▷
To be safe, stairs need to be well lit. Shatterproof lights have been sunk into the stair risers to illuminate the area without glare.

◁ **UTILITY AREA IN HALLWAY**
Noisy machines can disrupt rest and conversation. This hallway offers a solution, by keeping equipment out of the living and dining areas.

STUDIO LIVING

INTRODUCTION

△ **SHIPSHAPE KITCHEN**
The galley of a motor yacht illustrates how to pack a complete mini kitchen, with sink, oven, microwave, and hob, into a tiny space.

Lıvıng ın one room can be hell. But it can also be fun if you are prepared to be adventurous with space and furniture. Of course "one room" can describe many different shapes and sizes, from a tiny "bedsit" to a galleried, open-plan apartment. However, the basics remain the same, and it is what you do with them that counts.

For many reasons, both social and cultural, family units are growing smaller and this, in turn, has created a rising demand for one-room apartments. Couples without children, single professional people, those wanting a city *pied-à-terre*, and separated or divorced people are among the large group of mainly city-dwellers for whom one-room living has become either a choice or a necessity.

Living in one space certainly has economic advantages, such as lower rent, heating, and lighting costs, but it also has enormous creative potential and it can challenge you to think very clearly about yourself and your lifestyle, and to crystallize aspects of your personality and your way of doing things. These will determine the layout of your living space, and the furniture and fittings that will make it work for you.

SOURCES OF INSPIRATION

Most of us have experienced life in a confined space, such as a tent, caravan, or boat, and have enjoyed it tremendously. What the experience teaches you is the importance of organization, how to reduce your needs to essentials, and how to simplify and streamline your actions. You also learn, through improvisation, how to adapt what you have for other purposes. In the same way, one-room living concentrates the mind and challenges your ingenuity and imagination – there is no room for superfluous baggage.

The inspiration for many of the ideas in this book can be traced to houseboats and barges, Pullman carriages, and cruise ships. Today's motorized homes are fitted with sophisticated furnishings that cleverly combine living room, kitchen, dining room, bathroom, and bedroom. When you think about it – and once you have discarded traditional notions of what you actually need in order to live comfortably – you realize that all the necessities for everyday life can be fitted into a few cupboards. A wall of fitted cupboards, containing kitchen, wardrobe, and bed (*see opposite*) has just been incorporated into a London mews flat, but many other elegant solutions to one-room living have been inspired by the Japanese approach to life in a minimal,

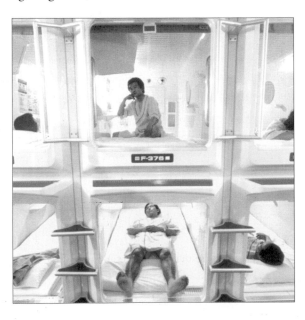

SLEEPING CAPSULES ▷
The Japanese, familiar with cramped, multi-functional living spaces, devised the capsule hotel as a one-night stop for travellers prepared to put basic amenities above luxury and space.

multi-functional space. Sliding, translucent screens provide a flexible way of dividing living areas, while taking up very little space. The futon has been accepted in the West as a simple sofa-bed (although in Japan a futon, without a base, is rolled up and stored during the day). The capsule hotel may not be to everybody's taste, but it does illustrate how to reduce sleeping accommodation to its most expedient level.

Technological changes in the workplace are another major influence on our living patterns. Innovations such as laptops, modems, and mobile phones, and the introduction of flexible working practices, have liberated us from a fixed workplace, and are blurring the boundaries between home and office, work and leisure.

All of these changes are reflected in a growing market for adaptable, multi-purpose, space-saving products, and manufacturers and designers have begun to tailor their designs to satisfy this new demand. Tapering baths, swivelling handbasins, and corner options on everything from showers and sinks to storage units; these are just some of the new product species that are emerging in response to the demands of our new way of living.

In this chapter we have included some of the best examples of such products and designs to stimulate your search for ways of making the most of a limited living space.

△ **FOLD-AWAY LIVING**
Most of the essentials of one-room living can be fitted into a few cupboards. This wall, finished in Italian-style plaster, hides a fold-out kitchen, a fold-down bed, and a fold-out wardrobe. The doors of the kitchen and the wardrobe contain built-in storage.

INDUSTRIAL SPACE ▽
The conversion of obsolete industrial buildings has created a new type of living space, with exposed beams and brickwork and double-height ceiling that allows for the construction of a gallery level and suspended storage.

EVALUATE YOUR ROOM

Examine your room objectively, picking out positive features that can be developed, and noting the weaker areas that need improvement.

☐ Are there spaces such as alcoves and chimney breasts or understair areas with potential for built-in shelving and cupboards?

☐ Is there room for a permanent sleeping area, or enough ceiling height to consider constructing a raised sleeping platform?

☐ How much sunshine and natural light does the room receive during the day? Which areas of your room benefit most from these?

☐ Would it be possible to enlarge the main window to full floor-to-ceiling height, or to extend it into a balcony or patio area?

☐ Can more windows be let into an external wall if necessary?

☐ Does your room have access to a garden, roof terrace, or patio? If not, are there ledges suitable for window boxes?

Whether your prospective living space is one room in a large, converted house, a flat with two or three tiny rooms, whose dividing walls can be knocked down to create one large space, or a spacious loft apartment in a converted industrial property, your first priority in planning how to use the space is to look carefully at your future home. Study its architectural features, noting the position of all plumbing, electrical, and gas supplies, the way light enters the building, and which window offers the best view. Try to work with the existing structure and services, not against them, and a plan will begin to take shape. Basic services can, of course, be moved if necessary, and remote pumping and macerator systems are available that allow you to fit a bathroom or kitchen into a location that conventional plumbing cannot reach.

Consider your heating options at the planning stage: radiators, a hot air system, or even underfloor heating – a Roman invention that is currently enjoying a revival. Think, too, about any structural changes that you might want to make, such as demolishing walls, building a

STARTING FROM SCRATCH

If you have the opportunity of starting from scratch, your apartment will be purpose-designed and unique to you. The "shell and core" method of loft conversion offers plumbed and wired living spaces ready to be personalized in this way.

❶ A Blank Canvas
Plumbing, drainage, and electrics are installed in the shell. Brickwork has been cleaned and ceilings plastered.

❷ Planning and Building
Living zones are planned and built on different levels using a variety of solid and translucent materials.

❸ A Personalized Space
The final loft space has living and working areas at varying heights, each contained and colour-defined.

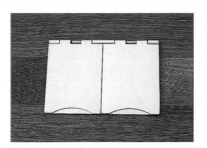

◁ **FLOOR SOCKETS**
A below-floor power circuit with flush-fitting, floor-mounted sockets provides flexibility in an open space, allowing lights, computers, and audio equipment to be moved around easily.

glazed extension, or enlarging or creating windows and doors. For this type of work, you will need to consult an architect who will deal with planning regulations, and help you to draw up plans and select materials.

Although overall size will influence what is possible, all one-room living spaces have certain requirements and problems in common. These centre on the basic functions of living – cooking, eating, sleeping, washing, working, and relaxing – and these areas and their requirements have been covered in detail in this chapter. To help focus your ideas, work through the studio living questionnaire (*see pp.252–253*).

LIVING IN LOFTS

This section on one-room living shows examples of a range of different studios and the ingenious ways in which their owners have adapted them

△ **USING BORROWED SPACE**
Lateral thinking can solve tricky problems. Here, a washing machine has been fitted into a tiny toilet area by utilizing "dead" space from the kitchen on the other side of the wall.

to their needs. We also include a number of loft apartments. Lofts originated in New York in the 1980s, when abandoned warehouses were discovered to have valuable residential potential. The loft movement's mission to salvage disused industrial buildings that might otherwise have been demolished, retaining as far as possible the original features and industrial dimensions, has been welcomed for helping to revitalize run-down inner-city areas.

You will find exciting lofts in this chapter as small as 80 square metres (861 square feet), in which the architect has succeeded in combining the living elements essential for a decent quality of life by employing all the tricks he knows for making small spaces appear larger: raised sleeping or work platforms, curved false walls, glass bricks, full-height and full-width mirrors, and frosted glass panels, to name just a few.

Today's designers are also rediscovering age-old furniture forms to suit current lifestyles. Folding, stacking, nesting, hinged, pack-away, and clip-together units can be assembled according to individual needs, and updated versions of old favourites, such as nesting tables, are appearing.

All these devices are invaluable when planning and furnishing a very limited space. A bed or work area on a raised platform releases useful floor space, as well as offering the chance of filling the area below with storage. If you seldom need a dining table, why not store a folded table and a set of trestles out of sight? And, if ceiling height permits, create vital long-term storage space by building a false ceiling to make an "attic", or a raised floor level to form a "cellar".

△ **"HOT SPRINGS"**
Radiators come in all shapes and sizes. This wall-mounted vertical model will fit into a corner or alongside a window.

(see p.219).

ABOUT YOU

Before designing your space, you must ask yourself some searching questions: your answers could determine certain choices you have to make *(see p.219)*.

☐ Are you basically an untidy person? Do you have a good storage system, yet have difficulty using it? Are you uncomfortable in a tidy environment?

☐ Are you a workaholic? Do you put your work before leisure, or even before cooking? Do you own a lot of electronic equipment, a library, or a vast amount of files?

☐ Do you entertain often? Is a good deal of your time reserved for cooking, dining, and socializing with friends and family?

☐ Are you a home-maker? Do you prefer to make things yourself rather than buying them in the shops?

☐ Do you have hobbies with special equipment that your living space has to accommodate, such as a workbench, or storage space for a surfboard or skiis?

DIVIDING AND DEFINING SPACE

Both physical and visual barriers can be used to separate different areas in a single, open-plan living space: half-height walls, translucent materials, varying floor levels, screens, and mobile shelving units – all of these can be employed in imaginative ways.

❶ Translucent fabrics

❷ Bamboo roller blinds

❸ Aluminium venetian blind

❹ Raised platform area

❺ Varying floor finishes

❻ Towel rail/room divider

❼ Different floor levels

❽ Half-height walls

❾ Double-sided shelving

◁ PRIVATE SCREENING
A screen can create instant privacy. This one, made of maple veneer panels with translucent, polypropylene hinges, appears to balance with no visible fixings.

One of the fundamental questions you must ask yourself when considering the idea of living in a one-room space is how to deal with the reality of having every aspect of your living arrangements exposed, either within earshot or within view, at all times: having to share the space for living, cooking, working, sleeping, and entertaining. Your solution will depend very much on the type of person you are, so before you start planning your layout you will have to ask yourself some very personal questions and answer them as truthfully as possible. Otherwise your scheme will backfire on you (see "About You" left).

Do you need to screen off certain areas for privacy or for peace and quiet, or would you enjoy an open-plan room? Depending on your attitude to these two central questions, you have a choice of dividing up your space in either visual or physical ways. Effective visual barriers can be remarkably simple: a change of flooring finish from carpet to tiles, a switch in flooring colour, a raised step to another floor level, or simply a large plant in a strategically placed pot. There are also ways of creating visual – but not solid – barriers for privacy, such as draped translucent fabrics, open, double-sided shelving, or vertical towel rails. Equally, there are ways of

creating solid barriers, perhaps for soundproofing purposes, without them being permanent, such as sliding partitions, screens, or units on castors.

Planning and storage are the keys to one-room survival, and this applies particularly to rooms that have to double as home work spaces. Once you have discarded unnecessary furniture and belongings, look for a modular storage system that suits your lifestyle, the nature of your work, and your personality. There has been a tremendous growth in well-designed storage systems, ranging from modular stacking boxes and baskets to industrial fibreboard containers on castors. Many of the high-tech storage containers available have been inspired by the extremely functional products that are to be found in industrial and catering equipment trade catalogues.

For those who like to keep in touch with nature and have difficulty in settling for a window-box-sized garden, plants offer another way of dividing one living area from another, as well as adding a hint of nature to an urban setting. A traditional jardinière (an ornamental plant stand) can act as a low-level divider, while trailing plants on a high-level shelf soon extend downwards to become a natural wall of foliage. Among the new designs available is the plant holder shown (see right), which consists of a suspended, vertical series of pop-together, transparent plastic bags, each with its own mini supply of water. This system can also be used as a decorative infill between areas of your living space – but for plants to flourish you must place it close to a good source of natural light.

HANGING GARDEN △
Clear plastic pockets and water sacs provide both an unorthodox indoor garden and an attractive vertical wall decoration, especially if the plants or herbs develop into a cascade of foliage.

BORROWED LIGHT ▽
One of the disadvantages
of building a gallery in a
converted loft is that there
may be areas with little
natural light. The use of
sandblasted glass panels in
this raised work area is one
way of allowing light to
reach those dark corners.

△ MIRROR IMAGES
Filling a narrow wall space
with a strip of mirror is an
effective way of creating the
illusion of a small window.
The mirror will reflect any
available light.

We take light for granted, yet it is a valuable tool
for changing the shape, colour, and dimensions
of a studio room. It influences the entire
atmosphere of a place and our own feelings as
occupants. Take every opportunity to maximize
the available natural light and experiment with
ways of using it to create a sense of spaciousness.

Light can be reflected around a room through
the use of pale-coloured paintwork and reflective
surfaces, such as mirror, glass, laminate, and
aluminium slatted blinds. Light can also be
transmitted into the darker parts of an interior
through clear and frosted glass, glass bricks,
translucent paper, fabrics, and blinds. Recessed
downlighters can create pools of light that act as
focal points, and spotlights can be arranged to
draw the eye in a certain direction, thereby
creating a feeling of space in a small room.

MANIPULATING SPACE

An external wall, or a roof that has been exposed
by removing a ceiling, provides the possibility
of creating another window or a skylight, or an
existing window can be enlarged to increase the
amount of natural light available. If this is not
an option, create the illusion of a window by
inserting a strip of wall mirror between doors or
cupboards. A framed, wall-hung mirror can also
convey the impression of an adjoining room.

You can also manipulate space through the use
of a variety of light fittings, and by the clever use
of colour and pattern. For example, some colours
seem to recede while others advance: dark paint
will appear to lower a ceiling and bring it nearer,
while a light, pale colour will make it recede.

When living in limited space, try to apply the
motto of the king of modernism, the architect
Mies van der Rohe: "Less is more", and cut back
on clutter. But sparseness need not be cold. A
light colour scheme in a minimalist-style interior
creates a feeling of airy space, but you can soften
the hard edges with wooden floors, personal
objects, and plants. Salvaged items and recycled
materials, such as reclaimed wood and multi-
coloured plastic sheet, can be sympathetic in a
home environment, and are especially valid at a
time when we cannot afford to waste materials.

Today there is more need than ever to
personalize your own space. Be bold, and go for
what you have always wanted. You are expressing
your personality and lifestyle and, after all, you
are the one who must live there.

SYLVIA KATZ

CREATING LIGHT AND SPACE

Light is particularly important in a small or one-room living space. It can be manipulated to change the feel and shape of a room, through the use of light fittings, mirror, and glass, and by a careful choice of surface finishes and colours.

❶ Illuminated glazed infill

❷ Glass block wall

❸ Sandblasted glass panel

❹ "Room" in a mirror

❺ Mirror-doubled space

❻ Reflected light

❼ Shimmering metal blinds

❽ Window-ledge garden

❾ Patio kitchen extension

ACTION CHECKLIST

Before you start any alterations or building work, check through the following brief guidelines, which will help you to draw up your plan of action.

☐ Have you made a list of existing furniture and fittings that you would like to use in your new studio space?

☐ Have you started to collect pictures and samples of designs and products suitable for studio living?

☐ If you plan to make structural changes for a studio conversion, have you been in touch with your local authority? Even putting up a partition may require planning permission.

☐ Have you budgeted carefully for your basic work programme and materials? Have you thought of setting aside extra for contingencies?

☐ Can you work out a schedule to coordinate the work of builders, plumbers, electricians and carpenters? Can you do any of the work yourself?

ASSESS YOUR NEEDS

THE FOLLOWING questions will prompt you to consider your lifestyle and needs, area by area, so that as you work through this chapter you will be able to identify the studio plans, elements, and style choices that suit you best.

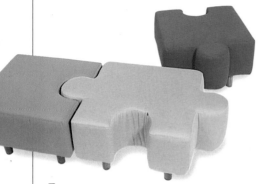

LIVING

The quality and comfort of life in a one-room interior depends on how much space you can create and how well adapted it is to your lifestyle.

☐ Do you find it easiest to relax in a small intimate area, or do you like the sense of freedom found in a large open space?
☐ Would you prefer to define different areas by varying the floor coverings and wall colours, or do you want to maintain a unified, open-plan space?
☐ Can you arrange your living space to make the most of natural light?
☐ If your space is limited, do you want to keep it uncluttered by using furniture that can be moved aside when it is not needed?
☐ When you have friends to visit, are they happy to relax on floor cushions, or would they prefer more conventional seating?
☐ If you have a large collection of books, can they be stored in high-level shelving in spaces that would otherwise be wasted?
☐ Do you have collections of objects that you wish to display? If so, can they be housed in alcoves or wall units, or would a mobile storage unit be more useful?
☐ Would a mini or portable audio unit be adequate for your needs, or do you have a system that needs special installation?
☐ Would different kinds of lighting for relaxing, reading, or working improve your enjoyment of these activities?
☐ How important is a garden to you? Would a window-box or indoor plant display provide a replacement?

COOKING AND EATING

The most important influence on the design of this area is whether you see cooking and eating as important activities or as transient necessities.

☐ Would you like to separate the kitchen in some way, or would you rather include it in the general living space?
☐ When you are working in the kitchen, would you like to face into the living area, or would you prefer an outside view?
☐ Would you like to close off the kitchen, or would you rather make a feature of it by displaying attractive equipment?
☐ Are you a convenience cook, who needs only a microwave oven and fridge, or do you need space and equipment to prepare adventurous meals for yourself and guests?
☐ Do you use some pieces of equipment more frequently than others? Can they be stored so that they are accessible, with heavy equipment stored at low levels?
☐ Do you like to sit down at a table for everyday meals, or are you happy with a more informal tray or breakfast bar?
☐ Would you like a dining table that can be extended when necessary, or could you manage with a folding or trestle table that can be put away when not in use?
☐ If space is limited, would a slimline or table-top dishwasher fit? Do you really need such equipment?

☐ If you spend a lot of time in the kitchen area, are you sure that the flooring is durable but "giving" and easy to clean?
☐ Is your cooking area in an unventilated or tight space? Have you considered an extractor fan or waste disposal unit?

WORKING

The design of your work area depends on whether you are happy working on the kitchen table, or whether you need privacy and a businesslike atmosphere.

☐ If you work from home, do you need a dedicated work space, or would a surface that can be folded away or double as a dining table suffice?
☐ Have you taken into account your realistic day-to-day and long-term work storage needs? Can you plan in sufficient file and shelf space near your work area for easy retrieval?
☐ Does your work require much specialist equipment? Can you arrange your work space so that there is access to ample power and telephone points?
☐ Would a purpose-built mobile computer table with shelves for printer and keyboard best suit your needs?
☐ Is good natural light or task lighting essential for your work?
☐ Can you concentrate easily or do you need some sort of barrier, such as screens or a room divider, to prevent distraction?
☐ Can you adjust your work furniture and equipment in order to achieve maximum comfort and efficiency?
☐ Do you want your work area to look like an office, or would you prefer it to blend in to your interior scheme?
☐ Would screening your work area give a more professional impression when clients visit you?
☐ Is it important to you that your household accounts are well organized and accessible?

WASHING

Your bathing habits will determine the siting and design of your bathroom. With imaginative planning, a bath can be installed even in restricted spaces.

☐ Which do you prefer: a shower or a bath? If space is limited, would you consider devoting the entire space to a luxury shower-room, or could you install a space-saving bath?
☐ Do you need a separate bathroom or could you incorporate a bath or shower cubicle into your living area?
☐ Can you make use of space above the bath and WC for bathroom storage? Do you have enough shelves and cabinets for toiletries so that the basin area does not become too cluttered?
☐ If your bathroom is likely to be used by visitors, have you considered how much of the contents you might prefer to conceal?
☐ Do you have the space for a large cupboard for spare towels, or will they have to be stored elsewhere?
☐ Have you made provision for clothes, such as hooks for bathrobes, a laundry hamper, and a bathroom chair?

SLEEPING AND DRESSING

Would you feel happier with a semi-private, defined "bedroom" area, or must the bed double as seating during the daytime, and the sleeping area be used for working and relaxing?

☐ Can you be bothered with the inconvenience of a foldaway bed, or one that doubles as seating during the day, or would you prefer a permanent bed, either on the floor or on a raised platform?
☐ Is privacy in your sleeping area important? Would curtains provide adequate screening, or would you prefer something more substantial?
☐ What do you like to keep by your bed? Have you provided for storage of your alarm clock, reading material, and so on?
☐ If you plan to erect a platform bed, is there a source of natural light and ventilation nearby?
☐ How much hanging, shelf, and drawer space do you need for clothes? How do you like to store out-of-season clothing?
☐ Would you like a dressing area with a full-length mirror and good lighting?
☐ Are you likely to have guests to stay? Do you have room to store a foldaway bed, or could you have seating that doubles as a bed, such as a futon, sofa-bed, studio couch, or truckle bed?

UTILITIES

In the early stages of planning, allocate spaces for cleaning-equipment storage and for clothes drying, as well as for plumbing in a washing machine.

☐ Will you need facilities to do your own laundry, or do you send it out?
☐ If space is limited would a half-size or table-top washing machine suit you?
☐ Will you need to install a clothes drying rack or pulley, or do you have a drier?

☐ Have you planned for a ventilated cupboard for storing bulky cleaning equipment, such as vacuum cleaners?
☐ Could you have a space-saving fold-out ironing table fitted into a kitchen unit, or do you have room for a full-size model?

STORAGE

A good storage system is an absolute necessity for studio living in order to reduce clutter and keep belongings in some degree of order.

☐ Do you prefer to hide clutter behind doors, or do you like the idea of using open containers, such as baskets and hanging wall pockets?
☐ Will you need space for long-term storage, such as gardening and sports equipment, tools, and DIY material?
☐ If you don't want a fitted appearance in your kitchen, can you adapt existing pieces of furniture for storage?
☐ Do you have equipment that requires storage at a controlled temperature?
☐ Will items in long-term storage need protection from dust and insects?
☐ If you have valuables, is it worth investing in a safe for security?

SPACE-SAVING BEDS

MANY OF THE IDEAS for fitting beds into small spaces, such as the truckle bed or the Japanese futon, are based on traditional designs. Other space-saving solutions, such as fold-away beds and raised beds with lockers below, originate from cabin and couchette fittings. A major question is whether the bed has to double as another piece of furniture, such as seating, during the day, or whether it can be be concealed when not in use.

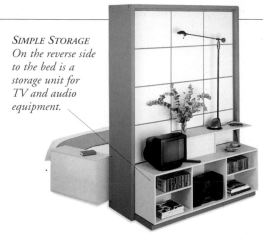

SIMPLE STORAGE
On the reverse side to the bed is a storage unit for TV and audio equipment.

FOLD-DOWN BEDS

The main advantage of a bed that folds up into the wall during the daytime is that it frees a considerable amount of living space. The bed is concealed behind a vertical surface that can then be used for decorative purposes. The disadvantage is that bedding must be packed away when the bed is not in use, which may prove inconvenient when carried out on a daily basis.

ADAPTABLE SCREEN/BED ▷
A good example of an adaptable, multi-purpose design, this screen/bed has shelving for audio equipment, CDs, and magazines on one side and, on the other, a hydraulically operated, pull-down bed. Pivoting side units on either side of the bed open out to create a contained sleeping area behind the screen, which is finished on both sides with a decorative panelled effect.

HANGING SPACE
Hooks set into the angled roof space create a small front-facing wardrobe.

DOOR SHELVING
The interior surface of the wardrobe door is fitted with useful storage shelves.

PAINTED MDF
The main structure of the unit is made from medium-density fibreboard (MDF).

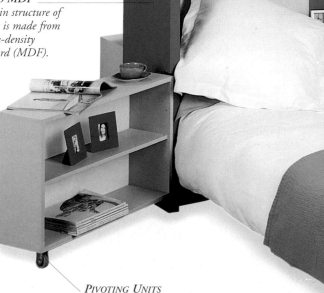

EASY OPENING
A hydraulic system enables the bed panel to be opened and closed with ease.

CONCEALED BED AND WARDROBE △
The pull-down bed and the wardrobe next to it are both completely concealed behind large panels. These have been treated with a special Italian-style tinted plaster finish to provide a neutral backdrop for furniture. The bed alcove, which includes a shelf for books and alarm clock, is illuminated by halogen spotlights.

PIVOTING UNITS
The side units pivot outwards, supported on rubber-tyred castors, to provide useful bedside storage.

BED CLOSED
*The bed is folded up
and the side units closed.*

PANELLED EFFECT
*A decorative effect is
achieved by covering
the vertical panels
with squares of 5mm
(³⁄₁₆ in) MDF.*

TRANSLUCENT BACK
*The side units and a
small bedhead alcove
are backed with
translucent plastic.*

HINGED BASE BOARD
*When the bed is folded up
this base board hangs flat.*

DUAL-PURPOSE BEDS

A bed is one of the most important and one of the largest items in any living space so, when space is limited, it is vital to choose one that earns its keep by doubling as seating or storage – or both – during the day, as well as providing a comfortable place to sleep at night.

VENTILATED BASE
*Air circulates
through holes to
the foam mattress
stored within.*

BED SUPPORT
*The hardwood
end pieces double
as frame supports
when the bed is
unfolded.*

△ **MULTI-FUNCTIONAL BENCH-BED**
Based on the delightfully simple principle of a box with a hinged lid, this space-saving bed, constructed in painted MDF with hardwood legs, can be used as a bench, a display shelf, or as a low table.

△ **ROOM WITHIN A ROOM**
The construction of this softwood platform bed has created generous study space below, with room for shelving and storage units.

UNDERBED STORAGE ▽
The space beneath a bed is ideal for storage – whether in deep drawers, mobile containers, or zipped bags – or, as here, for a spare bed.

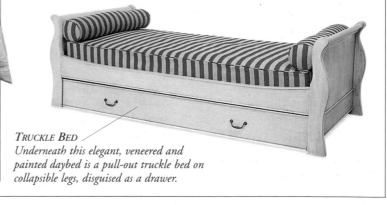

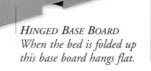

TRUCKLE BED
*Underneath this elegant, veneered and
painted daybed is a pull-out truckle bed on
collapsible legs, disguised as a drawer.*

FLEXIBLE FURNITURE

WHEN SPACE IS LIMITED, multi-functional furniture is the most practical choice. Look for sofas that convert to beds and for folding and stacking chairs that can be hung on the wall or stored in a corner when not in use. Nesting tables are intrinsically space saving, while portable pieces are extremely versatile. Make use of any spaces inside and under seating by packing with storage containers.

FLEXIBLE SEATING

Two types of seating are particularly well suited to one-room living: modular pieces provide maximum flexibility and function, as well as comfort, whereas minimal seating, which can be folded up or stacked when not in use, is ideal for maximizing the use of limited space.

INTERLOCKING PIECES
The sections of this fabric-covered foam seating system also fit together to form a block that can be laid horizontally, to provide an occasional double bed, or arranged vertically, to form a sculptural screen.

SIMPLE CONSTRUCTION
Polyurethane foam is cut to shape and covered in stretch jersey fabric.

FOLDING CHAIR △
An up-to-date version of an old favourite, this brushed aluminium chair with canvas seat and back is comfortable, lightweight, and easily stored when not in use.

CONVERSATION PIECES
Modular seating allows for the separate pieces to be arranged to meet the demands of any social occasion.

MODULAR SEATING △
Designed originally in the 1960s, these fabric-covered foam shapes are both practical and fun. As well as offering endless seating permutations to suit a variety of lifestyles and interiors, they can double as a spare bed (*see above*).

CONVERTIBLE SEATING ▷
Sofas that convert to beds are available in many shapes and sizes, including the traditional folding version with integral mattress, and futons on folding bases. Shown here is a studio couch that opens sideways to become a single bed.

ADAPTABLE TABLES

While there is always a need for small side tables, in restricted living spaces the emphasis must be on adaptable units that not only provide convenient surfaces but also double as stools or storage units. Look for designs that offer extra flexibility, such as nesting and folding tables, or units on castors that can be moved easily from one part of the room to another as required.

△ **SPACE-SAVING SEATING**
When not in use this ingenious version of the truckle bed slides under the low-level platform unit – which serves as a seating area – leaving the spaciousness of the interior undiminished.

VARIABLE HEIGHT
Simple adjustable vertical supports increase the usefulness of this small table.

◁ **ADJUSTABLE TABLE**
With a base that is large enough to provide stability in all positions, a simple height-adjustable table can be used as a small dining-table or plant stand.

△ **NESTING TABLES AND CHEST**
Space-saving nesting tables are widely available. This imaginative Italian design has extended the idea to include a small chest of drawers.

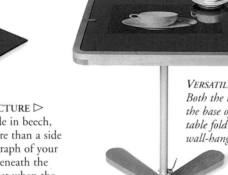

VERSATILITY
Both the top and the base of this table fold flat for wall-hanging.

WALL-HUNG TABLE/PICTURE ▷
This unusual design, made in beech, steel, and glass, offers more than a side table: a picture or photograph of your choice can be displayed beneath the clipped-on glass top so that when the table is folded up it can be hung on the wall as a work of art.

△ **OPEN TABLE**   △ **FOLDED TABLE**

REMEMBER

■ Choose modular furniture that allows you to arrange the pieces to suit your particular requirements.

■ Look for mechanisms and fittings that transform single items into multi-functional pieces of furniture.

■ Hide clutter in storage boxes and drawers fitted into all available space in and around furniture.

■ Choose furniture that is well designed and well made: cheaper products can be a false economy unless intended for a limited life.

■ Maximize the use of walls for storage by hanging up furniture and other items.

BEECH FRAMEWORK
The main structure of the unit is made from polished beech-veneered plywood.

ALUMINIUM ADDITIONS
Sheet aluminium has been cut and folded to form the drawers and legs.

TABLE-CHEST ▽
Look for multi-purpose designs, such as this beautifully made, beech-veneered table-chest. The clever use of hinges allows for easy adaptation from space-saving chest of drawers to low table, without disturbing the contents of the two aluminium drawers.

TABLE WITH STORAGE
Innovative design allows the unit to be easily adapted from chest to table.

COOKING AREA

CARAVANS AND BOATS provide excellent examples of the super-organization and streamlined, logical planning that are the key to successful cooking in a small space. The first step is to take account of how you shop and cook, so that you can make informed decisions about what equipment you need.

COOKERS AND FRESH-FOOD STORAGE

Limit yourself to two rings or burners – unless you honestly think that you need more – and opt instead for cooking methods that are both space- and energy-saving, such as multi-tiered pans, slow cookers, and microwave ovens. However little cooking you do, you will need storage for perishable food. Fridges come in all sizes and styles, including table-top and slimline models.

△ **TRIPLE SAUCEPAN SET**
Cook a complete meal on one ring in this classic three-part saucepan – an economy that is as relevant today as when the set was first designed.

△ **MULTI-TIERED COOKING**
Based on the Indian and Chinese method of stacking containers over one heat source, this is a supremely efficient cooking system.

COMPLETE KITCHEN ▷
As a ready-assembled unit, this self-contained mini kitchen is ready to be fitted and connected to power sources and plumbing. It provides a neat solution to food preparation in a very restricted space.

HEAVY DOORS
Each of the extra-wide doors is hung on four hinges and reinforced down the hinge side.

KITCHEN SINK
Neatly incorporated into the unit are a small sink, drainer, and two hot plates.

HIDDEN KITCHEN
Two large doors, each lined with shelves from top to bottom, open out to reveal a self-contained, fully fitted kitchen.

BUILT-IN MICROWAVE OVEN
The inclusion of a microwave oven is a boon to those with busy lifestyles, and extends the range of cooking options.

FULL-SIZE FRIDGE
Although the whole unit measures only 1000 x 600 x 900mm (39 x 23 x 35in), refrigerator capacity is not reduced.

WALL OF DOORS
The external doors of the kitchen, as well as other units along this wall, have a special marmorino plaster finish, made with lime and marble dust.

△ KITCHEN IN A CUPBOARD
The generous dimensions of this elegant cupboard kitchen provide ample storage space for china and non-perishable supplies on the shelves that line the inner surface of the doors. Downward-flowing light from a narrow glazed roof light illuminates the kitchen worktop.

MOBILE WORKSURFACE ▷
A mobile food preparation surface, such as this maplewood trolley, is very useful in small spaces. This model, of standard worktop height, has a deep drawer, a hanging rail for utensils, and a pull-out shelf.

WORKTOP HEIGHT

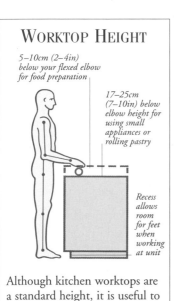

5–10cm (2–4in) below your flexed elbow for food preparation

17–25cm (7–10in) below elbow height for using small appliances or rolling pastry

Recess allows room for feet when working at unit

Although kitchen worktops are a standard height, it is useful to have a lower surface for certain food preparation processes.

TABLE-TOP APPLIANCES
An increasing choice of scaled-down, table-top versions of standard kitchen appliances, including fridges and cookers, is becoming available. To this can be added a range of table-cookers: electric grills and griddles, slow-cook woks, and even a mini electric oven that bakes, roasts, and grills.

△ CLASSIC COMPACT COOKER
Designed to sit on a kitchen worktop, or on an optional fold-flat stand, this updated version of a classic compact cooker includes two hot plates, an oven, and a grill.

△ TABLE-TOP SLOW COOKER
Slow cookers present great possibilities for imaginative and economical one-pan cooking, and many are attractive enough to be brought to the table for serving.

△ MINI FRIDGE
If space is tight, look for a mini fridge like this model, which features an ice-box, temperature control, and room for several bottles in the door, but is small enough to fit on a worktop.

Dining Area

The extent of your enjoyment of food and cooking, and your preference for eating at speed or dining at leisure, must exert a strong influence on your choice of furniture and fittings for this area. But, with planning and imagination, the difficulties of eating and entertaining in a tight space can be resolved, so that dirty dishes are quickly cleared from view and extra tables and chairs can be folded away or stacked in a corner when not in use.

Versatile Breakfast Bars

If you prefer a simple, informal eating area for everyday use, breakfast bars provide a neat and space-efficient option. Choose from a traditional, fixed peninsular bar, a kitchen counter with diner-style high stools – which may partially separate the cooking and living areas – or a hinged, wall-hung table that can be fitted in any suitable wall space and supported by a leg or a bracket that folds flat after use. If possible, site your breakfast bar where you can enjoy the morning sun.

△ **Pull-out Breakfast Bar**
Concealed behind a false drawer front, this pull-out breakfast bar with drop-down leg supports is an ingenious extension of the worktop. It can be quickly set up, and concealed when not in use, yet takes up only the space of one drawer in a standard kitchen unit.

◁ CORNER TABLE FOR TWO

When living in a restricted space, do not overlook any space, however small or awkwardly shaped: small tables can be designed to fit into the most surprising places. This example, supported on one leg, is built into a small, unused corner space.

▽ HIGH-TECH SOLUTION

An elegant method of concealing the cooking area in a studio or loft is to install a blind. In this high-tech loft, the kitchen area is screened off by a remote-controlled aluminium venetian blind. A dramatic lighting effect is created by switching on the kitchen counter downlighters when the blind is lowered.

FOLDING AND STACKING TABLES AND CHAIRS

Furniture that can be packed away saves a lot of space and reduces clutter, while a block of colourful stacking chairs can form an attractive interior feature. Folding chairs can be propped against the wall or hung decoratively on hooks or Shaker peg rails, liberating valuable floor space. Echoes of camping equipment are evident in these designs, which are based on adaptability and the use of strong, lightweight materials.

STACKING CHAIRS
Several of these chairs can be stored in a small area.

SUPPLEMENTARY SEATING △

Stacking chairs are a neat solution to additional seating requirements for those living in small spaces.

EASY STORAGE
A folding table can be propped against the wall or stored in a cupboard when not in use, while stacking chairs take up little space.

◁ LIGHTWEIGHT FURNITURE

A lightweight aluminium folding table and stacking chairs, which complement the aluminium blinds running the length of this minimalist loft, can be easily hidden away after use, leaving the uncluttered spaciousness of the apartment to be appreciated.

REMEMBER

■ Choose a kitchen bar for convenient everyday eating, bringing out a folding or trestle table for more formal dining.

■ Try to position the dining area in the sunniest part of the room to benefit from the morning or afternoon light.

■ Analyse your cooking and eating patterns carefully, and select furniture accordingly.

■ Look for imaginative ways of screening off the cooking area and of storing tables and chairs when they are not in use.

OUTDOOR-INDOOR EATING ▷

Garden-style folding furniture, bathed in light streaming through the full-width window, creates a sense of the outdoor patio area extending into the interior.

WASHING AREA

WHEN PLANNING YOUR BATHROOM, think beyond the limitations of the existing hot and cold water supply and waste stack positions: pipework can always be moved, thereby providing many new possibilities for the location and size of your washing area. Choose from a wide variety of space-efficient designs – from corner baths and showers to modern sitz baths.

BATHS AND SHOWERS

Showers are convenient, economical, fast, and ideal in restricted spaces. For those who prefer a relaxing bath, however, a range of ingenious designs allows a tub to be fitted into the most awkward area. Some baths are wider at one end than the other, while others fit neatly across a corner.

SHOWER-ROOM ▷
Although there is enough space to fit a bath in this high-tech shower-room, with its salvaged steel basin and exposed pipework, the entire width has been fitted instead with a custom-made steel shower tray, with an extra-large shower rose. A frosted glass panel allows natural light to enter.

CREATIVE SOLUTION ▷
This sunken bath is a unique space-saving feature: with the bed rolled back and the blinds down, a private bathing area is created, with interesting light effects produced by the underwater lighting. There is generous storage space beneath the decking constructed from reclaimed Scottish pitch pine.

REMEMBER

■ When choosing a shower, make sure that the unit suits the water pressure and flow rate of your plumbing system.

■ Standards for wc valves vary from country to country, so check that you have selected the appropriate system.

■ Remember to leave adequate space for movement and accessibility around fixtures such as towel rails, sinks, and shower units.

■ A ventilation fan must be fitted in an internal bathroom or shower-room to prevent damp and condensation.

■ Hide the unsightly clutter of pipework and cisterns behind fitted cupboards and semi-recessed vanity units.

■ Luxuriate in the sensation of washing in sunlight by positioning your shower or bath under a window or skylight.

■ When planning a bathroom, consider the benefit of fitting a heated towel rail.

CORNER SHOWER UNIT △
Showers are ideal when space is limited, as they can be fitted into any corner or incorporated into wardrobe units. Shower panels must be made of toughened safety glass.

SPACE-SAVING BATH △

Providing a compromise between a shower and a bath when space is limited, the sitz bath is an option for those who prefer bathing in comfort. Traditional in design, it takes up little space and is ideal for a small bathroom, bedroom, or even under the stairs.

REMOVABLE LEGS
The legs can be removed and the bath fitted into a built-in unit.

UNDER-BED STORAGE
Deep storage drawers are built into the space beneath the double bed.

SMOOTH MOVEMENT
The rubber rollers of the bed run in channels, making it easy to move despite its weight.

BATH SHELF
A generous shelf space for storing toiletries has been built around the bath, like the deck of a boat.

BATH LIGHT
The bath water, lit up by an underwater light installed in the base, throws reflections onto the ceiling.

CLEVER BASINS

Basins come in an exciting variety of shapes and sizes, as well as being made of different materials, but in small bathrooms it is crucial that you select a model that is large enough for your needs yet avoids wasting space. For example, a basin can be wall-hung on brackets or semi-recessed into a cupboard unit, both options allowing for storage space below.

SWIVEL BASIN
When the wc is in use, the basin is swivelled to one side.

SHARED SPACE
The handbasin fits neatly above the wc.

ADAPTABLE DESIGN △

The pre-plumbed panel of this clever, space-saving unit with swivelling handbasin contains hot and cold water and waste pipes, and allows for an individual choice of basin and wc to be installed.

BRIGHT CORNER
White paint and a sunny position ensure that this corner is bright with reflected light.

EXTRA STORAGE
Additional storage space has been created under the vanity basin in the remodelled wall.

△ CREATIVE WALLS

This wall looks like an original feature, but it has been newly constructed, with a small vanity basin, glass shelf, and cupboard built into an alcove where they are almost invisible from the rest of the studio apartment.

SPACE DIVIDERS

AREAS OF PRIVACY can be achieved in a single living space by a clever use of screening devices. Draped translucent fabric, blinds, sliding or opening panels, and simple folding screens are the traditional methods. Mobile storage units offer a flexible approach to dividing spaces, while remote-controlled, aluminium venetian blinds add a dramatic high-tech touch.

MULTI-PURPOSE ROOM DIVIDERS

Screens and panels make excellent room dividers but, when using them in a limited space, be sure to make the most of both sides: the front and back can be treated in different ways, either decoratively or as a support for shelving, cupboards, or clothes hanging rails.

△ SLIDING DOORS
Sliding doors and panels take up less space than double or folding doors. These top-hung panels, which are fitted from top to bottom with shelves to maximize their use, glide together to block off the work space on the far side.

"SCREENROBE" ▷
Today's designers are producing inventive solutions to the problems of small-space living, such as this dual-purpose, cherry-wood wardrobe with maple-veneered MDF (medium-density fibreboard) doors and hinged side screens. In this version, two units – one with shelves and the other with hanging space – stand together; the folding panels at either side can be opened to create a simple screen, or closed and folded flat against the wardrobe.

WARDROBE
With the screens closed, the unit is a wardrobe with plentiful shelving and storage space.

SCREEN
With the side panels open, and wardrobe doors closed, a solid screen is formed.

SCREENS AND BLINDS

There are many ways of creating screens: Japanese-style sliding screens and natural bamboo blinds can form space-saving room dividers, while reflective aluminium slatted blinds offer a stylish alternative. Translucent materials, including fabrics such as muslin or silk, plastics, glass bricks, and sandblasted glass, are ideal for allowing light into internal spaces without loss of privacy.

◁ HIGH-TECH SCREEN
This remote-controlled aluminium venetian blind is one of several used to divide the space in a loft apartment. The screen is light and reflective, so the interior space created does not appear boxed in.

TRANSLUCENT SCREENING ▽
It is important, in one-room living, to maintain a sense of space and light, and this is achieved here by using a translucent screen to separate what might otherwise remain a dark understairs area.

△ MAXIMIZING LIGHT
Sandblasted glass is an attractive option for fixed and sliding screens. It makes the most of the available natural light by subtle transmission and diffusion and also permits the creation of ever-changing patterns of light and shadow, which help to enliven flat surfaces.

HANGING RAIL
A movable rail can be pulled to the outside of the wardrobe behind the screen, providing useful hanging space and a dressing area.

HINGED PANELS
The side panels are hinged to open outwards, and to fold flat against the sides of the wardrobe.

EASY MOVING
A vertically sliding leg allows the screen panel to be positioned on an uneven surface.

COMPACT ROOM PLAN

TWO ROOMS ON THE GROUND FLOOR of a city terraced house
have been transformed into a studio space that, despite
occupying only about 42 square metres (450 square feet),
gives an overall impression of light and space. The carefully
considered colour treatment of surfaces in the kitchen is
enhanced by the otherwise white interior, as are the
collections of coloured glassware displayed in the studio.

INTERNAL ROOM
DIMENSIONS:
5m (16ft) WIDE
9m (29ft) LONG

*Sleeping platform, with kitchen
unit and dining area below*

Bay window

Boiler

Washing machine

Cooking area

*Bathroom,
with storage
area above*

①   **②**   **③**   **④**

*Hanging
rails*

*Stacking
wire storage*

*Entrance hall, with
storage above*

Living area

△ BIRD'S EYE VIEW
Parts of the original dividing wall remain, but the effect
is of a single space, with the advantage of natural light
from three sides. Although functional areas have been
reduced to a minimum, there is no loss of comfort.

SHARED WINDOW
*One window is shared between the
living area below and the sleeping
platform above.*

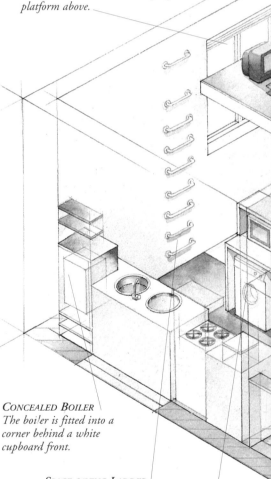

CONCEALED BOILER
*The boiler is fitted into a
corner behind a white
cupboard front.*

SPACE-SAVING LADDER
*Sturdy rungs, originally from a
ships' chandler, provide access to
the sleeping platform.*

PURPOSE-BUILT UNIT
*A washing machine, microwave,
fridge, and vegetable rack are all
housed in a purpose-built unit.*

DESIGN POINTS

■ Whenever possible, try to
construct a sleeping platform
alongside a window to ensure
good ventilation and a source
of natural light.

■ Even in a very small living
area, it should be possible to
find space to display collections
of objects; look especially at
any tall, narrow gaps.

■ A simple worktop and a pair
of folding or stacking trestles
provide a worksurface or a
dining table for entertaining
guests, and can be stored
unobtrusively until required.

■ Check with an architect on
fixed structural features, then
look for imaginative ways of
incorporating them into your
overall plan.

△ ❶ PLATFORM ABOVE THE KITCHEN
The ceiling is about 3 metres (10 feet) high, allowing
for a sleeping platform large enough to hold a television
and books by the bed. Natural light and ventilation are
provided by a window shared with the area below.

◁ ❷ OCCASIONAL DINING FURNITURE
When a dining space is needed, the worksurface is folded away and a dining table assembled from a simple table-top and trestles, which are easily stored, along with the stacking chairs, when not in use. The flat, painted kitchen unit conceals a fridge, washing machine and microwave oven.

VERTICAL LIGHTING
A 1970s Italian lamp runs on a cable from ceiling to floor, through a hole in the platform.

WINDOW FEATURE
Original large bay window provides natural light that is reflected throughout the interior.

MODULAR SEATING
Foam seating units interlock to double as a spare bed when required.

△ ❸ INSTANT WORKSTATION
A simple workstation is quickly assembled by lifting the horizontally hinged table-top and supporting it on another panel, which is hung vertically. When not in use, the panels fold unobtrusively against the kitchen unit, which not only provides a useful shelf, but also screens off much of the cooking area.

FOR MORE DETAILS...

Stacking baskets
SEE PP. 102

Modular foam furniture
SEE P. 256

Stacking chairs SEE P. 261

FLEXIBLE SHELVING
A modular shelving system, packed with books, CDs, and audio equipment, can be added to as necessary.

STORAGE SPACE
A hatch leads to storage space above the entrance lobby and bathroom.

ENTRANCE LOBBY
Access to the apartment from the communal hallway is via a lobby, which also houses shoe storage.

COMPACT BATHROOM
The bathroom has just enough room for a bath with fitted shower, wc, and handbasin.

MINIMAL WARDROBE
Two hanging rails, one above the other, and a mobile stack of wire baskets constitute the wardrobe.

△ ❹ MODULAR STORAGE RACK
Storage of books, magazines, telephone/fax machine, and mini sound system is all contained within a modular metal rack system along one wall.

COMPACT ROOM IDEAS

△ KITCHEN IN A CUPBOARD

An imaginative variation on the kitchen-in-a-cupboard theme is to recycle a secondhand wardrobe. Here, a small sink has been plumbed in, with shelving and drawers underneath. Tiling and shelves complete this neat, hide-away unit.

△ REMODELLED ROOM

A deep, false wall provides a practical way of creating a room within a room. Here, above a large amount of storage space and a doorway, a spacious bedroom has been created, the whole structure lightened by being painted completely white.

△ CORNER KITCHEN

A compact kitchen, with a sink, small hob, and extractor fan, has been fitted into this corner, with suspended shelving above.

COLOUR COORDINATION ▷

Many space-creating features, such as a convertible sofa-bed, folding chairs, and a glass-topped table, are demonstrated in this small studio, which also illustrates the way in which colour can be used to enhance the sense of space.

OPEN-PLAN ROOM PLAN

METICULOUS PLANNING along strong horizontal axes gives this studio, which measures only 5 x 8.5 metres (17 x 28 feet), a feeling of calm spaciousness despite its busy urban location. The functional areas are defined by varying floor levels and by boxed-in vertical supports, but the horizontal flow of space is maintained, with no view being blocked by a full-height wall.

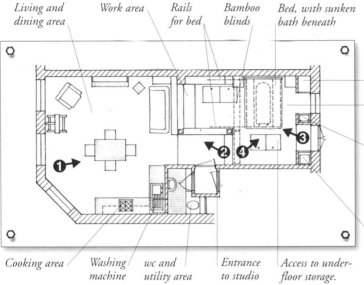

Living and dining area *Work area* *Rails for bed* *Bamboo blinds* *Bed, with sunken bath beneath*

INTERNAL ROOM DIMENSIONS: 5m (17ft) WIDE 8.5m (28ft) LONG

❶ ❷ ❹ ❸

Wardrobe

Sleeping area

Vanity unit built into remodelled wall

Boiler

Cooking area *Washing machine* *wc and utility area* *Entrance to studio* *Access to under-floor storage.*

FOR MORE DETAILS...

Fold-away ironing table SEE P. 239

Bath under bed SEE PP. 262–3

Screens and blinds SEE P. 265

△ **BIRD'S EYE VIEW**
A vast amount of concealed storage space has been planned into this studio, as well as an ingenious, double-function sleeping and washing area.

DUAL-PURPOSE TABLE-TOP
A folded table-top extension, which fits over the dining table, makes up the front of this storage cupboard.

ARTISTIC FOCUS
An artist's easel provides a clue to the interests enjoyed by the occupant of this serene studio.

◁ ❶ **UNBROKEN VIEW**
The dining area is located at the junction of the two major axes, accentuating the length of the interior. Since no solid wall interrupts the view, the sitting, working, cooking, and sleeping areas are all visible.

FLEXIBLE SEATING
When not in use, these lightweight folding metal chairs with wooden slats can be easily stored.

◁ ❷ RAISED WORKSTATION
The centrally placed work area is on a raised level that not only separates it from the living and dining areas, but also provides extensive underfloor storage space.

SCREENING OPTIONS
Two bamboo blinds screen off either the sleeping/washing area or the entire end section of the studio.

STUDY AREA
A large bookshelf along the side wall emphasizes the horizontal accent.

UNDERBED STORAGE
Although the bed contains large, built-in storage drawers, it can be easily rolled over the sunken bath.

VANITY UNIT
A small basin and cupboard are concealed in the remodelled end wall.

△ ❸ HORIZONTAL AXES
The interior of the apartment is illuminated by reflected light from windows at both ends of the room, although privacy in the bathing and sleeping area can be created by lowering the bamboo blinds.

CONCEALED BOILER
Hidden in the remodelled wall is a combination boiler, which obviates the need for a bulky hot water tank.

UNDERFLOOR STORAGE
Marine-style hatches give access to long-term storage space beneath the raised timber flooring.

BUILT-IN TOOL CHEST
The stair-tread lifts up to reveal additional storage space that is ideal for tools.

DEAD SPACE
A washing machine, accessed from the toilet/utility room, fills the otherwise inaccessible space in the kitchen unit.

DESIGN POINTS

■ Create a sense of warmth and cohesion in an open-plan interior by choosing natural materials such as wood, bamboo, and plain cotton.

■ Forget tradition when fitting plumbed-in equipment: it may be cheaper to take the machine to the plumbing rather than the plumbing to the machine.

■ To increase a sense of space and avoid claustrophobia, limit dividing walls to half height.

■ Vary floor levels to create spatial variety and to provide underfloor storage space.

■ Avoid condensation in a windowless internal bath area by fitting an extractor fan.

FOLD-AWAY IRONING BOARD
An extending ironing board occupies minimal space in the fitted kitchen unit.

❹ JAPANESE-STYLE BATHROOM ▷
A spacious bathroom is created by lowering the blinds and rolling back the bed to reveal the sunken bath. The remodelled end wall contains a wardrobe, cupboards, and vanity unit.

OPEN-PLAN ROOM IDEAS

△ HALF-WALL DIVIDER
The upstand at the back of this kitchen worktop successfully separates the preparation and cooking areas from the main living space, without blocking them off entirely.

◁ UNDERFLOOR STORAGE
Constructing a new, raised floor level is a way of creating a room within a room, as well as providing a large amount of useful and easily accessible long-term storage space.

△ SPACE-DEFINING DEVICES
Functional areas are defined here by devices such as blinds, half-height walls, and different floor levels. The bathroom is visually separated, with minimal privacy, but remains part of the main living area.

HIGH-LEVEL READING AREA ▷
If ceiling height permits, the construction of a gallery releases living space. Here, a library above a bank of roomy cupboards has been created. Painted white, they merge successfully into the general structure.

LARGE ROOM PLAN

WITH THE ORIGINAL TILING RESTORED and the aggregate pillars and ducting left exposed, the industrial aesthetic is retained in this loft in a converted riverside warehouse. The effect is softened, however, by the use of colour and the introduction of antique furniture. As the ceiling is not high enough to construct another floor, a galleried work area has been created above a bank of built-in kitchen cupboards.

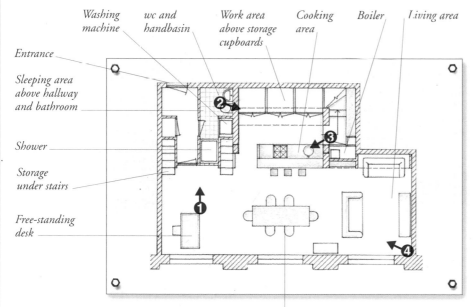

Washing machine • wc and handbasin • Work area above storage cupboards • Cooking area • Boiler • Living area

Entrance

Sleeping area above hallway and bathroom

Shower

Storage under stairs

Free-standing desk

Dining area

BIRD'S EYE VIEW △
Three large windows, providing a view of the river and a source of natural light, are a major feature in this loft and formed the main influence on the plan, which packs all services against the inner wall.

INTERNAL ROOM DIMENSIONS:
7m (24ft) WIDE
11m (36ft) LONG

FITTED WARDROBE
Along the back wall, a fitted wardrobe and cupboards are painted a cheery bright yellow.

PLATFORM BED
The bed is sunk into the platform and surrounded by a wide ledge.

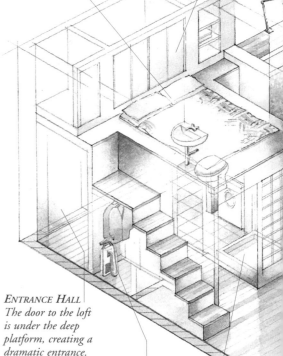

ENTRANCE HALL
The door to the loft is under the deep platform, creating a dramatic entrance.

BELOW-STAIRS STORAGE
In the entrance hall, under the stairs, is a space for coats and cleaning equipment.

SHOWER CUBICLE
Alongside the utility area is a large shower with natural light transmitted through glass bricks.

FOR MORE DETAILS...

Loft conversion in progress SEE P. 246

Workstation with glazed panels SEE P. 250

Glass brick panel in internal shower-room SEE P. 251

◁ ❶ **COLOURFUL ENTRANCE**
Above the entrance to the loft is a symmetrically planned sleeping platform with built-in wardrobes behind. The bathroom, utility area, and shower cubicle are underneath, with natural light entering through the glass brick wall. Two sets of deep steps conceal long-term storage.

◁ ❷ HIGH-LEVEL WORKSTATION

The long work desk, which has been built on a raised platform above the walk-in kitchen cupboards, offers an overall view of the loft interior and of the river, as well as providing a quiet work space that is separate yet still part of the whole.

❸ DUAL-PURPOSE BREAKFAST BAR ▷

The food preparation and washing-up areas are screened by an oak upstand that functions as both a breakfast bar and a space divider. The bar is fitted with small strip lights that give a decorative effect as well as useful illumination.

WALL OF STORAGE
Bookshelves, holding magazines, books, and storage boxes, have been fitted into one entire wall of the loft.

EXTRA LIGHT
Sandblasted glazing panels along the lower front of the desk allow light into the darkest part of the work platform.

INDOOR GARDEN
A shelf of plants introduces a natural detail to the industrial scale of the loft space.

WALK-IN LARDERS
Capacious walk-in cupboards contain a microwave and freezer as well as other kitchen equipment and food.

OLD AND NEW
A large renovated antique wardrobe adds a personal touch.

DESIGN POINTS

■ When planning a loft space, aim to work with, not against, the existing structure and, if possible, try to accommodate the existing services.

■ Opt for glass bricks instead of a solid wall to allow light into a dark interior space while still preserving privacy.

■ If you work from home, try to separate the work space from the main living area.

■ Sensitively handled colour is a useful device for defining function, shaping space, and providing a focus.

■ Salvaged or antique furniture adds individuality to an industrial-scale interior.

OAK WORKTOP AND COUNTER
All the kitchen appliances are built-in behind the worktop and counter, which are made of oak – the same wood as the flooring.

ANTIQUE DESK
An antique "partners' desk", at right angles to the dining table, commands a long view of the loft.

❹ COLOUR-CODED AREAS ▷

With the different living zones clearly colour-coded – blue for the bathroom, yellow for the sleeping and work spaces, and salmon-pink for the kitchen and living areas – the effect is reminiscent of an abstract Cubist interior.

LARGE ROOM IDEAS

△ **DISTINCTIVE FEATURE**
A sense of scale has been given to the interior by this dramatic roof truss – an original architectural feature that has been retained and incorporated into the shelves and worktop. The kitchen area is defined by studded rubber flooring and screened by a sliding door that becomes part of a wall of cupboards when closed.

△ **FULL-HEIGHT SCREEN**
Painted in a strong colour, against which red and white furniture and a collection of ceramics stand out in contrast, a blank, full-height wall screens off the kitchen area while still allowing a flow of air and space. A small painting provides a focus.

◁ **SCULPTURED LIVING**
In this minimalist interior, living elements – contained along one side of the loft behind blocks of fitted storage – are reduced to abstract sculptural forms. The use of soft colour and a natural timber flooring averts any impression of coldness.

CREATED LIGHT AND SPACE ▷
Although this corner kitchen has no natural light source, a sense of light and spaciousness has been achieved. A glass shelf with a stainless steel hanging rail is suspended above the island bar, with additional glass and metal fixtures along the rear wall. Colour has been used to define a large flat expanse of architrave.

GALLERIED ROOM PLAN

A SHELL-AND-CORE CONVERSION in part of a redeveloped warehouse, this space, measuring 53 square metres (570 square feet), has been fitted out by architects specializing in loft design. The use of strong colours softens the industrial rawness of exposed ducting and brickwork, and only the bed deck, floating dramatically above the kitchen/dining section, breaks the curve of the wall containing the functional areas.

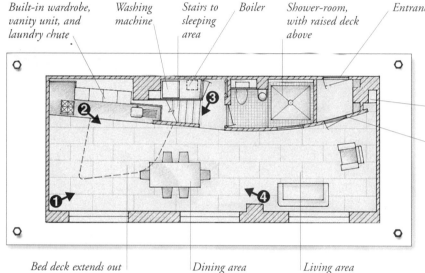

Built-in wardrobe, vanity unit, and laundry chute

Washing machine

Stairs to sleeping area

Boiler

Shower-room, with raised deck above

Entrance

Shelves in narrow alcove

Built-in functional areas behind curved wall

Bed deck extends out above kitchen area

Dining area

Living area

BIRD'S EYE VIEW △

All the service elements are tucked away behind the curved wall, leaving a clear living space that has the benefit of natural light from three windows.

INTERNAL ROOM DIMENSIONS:
4.6m (15ft) WIDE
11.6m (38ft) LONG

BED-DECK ILLUMINATION
Halogen lamps are clamped at low levels to the balustrade surrounding the bed deck.

WALL OF STORAGE
The built-in storage unit, made of MDF, has a space-saving, pull-out clothes rail and shoe shelves.

FOR MORE DETAILS...

Hobs with overhead extraction
SEE P. 35

Built-in wardrobe
SEE P. 105

Shower-room SEE P. 262

Vertical space-saving ladder
SEE P. 266

◁ ❶ SPACIOUS LINES

A continuous, uncluttered stretch of birch-faced ply flooring follows the elegant line of the service wall, whose double height makes the living space appear larger than it is. The loft height is also accentuated by light reflected onto the main end wall from concealed strip lighting in a narrow alcove.

EXTRACTOR HOOD
Above the hob, a suspended sheet of etched glass provides an unusual and attractive hood for the extractor ducting.

NATURAL MATERIAL
A slate worktop, with integral grooved draining board, is fitted over the kitchen units.

◁ ❷ OVERALL VIEWS

This is a loft with exciting perspectives in all directions: from the bed deck, beyond the wall-mounted television, the main loft space is visible, while the second deck, with shower-room below, can be seen to the left.

SECONDARY DECK
A raised deck above the shower-room can be used as a guest room or for storage.

CLOTHES-CARE SOLUTION
Leading to the utility area and washing machine below is a useful laundry chute.

VERTICAL LADDER
Access to the raised deck is constructed from scaffold sections.

❸ CONTRASTING FEATURES ▷

Behind the facade, the warm, colourful sleeping area, reached by narrow steps, provides a contrast to the expanse of raw brickwork and large-scale original windows in this industrial space.

PERFORATED METAL SCREEN
A panel of perforated metal, spot-lit from behind and floating proud of the wall, allows light into the deck area.

NATURAL LIGHT
Light filters into the bathroom through a frosted glass window.

REFLECTED LIGHTING
Light from the strip lighting behind these narrow vertical shelves is reflected back into the main living area.

DESIGN POINTS

■ It is possible to fit all the functional areas into a tight plan, as long as the living area maintains a free flow of space.

■ Colour plays an important part in shaping an interior: a cool, minimalist, industrial-style loft can be humanized by an expanse of strong colour.

■ A wardrobe with short, pull-out hanging rails can be fitted into a shallower space than one with a single end-to-end rail.

LUXURY SHOWER-ROOM
Although wide enough for a bath, the area is fitted with a stainless steel shower tray and an extra-large shower head.

❹ SLEEPING BALCONY ▷

Perched on an exposed steel beam above the kitchen area is a bed deck with a balustrade of perforated aluminium. It appears like a theatre balcony, lit by mini halogen lamps, yet the deck provides a comfortable sleeping platform with built-in storage alongside.

SERVICE PANELS
Access to lighting transformers under the bed deck is provided by removable panels.

GALLERIED ROOM IDEAS

△ **VERTICAL ACCESS**
The industrial impression of a steel ladder leading up to the sleeping platform in this loft apartment is softened by the lavender paintwork.

◁ **NATURAL CHOICE**
Bamboo blinds, basketware, wood fittings, and a soft carpet provide warm natural colours and textures that harmonize with the exposed brick walls and ceiling beams.

△ **CORNER KITCHEN**
A mini kitchen has been neatly slotted into the corner beneath the narrow gallery. Boldly painted sliding doors allow the paraphernalia of plumbing, ducts, and kitchen storage to be quickly concealed from view.

RUSTIC CHARM ▷
This homely kitchen, brightened by natural light, fits neatly under a wide gallery. It illustrates the delightful effect that can be achieved by furnishing a kitchen with old items of furniture instead of fitted units.

LOFT PLAN

THE DISTINGUISHING FEATURE of this minimalist, high-tech loft is the use of remote-controlled, aluminium slatted blinds to divide up the space at different times of the day, while still allowing light to filter through. The device introduces an element of fun and adds to the astonishing illusion of space created by an entire wall of mirror. All the light sources are concealed so that this studio is filled with reflected light.

△ ❷ KITCHEN SCREENING
With the blind lowered and the slats only partially closed, reflections from downlighters play on the polished granite countertop, animating the kitchen area behind.

Cooking area · Entrance · Dual-function door to entrance lobby or sleeping area · Remodelled curved wall

Washing machine

Bathroom

Boiler

Dining area, with venetian blind to screen off kitchen

Storage cupboard

Living area

Sleeping area

Blinds along entire length of external wall

Working area

Blinds for screening

INTERNAL ROOM DIMENSIONS:
6.7m (22ft) WIDE
8.1m (26ft) LONG

△ BIRD'S EYE VIEW
The kitchen, bathroom, and storage areas are sited along the internal wall, while the uncluttered, main living space of the loft enjoys the natural light flowing in from the large windows.

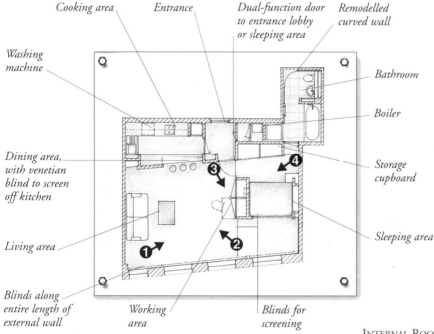

ALCOVE SHELVING
Shelving is tucked into a corner alcove, below a lowered ceiling with concealed lighting

BREAKFAST BAR
A polished granite worktop provides a dining bar between the kitchen and the living area.

DESIGN POINTS

■ A sequence of blinds can dramatically alter an interior space, creating new areas and separating off others.

■ Mirror is a powerful source of illusion. The larger it is, the more effective, but even a small framed mirror can give the impression of a room beyond.

■ Balance the cool effect of a minimalist, high-tech loft with the warmth of a timber floor. Parquet laid at right angles to the main axis will appear to widen an interior space.

◁ ❶ SHIMMERING REFLECTIVE WALL
The entire external wall of the loft is fitted with aluminium blinds. These create a shimmering wall that is reflected in the mirrored end wall, visually doubling the space. A bright red table adds a splash of colour to this cool interior.

KITCHEN BLIND
A blind screens off the entire kitchen and dining space.

CURVED WALL
A gently curving false wall leads you round into the lavatory area.

❸ **INSTANT OFFICE** ▷
A small home office is quickly assembled out of the bank of storage by opening one cupboard door as a gate-leg support and dropping down another as a work surface.

DUAL-FUNCTION DOOR
The entrance door can be used to close off access to the bedroom and bathroom.

STORAGE BANK
A bank of cupboards provides generous storage space and screens the sleeping area.

BEDSIDE STORAGE
A useful set of narrow shelves is concealed at either side of the bedhead.

CREATING SPACE
Remote-controlled venetian blinds screen off the bed and create a private or spare bedroom area alongside.

MIRROR ILLUSION
An end wall completely filled with mirror visually doubles the length of the studio and increases the light level.

FOR MORE DETAILS...

Curved bathroom wall
SEE P. 251

Mirrored wall SEE P. 251

Granite breakfast bar
SEE PP. 260–261

Blinds as screens SEE P. 264

FOLD-DOWN DESK
A useful home office space, created out of two cupboard fronts, is hidden from view when not in use.

❹ **PRIVATE SLEEPING AREA** ▷
The bed, with storage drawer underneath, is shielded by a bank of cupboards featuring a small, square, Japanese-style display cavity. By lowering a blind on the left-hand side, and swinging round the entrance door to close off the other side, a private sleeping area is created.

WALL OF BLINDS
Remote-controlled aluminium venetian blinds, covering four windows, line the entire external wall of the loft.

LOFT IDEAS

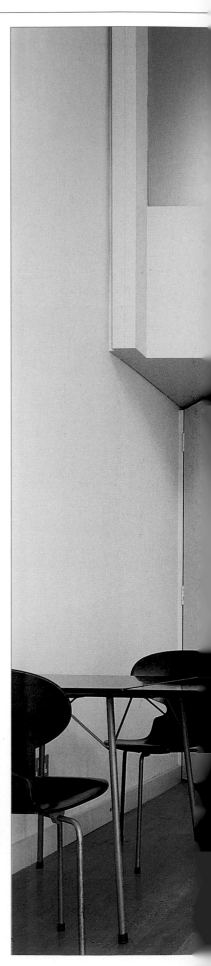

◁ **TOWEL-RAIL ROOM DIVIDER**
Decorative in shape, colour, and finish, towel radiators are no longer merely functional items, but play an important role in bathroom design. A free-standing vertical panel or ladder-style radiator, for example, can act not just as a towel rail and room heater but also as a room divider in an open-plan loft space.

DIVIDING LOFT SPACE ▷
Several ways of dividing space are illustrated in this minimalist loft. Extra-wide folding panels can be rapidly pulled across to conceal the kitchen, which is built under a gallery that divides the vertical space at one end of the room. A panel of translucent glazing allows light into a private area of the gallery, while a curved metal balustrade partially screens the open section.

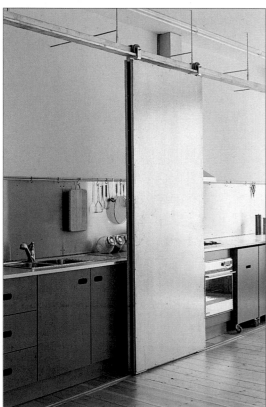

△ **INDUSTRIAL SLIDING PANELS**
Suspended, factory-style sliding panels offer a high-tech alternative to folding doors and blinds for screening off areas within a room. They take up less space than any folding system and can be faced with a choice of finishes, from metallic laminate to cork, paint, and plastics.

△ **PART-GLAZED SCREEN**
A quiet home-working space has been created here by placing a solid white screen behind the sofa. Above the screen is a glazed panel that allows the light and the line of the flush wall cupboards to flow through, following the direction of the flooring planks.

NATURAL LIGHT

YOU CAN TRANSFORM the character of your home by making good use of natural light. This light is superior to artificial light in two important ways: it is evenly distributed and therefore doesn't cast as many shadows; and, because it is less intense, it is less tiring on your eyes.

Each room will receive a different amount of light depending on its position in your house and the time of day. Decide how the available light can be used to best advantage in each case and how it can be modulated to suit your needs.

Window treatments allow you to modify the strength and amount of natural light that falls in each room. Consider the atmosphere or mood you want to create, how much privacy you need, and the function and style of the room when selecting blinds, curtains, or shutters.

CONTROLLED EXPOSURE
Evenly diffused natural light floods in through large skylights in the high ceiling.

POINTS TO CONSIDER

■ Sunny rooms get hot and stuffy without good ventilation so venetian blinds or louvred shutters, which let air in but keep sunlight out, are a good choice.

■ Blinds with an aluminium backing reflect heat back out through the window, helping to prevent uncomfortable heat build-up.

■ Check which way your room faces. If you need protection from both low winter sun and high summer sun, venetian blinds provide an attractive and flexible option.

■ A roller blind is a cheap and effective option if you require privacy only at night, and do not need to regulate the sunlight.

■ Before opting for frosted glass, check the effect by placing tracing paper over the window.

■ Even if your windows are very high, or unusually shaped, roller blinds can be made to measure and specially fitted with strings or hooks so they can be operated from below.

■ If a skylight is the only source of natural light in the room, make sure that it can be opened easily to provide ventilation.

■ A small window in a large room can make for a gloomy atmosphere. One option is to enlarge the existing window; or, if you would prefer a different aspect, consider installing a new window on another wall.

■ As long-term exposure to sunlight will eventually fade soft furnishings, books, and pictures, make sure that where possible you install blinds or screens to filter out the strongest rays. Try not to place vulnerable items in direct sunlight.

WORKING WITH NATURAL LIGHT

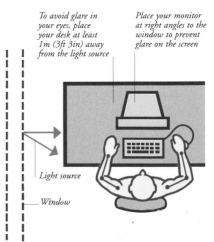

To avoid glare in your eyes, place your desk at least 1m (3ft 3in) away from the light source

Place your monitor at right angles to the window to prevent glare on the screen

Light source

Window

If you work at home, access to natural light is vital for a comfortable work environment. However, direct sunlight can cause glare on your computer screen. To avoid eyestrain and headaches, site your workstation at right angles to the light source and a short distance away, and install blinds or shutters.

OPAQUE GLASS

This glass can be plain, or have a textured, acid-etched, or sandblasted finish, to echo the theme of a room.

ADVANTAGES
• Obscures the view from passers-by.
• Makes curtains or blinds unnecessary.
• Allows maximum daylight to filter through.

DISADVANTAGES
• Hand-finished designs can be expensive.
• Can look cold and clinical.
• Does not retain heat in winter.

ROLLER BLINDS

Offering a limitless choice of colours, patterns, and textures, roller blinds draw attention to the window area.

ADVANTAGES
• Easy to fit.
• Take up a minimum amount of space.
• Huge choice of colours and designs.

DISADVANTAGES
• Block out light if you want daytime privacy.
• Difficult to clean and dust.
• Some spring mechanisms can jam in use.

VENETIAN BLINDS

These blinds allow a total or partial sun block and can be adjusted to suit winter and summer sunlight.

ADVANTAGES
• Adjustable control of sunlight and privacy.
• Available in wood, aluminium, or plastic.
• Allow good air circulation.

DISADVANTAGES
• Can suggest an office environment.
• Slats are difficult to clean and attract dust.
• Cheaper versions will warp and break.

VERTICAL BLINDS

Although strongly reminiscent of commercial office decor, vertical blinds are highly effective in controlling light.

ADVANTAGES
• Made in long lengths to cover large areas.
• Allow good air circulation.
• Can be backed to control glare and heat.

DISADVANTAGES
• Not a particularly attractive option.
• Lack the flexibility of venetian blinds.
• Overtly commercial look.

SHUTTERS

Shutters offer an interesting alternative to curtains or blinds. Added light control is provided by those with adjustable slats.

ADVANTAGES
• Slatted models still allow ventilation when shut.
• Locked shutters add extra security.
• For privacy, use only on lower part of window.

DISADVANTAGES
• Expensive as they have to be custom-made.
• Not suitable for oddly shaped windows.
• Can cut out too much light in winter.

CURTAINS

These add interest and colour, they emphasize your taste and style, and frame an otherwise plain window.

ADVANTAGES
• Can co-ordinate with the colour scheme.
• Help create a warm, homely atmosphere.
• Provide insulation against the cold.

DISADVANTAGES
• Have to be completely shut to block sunlight.
• Attract dust and are difficult to clean.
• Expensive over a large area, especially if lined.

ARTIFICIAL LIGHT

LIGHTING CAN BE DRAMATIC OR SUBTLE. It can draw the eye towards a particular focus or make parts of a room disappear. Even a dimmer switch can completely alter an interior space. The ideal is a balance between ambient and task lighting, but lights should always be selected with a specific function in mind, and knowing their effect on surrounding surfaces and materials. The days of the single, central pendant bulb are long gone, and a stream of exciting, adaptable systems offer scope for imaginative ideas for shaping space and providing a good level of visibility.

FLOOR-STANDING LAMP

The universal joint connecting the arm to the support of this simple, elegant lamp provides maximum flexibility.

ADVANTAGES
• Light can be directed to where it is needed.
• Height and angle of light are easily adjusted.
• Ideal as a portable, floor-standing reading light.

DISADVANTAGES
• Light is not easily directed upwards.
• Trailing flex can be hazardous.
• Can take up valuable floor space.

COMBINATION OF LIGHTING
A variety of lights, including uplighters, ceiling light, and wall-mounted spot, define different areas.

ANGLEPOISE

Precisely balanced, either on a cast metal base or clamped to a worksurface, this lamp is designed to rest in any position.

ADVANTAGES
• Ideal task light for working or reading.
• Can be angled to cast a pool of light.
• Very safe, weighty, cast metal base.

DISADVANTAGES
• Nuts holding light in position may loosen.
• The flex must be kept safely out of the way.
• Shade can become hot after lengthy use.

POINTS TO CONSIDER

■ Consider fixed lighting at the planning stage of a room, so you can arrange the electrical wiring system before you start decorating. Sockets can then be added for lamps and lighting effects.

■ When choosing lamps and fittings be aware of the type of light provided by different bulbs. Traditional tungsten bulbs give a warm colour cast, but get very hot. Halogen bulbs provide the most natural colour balance, while flourescent bulbs give off a cool, somewhat harsh light.

■ If reducing energy consumption is an important priority, choose lamps and light fittings that use long-life, compact flourescent bulbs. These consume 20 per cent less energy, give out less heat, and need less frequent replacement than tungsten bulbs.

■ Stairways and entrances and access to ancillary spaces, such as halls and cellars, must be properly lit. Lights need not be wall- or ceiling-hung, but can be mounted at low levels so that the focus of illumination is on the stair-treads.

PENDANT

Attractive in its functional simplicity, this lamp creates a warm, cosy pool of light to highlight a seating or dining area.

ADVANTAGES
• Creates a homely atmosphere round a table.
• Helps to create a focal point in the room.
• Height can be adjusted to suit.

DISADVANTAGES
• Requires a translucent bulb to avoid dazzle.
• Permanent fixture, so cannot be moved.
• Cannot be angled to give a directional beam.

TABLE LAMP

Ideal for a bedside table or living room occasional table, this traditional-style lamp provides soft diffused lighting.

ADVANTAGES
• Can be easily moved around.
• Less expensive than a floor lamp.
• No glare, as the bulb is not exposed.

DISADVANTAGES
• Light level too low to serve as a task light.
• Area illuminated may be quite small.
• Takes up table-top space.

WALL-HUNG UPLIGHTER

Uplighters throw soft, even, reflected light around a room, creating relaxing ambient lighting for living areas.

ADVANTAGES
• Can enhance architectural features.
• Translucent shade produces diffused light.
• Bulb and wiring are concealed.

DISADVANTAGES
• Electrical wiring must be concealed in wall.
• Not suitable for reading or working.
• Cannot be moved around the room.

MINI DOWNLIGHTERS

Low-voltage halogen fittings are now so small that they can be totally concealed in recesses on the underside of a shelf.

ADVANTAGES
• Are totally hidden and do not dazzle.
• Create bright, even lighting on worktops.
• Not hot enough to damage shelving.

DISADVANTAGES
• Difficult to conceal the wiring.
• A position has to be found for the transformer.
• Gloves needed to handle the bulbs.

BARE-WIRE SYSTEM

Mini low-voltage halogen spotlights rest on parallel tensile wires, which act as the track between two points.

ADVANTAGES
• Lights can be easily moved along the cables.
• Halogen light has minimal effect on colours.
• Light can be directed onto a worktop.

DISADVANTAGES
• Transformer needed to convert electric current.
• Light can be dazzling.
• Transformer must be fitted by an electrician.

DIFFUSED LIGHTING

Non-directional lighting offers a soft, ambient atmosphere that is successful in both hi-tech and traditional rooms.

ADVANTAGES
• Creates a relaxing ambience.
• Can disguise less than perfect surfaces.
• Useful for small spaces, as sits flush to the wall.

DISADVANTAGES
• Cannot be used for task lighting.
• Can be expensive.
• May need additional light sources.

SOFT FLOORING

A RELATIVELY PERMANENT fixture, flooring must be chosen carefully when planning a room. Your decision must encompass practical considerations, such as cost and the extent of use in different areas, as well as personal style preferences. Carpets, for example, are soft and comfortable to tread on with bare feet but can rot in damp conditions such as a steamy bathroom. Materials such as vinyl, while not as long-lasting as natural substances, are cheaper and easy to replace when worn. Experiment in each room with sample tiles and swatches before making a final decision.

CARPET

Carpeting varies from expensive wool mixtures to cheaper synthetic blends, but all offer great comfort underfoot.

ADVANTAGES
• Range of finishes from velvet to shag pile.
• Extensive choice of colours and patterns.
• Damaged carpet can be easily replaced.

DISADVANTAGES
• Regular cleaning needed to prolong carpet life.
• May need periodical re-stretching.
• Synthetic fibres react badly to burns.

FLOORING AS A ROOM DIVIDER
A change of colour and texture is an effective way of defining two different areas in a single space.

VINYL

A cheap, flexible plastic that is produced in sheet or tile form. It is available in a huge range of colours and patterns.

ADVANTAGES
• Soft and quiet underfoot, and non-slip.
• Inexpensive and easy to lay on a flat surface.
• Hardwearing and waterproof.

DISADVANTAGES
• Tends to discolour with age.
• Reflects light poorly and looks artificial.
• Ripples may form if laid on an uneven floor.

POINTS TO CONSIDER

■ No matter how good the flooring you choose, incorrect fitting or laying will result in an uneven surface that will wear badly. Always have flooring installed professionally.

■ If you are planning neutral-coloured walls to create a feeling of space, consider a natural-coloured floor to add warmth.

■ Would you like to create space by dispensing with radiators? Underfloor heating provides an alternative, but check that the flooring is suitable.

■ While the luxury of walking on carpet is appealing, carpet can be difficult to clean and maintain, and may not be practical in all areas of the house.

■ Bear in mind that plain-coloured flooring shows up marks more quickly than floors with a patterned surface.

■ Busy or large-scale floor patterns may overpower the rest of the room, especially if the room is small and the furniture and fittings are plain.

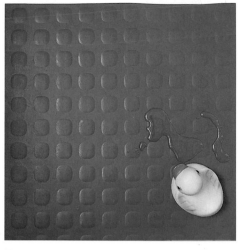

NATURAL FIBRE MATTING

Plant-fibre matting, such as seagrass, coir, sisal, or jute, offers a warm, natural look and can be loose laid or fitted.

ADVANTAGES
• Hard-wearing and sound-absorbent.
• Decorative weaves and colours available.
• A natural alternative to carpet and synthetics.

DISADVANTAGES
• Borders must be bound to prevent fraying.
• Not suitable for kitchens or in direct sunlight.
• Difficult to clean thoroughly.

CORK TILES

Manufactured by compressing cork, this flooring is inexpensive but rather dull in comparison to other natural floorings.

ADVANTAGES
• Warm and soft underfoot, and extremely quiet.
• Inexpensive and easy to lay without expert help.
• Sealed cork tiles are stain-resistant.

DISADVANTAGES
• Colour, texture, and pattern is uniform.
• Tiles are only stuck down with glue so may lift.
• Tiles damaged by water will need replacing.

RUBBER

Stud rubber flooring is available in sheet or tile form. It is extremely hardwearing and is water-resistant.

ADVANTAGES
• Virtually indestructable.
• Quiet and warm to walk on.
• Waterproof surface has anti-slip finish.

DISADVANTAGES
• Expensive to buy.
• Only stocked by specialist floor suppliers.
• Must be installed by an experienced fitter.

TEXTURED VINYL

Tough, waterproof, and non-slip, textured vinyl is available in a wide range of colours and textures.

ADVANTAGES
• Feels warm and absorbs sound.
• Durable and requires minimal maintenance.
• Easy to cut round awkwardly shaped walls.

DISADVANTAGES
• May be marked by furniture without castors.
• Can be stained by shoe polish and fibre pens.
• Abrasive cleaners can cause discoloration.

VINYL TILES

With all the advantages of sheet vinyl, vinyl tiles are available in a range of colours and can look good anywhere.

ADVANTAGES
• Spare tiles can be kept to repair worn areas.
• You can create your own unique pattern.
• Tiles are quick and easy to lay.

DISADVANTAGES
• Corners may break if not stuck down firmly.
• May not be waterproof if edges are not close.
• Can be stained by waxes, polishes, and solvents.

LINOLEUM

Produced from natural ingredients, such as linseed oil, linoleum comes in sheets or is hand-cut for intricate patterning.

ADVANTAGES
• A quiet, warm surface that cushions your feet.
• Manufactured from all-natural substances.
• Durable and low-maintenance.

DISADVANTAGES
• More costly than vinyl and needs expert fitting.
• Water can seep under unsealed edges.
• It may scuff or mark if not kept well-polished.

HARD FLOORING

LOFTS, KITCHENS, AND BATHROOMS tend to feature hard floor finishes, such as wood, stone, and timber. Hard floors do increase sound levels in a room but these can be muted by adding rugs and other soft materials. Wooden floors are warm, easy to sweep clean and good value, but long-term durability and water-resistance can be a problem. Limestone and slate are hard-wearing surfaces, but can be cold and hard on the feet. Underfloor heating, which is enjoying a revival, is compatible with most types of hard floorings, particularly ceramic, stone, and well-seasoned hardwood.

WOOD

The colour, grain, and warmth of wood make it a popular choice in all rooms, but bathroom floors must be sealed.

ADVANTAGES
• Plank or stripwood is simple to install.
• Mellows and improves with age.
• Works well in modern and traditional settings.

DISADVANTAGES
• Needs regular maintenance to look its best.
• Water penetration can swell and lift planks.
• Noisy when walked on in shoes.

HAND-COLOURED TILES
A highly imaginative use of colour turns a patchwork of tiles into a kaleidoscope of tones.

TERRACOTTA TILES

Both new and reclaimed terracotta tiles are available. In time, new tiles develop the rich patina common to old ones.

ADVANTAGES
• Clay is warmer than stone underfoot.
• Variety of colours, textures, shapes, and sizes.
• Sealed tiles are water- and stain-resistant.

DISADVANTAGES
• Unsealed tiles are porous and stain easily.
• Difficult to find matching old tiles in quantity.
• High-quality tiles can be expensive.

POINTS TO CONSIDER

■ Think carefully about your selection of materials for furniture, soft furnishings, cabinet finishes, worksurfaces, and appliances before making a final decision on the type of flooring. This way you can ensure that all the elements complement one another. Do not forget to take into account the floor in adjacent rooms; too many changes of finish from one room to the next in a small home can appear fussy and tiresome.

■ Bear in mind the cost of laying the floor as well as the purchase price of materials. Most floors should be laid before cabinetry and appliances are installed. Ensure the new flooring is well protected during other building work and installations.

■ The amount of day-to-day maintenance you are willing to undertake may influence your floor choice. Some materials, such as wood, require more care, especially around a sink, where water can damage the varnish.

■ Decide whether the room is large enough to accommodate two floor finishes. For example, you may prefer limestone tiles around an activity zone, and wood flooring in an area with less traffic.

■ If you choose tiled flooring, bear in mind that large rooms need large, plain tiles; small, patterned tiles will look too busy. Flagstones and large terracotta tiles particularly suit the proportions of larger rooms.

COLOUR-WASHED WOOD

Wood has its own charm, but a soft paint wash can brighten up weathered boards or mask poor-quality timber.

ADVANTAGES
• You control the colour depth and tone.
• Colour can be re-applied at any time.
• Compatible with underfloor heating.

DISADVANTAGES
• Expands in reaction to water and humidity.
• Is not impact-resistant and can splinter.
• Tends to amplify sound levels in room.

WOOD LAMINATE

Made from pressed, resin-impregnated papers, laminates offer an immense variety of colours, patterns, and textures.

ADVANTAGES
• Extremely hard-wearing and durable.
• Hygienic, stain-resistant, and easy to maintain.
• Patterns and colours do not fade.

DISADVANTAGES
• Hard surfaces can be noisy.
• More difficult to repair than carpet or vinyl.
• Surface can bubble or peel from the edges.

LIMESTONE

Along with other natural stones, pale grey limestone has a characteristic grain and texture that improves with age.

ADVANTAGES
• Natural colour blends with all room styles.
• Easy-to-clean surface.
• Extremely hardwearing.

DISADVANTAGES
• Expensive to buy and install.
• Cold to walk on barefoot.
• Slippery when wet.

SLATE

Popular because of its natural variations in colour from grey to green and purple, slate is precision-cut into sheets or tiles.

ADVANTAGES
• Wide range of colours and sizes of slate available.
• Choice of smooth or rough natural finishes.
• Wears well over the years and is waterproof.

DISADVANTAGES
• Large pieces are brittle and may crack or peel.
• Cold underfoot.
• Large sheets of slate are expensive.

GLAZED CERAMIC TILES

The most hardwearing and impermeable of all flooring materials, glazed ceramic tiles do not need sealing for protection.

ADVANTAGES
• Low maintenance and almost indestructible.
• Mass-produced, so easy and inexpensive to buy.
• Available in a huge range of bold colours.

DISADVANTAGES
• Hard on feet and slippery when wet.
• Grout between tiles can be difficult to clean.
• Strong-coloured glazes can be overpowering.

MARBLE

Marble flooring has a timeless quality, making it a desirable choice for both contemporary and traditional rooms.

ADVANTAGES
• Low maintenance and hardwearing.
• Natural beauty does not deteriorate with age.
• Smooth surface will not harbour dust or dirt.

DISADVANTAGES
• Slippery when wet and may stain.
• Expensive to buy and fit.
• Requires a strong sub-floor below.

WALLCOVERINGS

THE MATERIALS YOU CHOOSE as wallcoverings will determine the character of each room in your house. Deciding on colour and texture are both important considerations, but selecting a wall finish is not simply a style issue. Consider room use, temperature, and lighting when making your selection. While wallpaper or paint may be suitable for a living area or bedroom, they are not always the best options for a kitchen or bathroom, which are often hot and steamy. In these rooms, hard-wearing, washable coverings, such as tiles, stone, and glass may be more appropriate.

PLASTER WALLS

Once a technique for preparing walls, bare plaster is now a popular wall finish and comes rough, polished, or stained.

ADVANTAGES
• Masks uneven walls, turning them into a feature.
• Durable and inexpensive finish.
• Provides an opportunity to add character.

DISADVANTAGES
• Rough plaster attracts dust and is hard to clean.
• Can look artificial if not well rendered.
• Requires a splashback around countertops.

HARDWORKING WALLS
Architectural glass bricks allow light to penetrate, while mosaic tiles are durable and easy to clean.

GLASS BRICKS

Ideal as a screen where natural light has to be "borrowed" from another living area, glass bricks suit a modern space.

ADVANTAGES
• Add an area of interest.
• Are extremely durable and waterproof.
• Allow light to filter through.

DISADVANTAGES
• Expensive.
• Need to be installed professionally.
• Can make a room feel cold and clinical.

POINTS TO CONSIDER

■ Paint is the most versatile and inexpensive of wall coverings and offers the opportunity to experiment with a wide range of finishes from sponging to stencilling. The effects and colours can be selected to achieve total co-ordination.

■ Pale colours reflect light from windows to create a feeling of space. They are ideal for brightening north-facing rooms or rooms with a low ceiling. Large mirrors placed opposite natural light sources will also give an impression of additional space.

■ Natural materials, such as wood panelling, create a warm, homely atmosphere and provide insulation.

■ Emulsion paints are not suitable for cold exterior walls, or steamy bathrooms and kitchens with poor ventilation, because they cannot withstand condensation and damp. Choose oil-based paints, such as egg-shell, or specially formulated vinyl paints with fungicides to limit mildew on these walls.

■ Stainless steel, ceramic tile, or stone are all heat- and water-resistant, making them ideal for kitchen splashbacks.

■ High walls can make a room feel cold. Balance the proportions of the room by selecting one type of wallcovering for the lower walls and another covering for the upper part of the walls.

PAINT

The most versatile wallcovering of all, paint can be chosen to co-ordinate with your furniture and soft furnishings.

ADVANTAGES
• Wide range of colours with durable finishes.
• Walls can be wiped clean with a sponge.
• Simple to retouch small areas or repaint room.

DISADVANTAGES
• Not tough enough to be used as a splashback.
• Gloss paints show up imperfections in walls.
• Painted walls may peel or become mildewed.

WALLPAPER

Ideal for disguising uneven plasterwork, wallpaper can insulate against cold and creates a comfortable, furnished effect.

ADVANTAGES
• Plastic-coated, wipe-clean papers are available.
• Wide range of colours and patterns.
• Easy to hang and provides fast coverage.

DISADVANTAGES
• Steam may cause wallpaper to peel.
• Difficult to repair small area once damaged.
• Can be expensive for a large room.

WOOD PANELLING

Useful for covering up uneven areas on walls and ceilings, painted wood panels will also help insulate heat and sound.

ADVANTAGES
• Easy to install without expert help.
• Hides irregular walls or uneven plasterwork.
• Absorbs kitchen noise.

DISADVANTAGES
• Good quality panelling not always available.
• Unsuitable material for sink and cooking area.
• Traditional look does not suit all room styles.

TILES

Ideal for covering large expanses of wall, or for behind a hob or sink, tiles are available in a wide range of colours.

ADVANTAGES
• Easy-to-clean flat surface and thin grouting.
• Heat-resistant, so suitable for cooking areas.
• Pale tiles covering large areas look inoffensive.

DISADVANTAGES
• Regular shape and surface can look boring.
• Can detract from character of room.
• Darker coloured tiles can be less hardwearing.

MOSAIC TILES

Available in easy-to-use sheets, mosaic tiles are water-resistant and durable, ideal for the kitchen or bathroom.

ADVANTAGES
• Add character and interest to all surfaces.
• Easy to lay.
• Offer interesting design opportunities.

DISADVANTAGES
• Intricate designs are time-consuming.
• Grout can harbour soap and dirt.
• Can look municipal if used over large areas.

GRANITE

This popular kitchen material is often used as a splashback above granite worktops. It works best in small areas.

ADVANTAGES
• Hardwearing and low-maintenance.
• Easy to clean, with few grouted seams.
• Continuity; it can match a granite worktop.

DISADVANTAGES
• Dark, cold appearance unsuitable for large areas.
• Complicated to fit around plug sockets.
• Expensive; has to be cut off-site, to a template.

SHELVING

THE MOST VERSATILE FORM of storage is shelving – whether freestanding, built in, or within furniture, it is the most flexible way of accommodating different objects. At its most basic, it is also one of the cheapest. Shelving that is sympathetic to the architecture of the room can be immensely appealing; if it is erected without any aesthetic consideration of the larger space, however, it can be detrimental. Select the type of shelving according to the style of room, the nature of the objects to be stored, and whether or not you require flexibility.

TIMBER

Hardwood is the most elegant, expensive material; softwood, such as pine, is less formal and cheaper. Ensure timber does not clash with other wood in the room.

ADVANTAGES
• Has a natural beauty that wears well.
• Very sturdy and does not need edging.

DISADVANTAGES
• Some hardwoods may be difficult to obtain.
• While hardwood is strong, pine is less sturdy.

POINTS TO CONSIDER

■ Analyse carefully what you intend to store on shelves. Measure your possessions by the metre, allowing for possible expansion.

■ Determine how large the objects to be stored are in relation to the shelf depth, and allow a few centimetres extra.

■ Do you want to build in lighting? Low-voltage downlighters and

spotlights are good for display; strip lights hidden behind a lipped front are also useful.

■ Assess how you will clean the shelves – this may affect your choice of material.

■ If shelving is to house electrical equipment, consider false backs to conceal the wiring or build electrical sockets into the units.

MDF (MEDIUM-DENSITY FIBREBOARD)

This popular, versatile material, when painted, is often used as an effective substitute for timber. MDF is sturdy when used in short spans, and does not warp as much as solid wood.

ADVANTAGES
• Can be cut into different shapes easily.
• Available in many different thicknesses.

DISADVANTAGES
• Health risk, so wear a mask when cutting.
• Must be painted or varnished.

MELAMINE-FACED BOARD

Easy to wipe clean, melamine-faced board is a practical choice for utility areas, kitchens, or bathrooms. If necessary, it can be easily and effectively upgraded by applying a timber trim.

ADVANTAGES
• Impervious qualities good in wet situations.
• Inexpensive and practical.

DISADVANTAGES
• Needs careful application of edging detail.
• Can look cheap, particularly if shiny.

PLYWOOD

As a cheaper alternative to timber, plywood is at present enjoying a fashionable image. It can be covered in different timber veneers, such as birch or oak, and may be used in wet areas.

ADVANTAGES
• Can be extremely strong.
• Available in a waterproof variety.

DISADVANTAGES
• Feels like a substitute for more expensive wood.
• Edging must be carefully detailed.

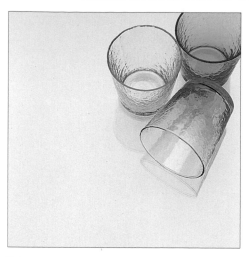

TOUGHENED GLASS

Glass shelves have a luminous quality, which can be enhanced by good lighting. They are particularly suitable for display purposes and in bathrooms.

ADVANTAGES
• Easy to wipe clean and does not stain.
• Decorative: can be clear, etched, or sandblasted.

DISADVANTAGES
• Expensive, as must be toughened.
• Shows fingerprints and may chip.

GALVANIZED METAL

Ideal for heavy utility areas such as garages and greenhouses, galvanized metal shelves are usually purchased in freestanding kit form, ranging from lightweight to heavy-duty shelving units.

ADVANTAGES
• Some kits designed for specific items, e.g. tools.
• Heavy-duty units can take a lot of weight.

DISADVANTAGES
• Will corrode over time and if damaged.
• Stylistically restrictive.

SHELF SUPPORTS

There are two basic types of fitted shelving: fixed shelves, which are often custom built; and adjustable shelves, which are usually available as a ready-made system and are more flexible, as the shelf heights can be altered. Below are some of the supports available: choice must be guided by the shelf material, the load, and the style of room.

FIXED SUPPORTS

WOODEN BATTENS
A good, basic support for shelving in an alcove or recess; ensure that the battens stop short of the outer edges of the shelf to make them less obtrusive.

SECRET FIXINGS
D-shaped brackets fixed to the walls slot into the short sides of the shelf and are concealed. An ideal minimalist solution for display shelving.

FIXED BRACKETS
These come in various forms, from a basic metal bracket to designer versions, as shown here. They do not need the support of side walls.

ADJUSTABLE SUPPORTS

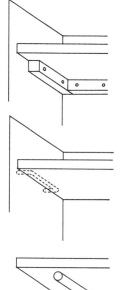

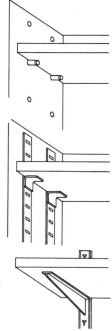

SLOTS AND DOWELS
Suitable for short shelf spans between two walls; the shelf rests on dowels plugged into holes at the sides. Unobtrusive, so ideal with glass shelving.

STRIPS AND CLIPS
Same principle as above, but saves setting out the holes and gives more flexibility. Metal strips are fixed to the side walls and shelves rest on metal clips.

RAILS AND BRACKETS
Good for large spans in utilitarian sites, brackets that slot into vertical tracks are very flexibile, easy to install, and do not need side walls for support.

SHELF SPANS

The load a shelf can carry depends on the type of material used, its thickness, and the distance between supports. For short shelves, a support at either end is sufficient, but for longer spans you may need to add some intermediate ones. The chart below shows the maximum span to allow between supports for medium loads, such as light books or china. For heavier loads, you will need less distance between supports. If your drill goes in with little resistance, your wall might not be able to bear heavy loads.

MATERIAL	THICKNESS	DISTANCE BETWEEN SUPPORTS
Timber	15mm (⅝in) 22mm (⅞in) 28mm (1⅛in)	50cm (19¾in) 90cm (35½in) 106cm (41¾in)
Glass Not suitable for heavy loads	6mm (¼in) 10mm (⅜in) 15mm (⅝in)	20cm (7¾in) 40cm (15¾in) 40cm (15¾in)
MDF **(Medium-density fibreboard)**	15mm (⅝in) 18mm (¾in) 25mm (1in)	50cm (19¾in) 70cm (27½in) 90cm (35½in)
Melamine-faced board	15mm (⅝in) 18mm (¾in)	40cm (15¾in) 60cm (23½in)
Plywood	12mm (½in) 18mm (¾in) 25mm (1in)	40cm (15¾in) 60cm (23½in) 80cm (31½in)

WORKSURFACES

SEPARATE ACTIVITY ZONES in a room will require worksurfaces manufactured from different materials. Your choice of material and the size of the surface will be lead by the task undertaken, as there is no one surface that can withstand scratches, stains and heat marks, and be hardwearing, easy to clean, and attractive. Compare the merits of each surface before making a selection.

POINTS TO CONSIDER

■ Terrazzo, granite, or stainless steel are ideal for the worksurface area surrounding the kitchen hob. All three are heatproof, hardwearing, and require little effort to maintain. If you are not planning to stay in your property for long, however, the cost of these materials may be a drawback.

■ Oiled hardwood, Colorcore, stainless steel, and Corian are water-resistant and soft in texture. They are useful for areas around kitchen draining boards, providing a cushioned landing for delicate china and glassware.

■ Chopping and food preparation is best performed on wood. Consider buying a series of different-sized blocks to lay on top of any surface, or install a slab of end-grain wood. Once regarded as a breeding ground for bacteria, wood is now known to be hygienic.

■ Oiled hardwoods make attractive and easy to restore general surfaces, when away from heat.

■ Granite or slate are both suitable surfaces for pastry-making because they are cool and smooth, so preventing pastry from sticking.

STAINLESS STEEL

A near-perfect worktop material, used in professional kitchens where performance is important. A brushed finish is best.

ADVANTAGES
• A non-corrosive and heatproof material.
• Wipes clean easily and is very hygienic.
• Brushed stainless steel wears particularly well.

DISADVANTAGES
• Highly polished surfaces scratch easily.
• A noisy surface to work on.
• Difficult to fabricate into curved shapes.

GRANITE

A natural material available in a huge range of colours and patterns. It is cut to size and polished to make worktops.

ADVANTAGES
• Natural beauty does not deteriorate with age.
• Almost impossible to scratch or chip.
• Heatproof, waterproof, and difficult to stain.

DISADVANTAGES
• Expensive as it is a hard stone to machine-cut.
• Weight requires base cabinets to be strong.
• Dark colourways can appear cold and murky.

SLATE

Many slates are too porous for kitchen use but a few newly available types have a high silica content that reduces porosity.

ADVANTAGES
• Smooth surface is cool and pleasant to touch.
• Relatively hardwearing if silica content is high.
• A cheaper alternative to granite and marble.

DISADVANTAGES
• Porous types of slate absorb oil and stain easily.
• A finish must be applied to reduce porosity.
• Colours can be dull and uninteresting.

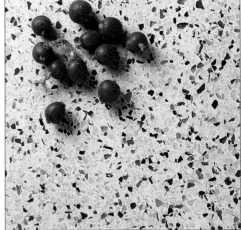

TERRAZZO

A lesser known material, made from a mixture of marble and granite chippings set in white cement, and then polished.

ADVANTAGES
• Comes in wide variety of colours and patterns.
• Can be made up to your exact specification.
• Hardwearing and waterproof.

DISADVANTAGES
• Costly and time-consuming to install.
• Not as hardwearing as natural stones.
• Bolder patterns may lose their appeal in time.

LACQUERED HARDWOOD

The beauty of wood makes it a popular choice. These worktops are coated with lacquer, above and below, for protection.

ADVANTAGES
• Wide range of different colours and grains exist.
• Worktops match the wood cabinet finishes.
• Reasonably priced.

DISADVANTAGES
• Liquid spillages eventually dissolve the lacquer.
• Knife cuts permanently damage the surface.
• Not as hardwearing as other wood finishes.

END-GRAIN WOOD

As its name suggests, this is wood turned on its end and glued together in blocks. It provides a good surface for cutting.

ADVANTAGES
• Very dense and wears evenly across the grain.
• Knife blades do not damage the end-grain.
• Blade is gripped on contact, making it safer.

DISADVANTAGES
• Central heating may cause the worktop to warp.
• Absorbs strong food flavours, such as garlic.
• Wood may contract in centrally heated homes.

OILED WOOD

Planks of solid hardwood that are glued together and brushed with linseed oil to prevent the wood from splitting.

ADVANTAGES
• More resistant to heat than lacquered wood.
• Flexible surface that can withstand knocks.
• Sanding and a coat of oil restores its beauty.

DISADVANTAGES
• Central heating may cause it to warp or crack.
• Chopping on this surface leaves deep incisions.
• Some oiled hardwoods are expensive.

FORMICA LAMINATE

A man-made material that has a paper centre and is built up with thick coats of lacquer to create a flexible sheet material.

ADVANTAGES
• Huge choice of bright colours and patterns.
• Waterproof and easy to wipe clean.
• Simple and inexpensive to manufacture.

DISADVANTAGES
• Cutting directly onto the surface causes damage.
• In time, the laminate can deteriorate.
• Once damaged, the worktop cannot be repaired.

COLORCORE

This material is made from layer upon layer of coloured paper, coated in a tough melamine-formaldehyde resin.

ADVANTAGES
• Knife cuts on worktops can be sanded away.
• Subtle range of colours is available.
• Waterproof and simple to wipe clean.

DISADVANTAGES
• More expensive than Formica laminate.
• Can become unstuck at the edges.
• Surface has no light-reflective qualities.

CORIAN

A synthetic resin best installed in heavily used areas, such as around sinks, where it can be seamlessly joined to worktops.

ADVANTAGES
• Rounded front edges are safer for small children.
• Joins between different sections are invisible.
• Sinks and worktops are made from one piece.

DISADVANTAGES
• Difficult to install without professional help.
• Over long periods, paler colours may yellow.
• Can work out as expensive as granite.

CONCEALMENT

CONCEALMENT IS A MAJOR ELEMENT of storage. Some items, though practical and frequently used, may detract from the aesthetic harmony of a room. Others might not actually need concealing, just protection from dust. You may also require storage that keeps personal belongings out of sight. Generally speaking, the majority of objects need to be concealed but should still be accessible without effort or disruption whenever required.

POINTS TO CONSIDER

■ Establish the reason for concealing items – for practicality, privacy, or aesthetics.

■ Try to anticipate how often you will want access to your concealed possessions. If you need them frequently, choose a method that requires minimum effort.

■ Take into account the amount of space required: side-hinged doors need a minimum of 60cm (23½in) clearance in front of them.

■ Do you require part-time concealment? If you need constant access to the objects and want to cover them up only occasionally for cosmetic reasons, blinds, screens, roller shutters, and curtains tend to offer the most useful methods of concealment.

■ Consider the practicalities, such as cleaning advantages and cost: avoid methods relying on a complicated mechanism unless you can afford the best quality.

FABRIC-FRONTED DOORS

To achieve a softer, more rustic look, replace solid door panels with wire mesh and pleated fabric. Particularly suitable for kitchens, bedrooms, and living areas.

ADVANTAGES
• Fabric design can tie in with other furnishings.
• Material can be changed as desired.

DISADVANTAGES
• More difficult to clean than solid doors.
• Side-hinged doors need clearance when open.

ROLLER SHUTTERS

Based on the pull-down principle of garage doors and bureaus, roller shutters hide items instantly, such as kitchen appliances, that are frequently used but that clutter up worksurfaces.

ADVANTAGES
• Useful for an immediate "tidy-up".
• Neat and do not intrude on the worksurface.

DISADVANTAGES
• Only suitable for modern-style kitchens.
• Expensive and difficult to source.

RETRACTABLE DOORS

Sliding back along the depth of kitchen units, retractable doors are completely hidden, leaving accessible shelves and open units to work on; when closed, they conceal the work area.

ADVANTAGES
• Allow dramatic transformations of view.
• Large areas of untidiness quickly hidden.

DISADVANTAGES
• An expensive, custom-made solution.
• Heavy doors need good-quality runners.

FOLD-BACK DOORS

These doors offer a space-saving solution for inaccessible corners, or in areas where you do not want the doors of a cabinet to protrude beyond a certain point in the room.

ADVANTAGES
• Do not need much clearance space.
• Fairly inexpensive solution.

DISADVANTAGES
• Central joints and hinging can be unattractive.
• Poor-quality models can come off tracks.

GLASS-FRONTED DOORS

Glass cabinets are particularly effective for storing glass and china. Sandblasted glass gives the same lucidity but offers a degree of opacity for less tidy owners.

ADVANTAGES
• Easy to clean.
• Display as well as protect contents.

DISADVANTAGES
• Items must be neatly arranged.
• Glass shows fingerprints.

TOP-HINGED DOORS

Most cupboards are side hinged, but in some cases top-hinged doors are more practical and look better, for example when a cabinet is wider than it is tall.

ADVANTAGES
• Useful for cabinets above normal reach.
• Can make use of space above a doorway.

DISADVANTAGES
• Require a stay to fix in open position.
• Awkward to operate above a certain height.

SLIDING DOORS

Most commonly used in wardrobes, sliding doors are particularly useful where there is restricted clearance space for open doors.

ADVANTAGES
• Save space as doors do not open into room.
• Discreet and unobtrusive.

DISADVANTAGES
• Only half of contents are visible when open.
• Dirt collects on tracks.

CURTAINS

The cheapest and most basic method of concealing is to use curtains to divide off an area that can be used for storage, such as under a table, or in an alcove, or even a whole section of the room.

ADVANTAGES
• Inexpensive and easy to achieve.
• Give a soft, informal look.

DISADVANTAGES
• Inconvenient to keep pulling back curtains.
• Not appropriate in formal rooms.

VENETIAN BLINDS

Available in a range of materials and colours, venetian blinds are particularly suited to minimalist or hi-tech interiors. They offer a quick and inexpensive way of cordoning off large areas of storage.

ADVANTAGES
• Altering slats gives good visibility.
• Available in metal and wood in many colours.

DISADVANTAGES
• Cleaning of blinds is labour-intensive.
• May be difficult to operate.

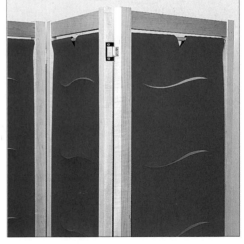

FOLDING SCREENS

Screens offer temporary concealment of large objects and pieces of furniture. They are now available in a variety of materials, and give a new dynamic to the architecture of the room.

ADVANTAGES
• Totally flexible and moveable.
• Can contribute to decorative scheme.

DISADVANTAGES
• No protection from dust and grime.
• Some materials may be difficult to clean.

INDEX

A

access:
ancillary spaces, 233
lofts and cellars, 230, 236, 237
accessories storage, 100–1
acrylic baths, 129, 131
adult bedrooms, 104–5, 108–9
adult storage plan, 106–7
Aga cookers, 36, 37, 48
airflow, bathrooms, 145
alterations, kitchen, 21
aluminium blinds, 248, 282, 283
ancillary spaces, 6, 12, 228–41
assessing your needs, 233
ideas, 240–1
lighting, 290
anglepoises, 290
antiques, 70
apothecary drawers, 60
architects:
bathrooms, 124
studio living, 251
architectural salvage, 156
archive storage, 200, 203
arm rests, task chairs, 189
armchairs, 70, 73, 75
armoires, 99
artificial lighting, 290–1
assessing your needs:
ancillary spaces, 233
bathrooms, 126–7
bedrooms, 93
home offices, 184–5
kitchens, 22–3
living areas, 73
studio living, 252–3
attic see also lofts:
bathrooms, 160
conversions, 187
audio-visual equipment storage, 79

B

back support, chairs, 188, 189
back-to-wall wcs, 141
balconies, 10, 12
living areas, 71, 72
studio living, 279
banquettes, 39, 64
bar stools, 38
basements, 187
basins, 12, 136–9
assessing your needs, 127
children's bathrooms, 163
double, 137, 166, 167
fitted bathrooms, 147, 148
studio living, 263

taps, 136, 138–9
undercounter storage, 136, 143
bath racks, 128, 159
bathrooms, 7, 12, 114–73
assessing your needs, 126–7
children's, 162–5
compact rooms, 266–7
dual-purpose, 158–61
en-suite, 90
fitted, 146–9
flooring, 294
galleried rooms, 278–9
heating and ventilation, 144–5
improvised, 154–7
large rooms, 274–5
lofts, 282–3, 284
open-plan rooms, 270–1, 272
shared, 166–9
shelving, 298, 299
storage, 142–3
studio living, 252–3, 262–3
unfitted, 150–3
unusual shape, 170–3
wallcoverings, 296
baths, 128–31
assessing your needs, 126
children's bathrooms, 163
dual-purpose bathrooms, 158–9
fitted bathrooms, 146
fittings, 126, 135
heated panels, 145
maintenance, 126
materials, 131
painting, 164
panelling, 155
shapes, 128–9
shared bathrooms, 166–7, 168–9
shared baths, 128–9
shower mixers, 134
specialist, 130–1
studio living, 262–3
sunken, 172–3
unfitted bathrooms, 150–1, 152
unusual shape bathrooms, 171, 172
waste outlets, 135
bedheads, 104–5
bedrooms see also sleeping areas, 88–113
accessories storage, 100–1
adults', 104–5, 106–7, 108–9
adult storage, 106–7
assessing your needs, 93
children's, 102–3, 110–3
children's storage, 102–3
clothes storage, 98–9
concealment, 302
dual-purpose offices, 210
furniture, 93, 96–7
lighting, 9

wallcoverings, 296
beds, 90–1, 93, 94–5
adult bedrooms, 104–5
child's, 92, 93, 111
children's storage, 102–3
fold-down, 245, 254–5
futons, 245, 254
platform, 210, 247, 255, 266, 274
sleeping balconies, 279
sofa beds, 191, 210, 256
studio living, 254–5
truckle beds, 254, 255, 256–7
bedside storage, 96–7
bedside tables, 104, 106–7
Belfast sinks, 40
below-deck ovens, 36
benches, 60
bidets, 141
assessing your needs, 127
shared bathrooms, 167
waste outlets, 135
bins, 33
blackboards, 52, 66
blinds, 288–9
aluminium, 248, 282, 283
bamboo, 248, 280
bathrooms, 167, 171
living area, 72–3
room dividers, 199, 214, 248, 264–5
studio living, 265
venetian, 204, 303
boilers, 266, 271
books:
kitchens, 49
living area, 81, 84
booster pumps, 119
bottles:
pull-out storage, 28
wine racks, 29, 49
box files, 200
boxes, storage, 203
bread-bin drawers, 25
breakfast bars, 38, 260–1
built-in storage:
clothes, 98
small bedrooms, 107
studio living, 278
wardrobes, 106
built-in tables, 38
bunk beds, 111

C

cabinets:
bathrooms, 123, 142, 143
bedside storage, 97
book storage, 81
doors, 303
living areas, 84–5
cable management, 194, 195, 202
capsule hotels, Japanese, 244, 245

wallcoverings, 296
carousel storage trays, 29, 238
carpets, 292
bedrooms, 90, 105
cedarwood, 166
ceilings, bathrooms, 171
cellars, 236–7
access, 230
ancillary spaces, 231
conversion, 231
improving, 233
wine, 237
ceramic basins, 139
ceramic disc taps, 119, 120, 135
ceramic flooring, 294–5
ceramic hobs, 34
ceramic tiles, 156, 296
chairs:
dining areas, 261
easy, 191
folding, 38, 190
home office, 189, 190
living area, 75, 256
stacking, 190
task chairs, 188–9
chaise longue, 75
chests:
adult bedroom, 104–5, 106
bedside storage, 96–7
games and pastimes storage, 79
home office, 203, 209, 212
living area, 76
children:
bathrooms, 162–7
bedrooms, 92, 110–1, 112–3
beds, 92, 95
cooking shelf, 66
storage, 102–3
chilled food storage, 26–7
china storage, 85
chopping boards, 30, 56
circular baths, 129
circular kitchens, 46–7
circular showers, 132
cisterns, 140–1
close-coupled wcs, 140
clothes storage, 98–9
adults, 104, 106–7
bedrooms, 91, 106–7
children, 111
clothes tent, 99
coffee table, 76, 85
coil radiators, 171
coir matting, 293
collections, 80
Colorcore worksurfaces, 300–1
colour, 8–9
bathrooms, 118
children's bedrooms, 112
living areas, 86
studio living, 250
column radiators, 144

compact room, studio living, 266–7
computers:
  computer desks, 194–5
  fitted desks, 192
  monitors, 194, 195
  safety, 195
  storing disks, 201
concealed computer desks, 195
concealment, 302–3
  staircases, 345
condensation, 145
condiment cupboards, 29
conservatories, 12, 71, 86
conversions:
  ancillary spaces, 231
  home offices, 216–9
cookers, 36–7, 258, 259
cooking:
  extractors, 34–5
  hobs, 34–5
  kitchens, 23
  ovens, 36–7
  studio living, 252, 258–9
co-ordinated linens, 92
copper baths, 131
Corian worksurfaces, 300–1
cork tiles, 293
corner basins, 137
corner baths, 129, 168, 172
corner cupboards, 29
court cupboards, 42, 48, 50
crockery, storage, 42–3
cup hooks, 43
cupboards see also larder
cupboards, 12
  adult bedrooms, 105, 107
  bedrooms, 93
  bedside storage, 96
  children's storage, 102–3
  clothes storage, 98–9
  corner, 29
  court, 42, 48, 50
  doors, 303
  hallways, 234, 240
  hardware storage, 42
  living areas, 73, 84
  lofts and cellars, 236–7
  non-perishable food storage, 28–9
  office-in-a-cupboard, 197
  over-counter units, 29
  remote office storage, 202
  utility areas, 238
curtains, 289
  clothes storage, 98–9
  concealment, 303
  landings, 235
  living areas, 73
  shower, 133
cushions, 86
  easy chairs, 191
  wedge cushions, 189

D

damp-proofing, 236
David, Elizabeth, 17
dead space, 220–3
deck-mounted taps, 138
decking, bathrooms, 166
dedicated rooms, 186, 204–7
deep bath tubs, 131, 172
desks:
  cable management, 194, 195
  computer desks, 194–5
  dedicated rooms, 204, 205
  dual-purpose offices, 209
  edges, 192
  executive offices, 224, 226
  fitted, 192
  freestanding, 193
  home offices, 192–5
  integrated offices, 214
  kitchens, 65, 66
  pedestal, 201
  storage, 200, 201
  writing, 85
diffused lighting, 291
dimmer switches, 151, 167
dining areas, 71, 72
  ancillary spaces, 232
  compact rooms, 266–7
  galleried rooms, 278–9
  kitchens, 65
  large rooms, 274–5
  lofts, 282–3
  open-plan rooms, 270–1
  studio living, 252, 260–1
dining rooms, 85
  dual-purpose offices, 208–9
  meeting areas, 198
disguised office units, 197
dishwashers, 40, 41
disk storage, 201
display, 80, 299
doors:
  adult bedroom plan, 105
  clothes storage, 99
  concealment, 302–3
  fabric-fronted, 302
  glass-fronted, 72, 303
  living area, 72, 83
  lofts, 237
  sliding, 170, 264
  shower, 133
double basins, 137, 166, 167
double-ended baths, 128, 129
double ovens, 37
double showers, 133
downlighters, 291
  bathrooms, 151, 155
  shelving, 298
  studio living, 250
drafting chairs, 189
draining boards, 40

drawers:
  accessories storage, 100–1
  adult bedroom storage, 104, 106
  apothecary, 60
  bread-bins, 25
  desks, 193
  entertainment storage, 78
  fridges, 26
  pedestals, 201
  plan chests, 203
  toy storage, 66
  trolleys, 203
  utensil storage, 42
drawing boards, 206, 221
dressers, 43, 48, 50, 53
dressing areas, 90
dressing rooms, 106–7, 158–9
dressing tables, 104, 210
drinks facilities, 205
dual-purpose bathrooms, 158–61
dual-purpose offices, 186, 208–7

E

eating areas see also dining areas, 23, 38–9
  compact rooms, 266–7
  galleried rooms, 278–9
  large rooms, 274–3
  lofts, 282–3
  open-plan rooms, 270–1
  studio living, 252, 260–1
electrical wiring, 298
  showers, 135
electricity meter, 233
electricity sockets:
  ancillary spaces, 233
  home offices, 205
  shavers, 167
  studio living, 247
en-suite bathrooms, 90, 119, 170
en-suite shower rooms, 91
entertaining, 70, 73, 82
entertainment, 76, 78–9
environmental concerns, 120
equipment storage, 22, 42
  home offices, 185
  kitchen appliances, 30, 45, 302
  racks, 62
  utility areas, 238
executive chairs, 189
executive offices, 224–7
extensions, 216
extractors, 45, 53
  bathrooms, 145
  hobs, 34–5
  ovens, 37
  studio living, 278
eye-level ovens, 37

F

fabrics, 8
  covered doors, 99, 302
  kitchens, 64
  sofas, 74, 74
  task chairs, 188, 189
false walls, 268, 271, 283
family kitchens, 64–7
fan heaters, 145
filing cabinets, 202, 203
  living areas, 77
filters, waste outlets, 135
fire prevention regulations, 235
fireplaces:
  kitchens, 64
  living areas, 70, 71, 72, 82
  seating, 74
fitted bathrooms, 146–9
fitted desks, 192
fitted kitchens, 52–5
fitted shelving, 299
flagstones, 294
floor coverings, 73, 184
flooring, 292–5
  ancillary spaces, 231, 232
  as room dividers, 248, 249
  bathrooms, 151, 154, 163
  bedrooms, 90, 92
  living areas, 71, 72, 83
  lofts and cellars, 236
  studio living, 282
  underfloor storage, 271, 272
  wood, 8
floor lights, 171
floor sockets, 247
floor-standing lamps, 290
focal points, 72, 73, 82
fold-down beds, 245, 254–5
folding furniture, 245, 261
  chairs, 190
  table and chairs, 38
food preparation, 22, 30–1
  rinsing sinks, 32–3, 53
food storage, 22
  chilled food, 26
  fresh food, 24–5
  non-perishable food, 28–9
  studio living, 258–9
foot-rests, 188, 189
formal meeting areas, 198
Formica worksurfaces, 301
four-poster beds, 94–5
freestanding desks, 193
freestanding food preparation areas, 31
freestanding fridges, 27
freezers, 26–7
French windows, 49
fresh food storage, 24–5
fridge drawers, 26
fridges, 26–7, 53
  studio living, 258, 259

front doors, 233
front rooms, 187
furniture see also chairs, desks,
tables etc.:
  bedrooms, 93, 96–7
  dual-purpose offices, 208
  home offices, 184
  integrated offices, 214
  living areas, 73
  unfitted kitchens, 48–51
futons, 245, 254

G

galleries:
  home offices, 222
  studio living, 272, 278–9
galley-style bathrooms, 170
games and pastimes storage, 78–9
garages, 187, 216
garden sheds, 187
gardens, 12
gas cookers, 61
gas hobs, 34–5
gas meters, 233
glass, 288–9
  basins, 139
  bedside chests, 97
  bricks, 143, 166, 296
  doors, 72, 83, 303
  floor panels, 240
  kitchen cabinets, 42–3
  shelving, 299
  tables, 77
grab rails, 129, 163
granite:
  splashbacks, 296
  worksurfaces, 34, 300
griddles, 34
grouting, 154

H

hallways, 6, 230–3, 234–5
  home offices, 222
  storage, 235, 240
halogen downlighters, 151, 155
halogen hobs, 34
hard flooring, 294–5
hardware storage, 42–3
hardwood, 298
  flooring, 294
  worksurfaces, 300–1
headboards, 93, 94–5
headrests, 189
heat exchangers, 145
heating:
  bathrooms, 144–5, 148
  bedrooms, 92, 93
  studio living, 246
  underfloor, 292, 294
high-level cisterns, 140
hip baths, 131

hobs, 34–5
  ceramic, 34
  gas, 34, 35
  halogen, 34
  height, 35
  induction hobs, 35
home offices, 8, 174–227
  assessing your needs, 184–7
  conversions, 216–9
  dedicated offices, 204–7
  desks, 192–5
  dual-purpose offices, 208–11
  executive offices, 224–7
  integrated offices, 212–5
  meeting areas, 198–9
  seating, 188–91
  storage, 200–3
  units, 196–7
  unusual space offices, 220–3
hot plates, 85
hydrotherapy baths, 130

I, J

improvised bathrooms, 154–7
improvised kitchens, 60–3
induction hobs, 35
industrial buildings, 246, 247
informal meeting areas, 198–9
insulation:
  loft, 236
  noise, 224
integrated offices, 186, 212–5
ironing boards, 239, 271
island units, 31, 56–9
  family kitchen, 65
  unfitted kitchen, 49
Jacuzzi showers, 119
jute matting, 293

K

kitchens, 12–13, 14–67
  compact rooms, 266–9
  concealment, 302
  equipment storage, 42–3, 258–9
  family kitchens, 64–7
  fitted kitchens, 52–5
  flooring, 294
  food preparation, 30–3
  food storage, 24–9, 258–9
  galleried rooms, 278–9
  hobs and cookers, 34–7
  home offices, 199
  improvised kitchens, 60–3
  island kitchens, 56–9
  large rooms, 274–5
  lighting, 9
  lofts, 282–3
  open-plan rooms, 270–1
  screening, 276, 282
  shelving, 298
  small kitchens, 44–7

studio living, 245, 252, 258–9
  unfitted kitchens, 48–51
  wallcoverings, 296
  worksurfaces, 300
kneehole desks, 193
knife storage, 30

L

ladders, 266, 279, 280
ladder-style radiators, 72
ladder towel rails, 145
lamps, 291
  tables, 76
  task lighting, 201
landings, 231, 232–3, 234–5
  home offices, 222
  utility areas, 240
larder cupboards, 20, 24–5
  family kitchens, 64
  improvised kitchens, 61
  unfitted kitchens, 49
large rooms, studio living, 274–5
laundry bins, 147, 163
laundry chutes, 278–9
laundry facilities, 239
le Corbusier, 106
less-abled people:
  showers, 133
  taps, 138
  wcs, 141
library, 272
light bulbs, 290
lighting, 8–9, 288–9, 290–1
  ancillary spaces, 231, 233
  bathrooms, 167, 151, 171
  bedrooms, 9, 92, 93
  bedside storage, 96–7
  clothes storage, 98–9
  combined with extractor fans,
    145
  integrated offices, 213
  kitchens, 9
  living areas, 70, 71, 73, 83
  lofts and cellars, 236
  meeting areas, 198
  shelving, 298–9
  stairs, 9, 240
  studio living, 250, 251
  task lighting, 201
limescale, 120
limestone flooring, 171, 294–5
linen boxes, 155
linen presses, 152
linens, co-ordinated, 92
linoleum, 151, 154, 293
living areas, 6, 9, 68–87
  ancillary spaces, 232
  compact rooms, 266–7
  concealment, 302
  family rooms, 82–3
  galleried rooms, 278–9
  integrated offices, 186, 212–5

large rooms, 274–5
living rooms, 84–5, 86–7
lofts, 282–3
open-plan rooms, 270–1
seating, 74–5
studio living, 252, 256–7
wallcoverings, 296
lofts, 6, 230–1, 236–7
  access, 232
  flooring, 294
  galleried rooms, 278–9
  home offices, 187, 216, 218
  improving, 233
  large rooms, 274–5
  studio living, 247, 282–3
loungers, 73
louvred shutters, 288
lumbar support chairs, 188, 189

M

mantelpieces, 84
marble:
  basins, 139
  baths, 131
  countertops, 136, 148–9
  tiles, 295
marine plywood, 147
mats, non-slip, 129, 163
matting, 293
MDF shelving, 298–9
meat safes, 25
meeting areas, 184, 198–9
  dual-purpose offices, 209
melamine shelving, 298–9
metal shelving, 299
mezzanines:
  bathrooms, 172
  home offices, 220–1
microwave ovens, 37, 258
Mies van der Rohe, Ludwig, 250
mildew, 120
mirrors, 296
  bathrooms, 143, 146–7
  bedrooms, 93
  studio living, 250, 251
mixer taps, 138, 139, 141
mobile computer desks, 195
mobile office units, 196
mobile storage units, 79, 201, 267
modular seating, 72, 74, 256
monitors, 194, 195
monobloc taps, 138
mosaics, 146, 170, 297
murals, 164
music areas, 73, 79, 82–3

N, O

needle showers, 119
nest of tables, 77, 83, 247, 257
noise insulation, 224
non-perishable food storage, 28–9

noticeboards, 62, 66
nursery, 110
occasional seating, 190–1
occasional tables, 76–7
office areas, 66
office units, 196–7
offices *see* home offices *and*
   work areas
opaque glass, 154
open fires, 73
open-plan rooms, 71, 72–3, 86
   studio living, 270–1
outbuildings, 186–7
   conversions, 186, 216–7, 218
oval tables, 39
ovens, 36–7, 258
over-counter units, 29

P

paint:
   bathroom floors, 159
   period restoration, 11
   wallcovering, 155, 156, 296–7
pan storage, 30, 31
panelling:
   baths, 155
   concealed plumbing, 159
   sliding, 284
pantry cupboards *see* larder
   cupboards
parquet flooring, 282
partitions, 83, 85
pedal bins, 33
pedestal basins, 136
pedestal storage, 201
pendant lamps, 291
peninsular units, 58
period restoration, 9, 11
pets, 53, 73, 82
phones see telephones
pillar taps, 135, 136, 138
pinboards, 62, 66, 196
plan chests, 203, 209, 212
planning details, 286–303
plants, 249
plaster, 296
   mouldings, 11
   ornate, 70
   wallcoverings, 8
plastic storage units, 100
plate racks, 56
platform beds, 247, 255, 266, 274
play areas, 70, 92, 102
plinth radiators, 145
plugs, bath, 135
plumbing:
   baths, 129
   concealing, 159
plywood, 147, 238, 298–9
pop-up waste systems, 135, 139
porcelain sinks, 40, 60
posture:

task chairs, 188, 189
   VDUs and, 195
pull-out storage, 28
pumps, shower, 119

R

racks:
   drainage, 41
   equipment, 62
   plate, 56
   shoe, 107
   tea-towel, 53
   vegetable, 25
radiators:
   bathrooms, 166
   children's rooms, 92
   coil, 171
   column, 144
   ladder, 72, 145
   plinth, 145
   studio living, 247
   towel rails, 144, 145, 284
ramp access, 233
reclining chairs, 75, 191
rectangular tables, 39
recycling waste, 33
refrigerators see fridges
remote office storage, 202–3
resin baths, 131
rim-mounted taps, 135
roll-top baths, 150–1
roll-top desks, 193
roller blinds, 171, 248, 288–9
roller shutters, 302
roof space conversions, 91
room dividers:
   blinds, 282, 283
   flooring, 248, 249
   home office, 199, 214
   kitchens, 50
   living areas, 72–3, 84
   multi-purpose, 264–5
   studio living, 264–5
round baths, 129
round tables, 39
rubber flooring, 293
rugs, 294

S

safes, 203
safety:
   children's bathrooms, 162, 163
   children's bedrooms, 92
   computers, 195
   mezzanines, 221
   showers, 120, 135
sanitary ware, 11
   see also basins, baths etc.
saucepan trees, 43
saucepans, 258
saunas, 158

Screenrobe, 264
screens:
   computer see monitors
   concealment, 303
   cooking areas, 276, 282
   integrated offices, 213
   living areas, 72–3
   meeting areas, 199
   privacy, 249
   room dividers, 264–5
   sleeping areas, 254
   studio living, 245, 276, 282
seagrass matting, 293
seating, 184
   dining areas, 261
   home offices, 188–9
   living areas, 70, 72–3, 74–5, 82
   long-term, 188–9
   meeting areas, 198, 199
   occasional, 190–1
   reading areas, 225
   studio living, 256–7
seats, wcs, 141
security, 216, 217
shared bathrooms, 166–9
shaver sockets, 167
sheds, 187
shelves:
   bookshelves, 49, 81
   children's cooking, 66
   children's storage, 102–3
   kitchen, 42, 62
shelving, 12, 298–9
   bathrooms, 123, 143, 166
   bedrooms, 93, 105, 110–1
   book storage, 81
   clothes storage, 98–9
   collection display, 80
   home office, 204, 205
   living areas, 73, 83, 84–5
   lofts and cellars, 236–7
   remote office storage, 202, 203
   stairways, 240
   studio living, 248
   walk-in wardrobes, 107
   workstation storage, 200, 201
shoe storage, 101, 107
shower rooms, 6, 12, 119, 132–3
   en-suite, 91
   studio living, 279
showers, 116–7, 132–5
   assessing your needs, 126–7
   booster pumps, 119
   children's bathrooms, 162
   double, 133, 168
   extractor fans, 145
   Jacuzzi showers, 119
   lighting, 145
   needle showers, 119
   shared bathrooms, 168
   studio living, 262
   unusual shape bathrooms, 171
   water temperature, 120, 135

shutters, 289
sideboards, 85
sinks:
   double, 32
   food rinsing, 32, 53
   island units, 58
   multi-purpose, 32
   porcelain, 40, 60
   sitting areas, 57, 64
   small kitchens, 44–7
   studio living, 258
   washing-up, 40–1
   waste disposal units, 33
sisal matting, 293
sit baths, 131, 263
skylights, 213, 218, 288
   bathrooms, 170
slate:
   flooring, 294–5
   worksurfaces, 300
sleeping areas *see also* bedrooms·
   assessing your needs, 253
   compact rooms, 266–7
   galleried rooms, 278–9
   large rooms, 274–5
   lofts, 282–3
   open-plan rooms, 270–1
   studio living, 254–5
sleeping balconies, 279
sliding doors, 170, 264, 284
slipper baths, 128, 131
slow cookers, 259
soak tubs, 130
sofa-beds, 191, 210, 256
sofa tables, 77
sofas, 73, 74, 256
soft flooring, 292–3
soft furnishings, 64
soft seating, 191, 199
softwood shelving, 298
spa baths, 130, 131
space dividers see room dividers
specialist baths, 130–1
splashbacks:
   bathrooms, 136
   kitchens, 36
spotlights, 250, 290–1, 298
stacking chairs, 190
stainless steel:
   basins, 139
   baths, 131
   secondhand fittings, 62
   sinks, 41
   tiles, 296
   worksurfaces, 300
staircases, 230
stairlifts, 233
stairs, 231, 234–5
   fire prevention regulations, 235
   improving, 233
   landings, 222
   lighting, 9, 290
   understair use, 222, 240, 274

stationery, 201
steam ovens, 37
steamers, 34
stencilling, 296
stone:
    flooring, 171, 294
    wall covering, 296
stools, 38, 190, 260
storage, 12
    accessories, 100–1
    ancillary spaces, 230–3
    bathrooms, 123, 127, 142–3
    bedrooms, 90–2, 93, 106–7
    bedside, 96–7
    below-stairs, 274
    built-in, 278
    child-proof locks, 162
    children's, 66, 102–3
    cleaning equipment, 52
    clothes, 91, 98–9, 237
    concealed, 147, 202, 302
    dual-purpose offices, 208–9, 210
    fitted bathrooms, 146–7
    food, 24–9, 258–9
    games & pastimes, 78
    hallways, 234–5, 240
    hardware, 42–3
    home offices, 185, 200–3
    integrated offices, 213, 214
    kitchens, 22
    living areas, 70, 84–5
    lofts and cellars, 236–7
    mezzanines, 221
    modular systems, 267
    office units, 196–7
    room dividers, 264–5
    shared bathrooms, 167
    shelving, 298–9
    sleeping areas, 254–5
    studio living, 249, 253, 258–9
    tables, 76
    undercounter, 136, 143
    underfloor, 271, 272
    utility areas, 238–9
    wardrobes, 158
    washstands, 137
strip lights, 298
structural alterations, 242–85
studio living, 242–253
    bathing areas, 262–3
    beds, 254–5
    compact rooms, 266–9
    cooking areas, 258–9
    dining areas, 260–1
    furniture, 256–7
    galleried rooms, 278–81
    large rooms, 274–7
    lofts, 282–5
    open-plan rooms, 270–3
    space dividers, 264–5
studios, 172, 218

study areas, 6, 103, 111
sunken baths, 172–3

T

table lamps, 76, 291
tables, 38–9
    bedside storage, 96–7
    built-in, 38
    dining areas, 260, 261
    dual-purpose offices, 209
    family kitchens, 65, 66
    home office, 193, 204
    living areas, 73, 76–7, 84–5, 256–7
    meeting areas, 198–9
    shapes, 39
tapered baths, 129
tapestries, 70
taps:
    basins, 136, 138–9
    bath fittings, 135
    bidets, 141
    ceramic discs, 119, 120, 135
    kitchen, 32, 40
    mixer, 138, 139, 141
    monobloc, 138
    replacing, 155
    shower mixers, 134
task chairs, 188–9
tea-towel racks, 53
teenage bedrooms, 103, 111
telephone handset design shower mixers, 134
telephones, 233
televisions, 70–3, 79
    family rooms, 82, 84
    seating, 74
terracotta tiles, 294
terrazzo worksurfaces, 300
textured vinyl, 293
thermostatic shower controls, 135
tiles, 294
    cork, 293
    grouting, 154
    vinyl, 292, 293
    wallcovering, 156, 296–7
timber:
    flooring, 294
    shelving, 298–9
tool chests, 271
towel rails:
    bathrooms, 144–5, 155, 167
    studio living, 248, 284
toy storage, 66, 102–3, 110
track lighting, 291
trestle tables, 193
trolleys:
    bathrooms, 142
    drawers, 201
    mobile computer desks, 195
    tables, 76, 85
truckle beds, 254, 255

tub chairs, 191
typist's chairs, 190

U–W

under-stair space, 233, 234, 239
unfitted bathrooms, 150–3
unfitted kitchens, 48–51
unusual shape bathrooms, 170–3
uplighters, 83, 290, 291
utensils, 42, 62
utility areas, 238–9, 240
    shelving, 298
    studio living, 253
utility cupboards, 52
utility rooms, 230, 233, 239
vanity units, 271
vegetable racks, 25
vegetables:
    fridges, 27
    pantry cupboards, 24
    rinsing sinks, 32, 53
venetian blinds, 288–9
    concealment, 303
    home offices, 204
    room dividers, 199, 214
    studio living, 248, 265, 282–3
ventilation:
    bathrooms, 145, 171
    pantry cupboards, 25
vertical blinds, 289
vinyl flooring, 292–3
visible storage, 43
walk-in wardrobes, 107
wall cupboards, 29
wall heaters, 145
wall-mounted sanitaryware:
    basins, 137
    bidets, 141
    taps, 135
    wcs, 141
wallcoverings, 296–7
    ancillary spaces, 232
    child's bedrooms, 92
    plaster, 8
wallpaper, 296–7
walls:
    false, 268, 271, 283
    half-height, 248, 272
    storage, 143
wardrobes, 91
    adult bedrooms, 105, 106–7
    bathrooms, 158
    clothes storage, 98–9
    concealed, 254
    doors, 303
    fold-out, 245
    room dividers, 264–5
    walk-in, 107
washing areas, 262–3
    assessing your needs, 253
    compact rooms, 266–7
    galleried rooms, 278–9

    large rooms, 274–5
    lofts, 282–3
    open-plan rooms, 270–1
washing machines:
    bathrooms, 160
    studio living, 271
washing-up, 23, 40–1
washstands, 137
waste disposal, 23, 32–3
waste outlets, 135, 139
waste recycling, 33
water conservation, 127
water consumption, 120, 140
waterfall spouts, 135
wcs 12, 140–1
    assessing your needs, 127
    children's seats, 141, 162
    cisterns, 140–1
    seats, 141
    under-stair spaces, 232
    water conservation, 127
    water consumption, 120, 140
wedge cushions, 189
whirlpools, 130
window seats, 235
windows, 288
    bedrooms, 93
    French, 20, 49
    home offices, 216, 218
    living areas, 73, 82–3
    studio living, 250
wine cellars, 237
wine racks, 29, 49, 238
wood:
    basins, 139
    baths, 131
    chopping boards, 30, 56
    decking, 166
    flooring, 8, 45, 90, 282, 294–5
    panelling, 61, 296–7
    shelving, 298
    treatments, 136
    wc seats, 141
    worksurfaces, 300–1
wood-burning stoves, 61
work areas:
    assessing your needs, 252
    compact rooms, 266–7
    galleried rooms, 278–9
    large rooms, 274–5
    lofts, 282–3
    open plan, 270–1
workstations, 184
    storage, 200–1
    studio living, 267
worksurfaces, 192–3, 300–1
    computer desks, 194–5
    cooking areas, 259
    office units, 196–7
    tables, 193
worktops, 30, 31
writing desks, 86

ACKNOWLEDGMENTS

ARTWORK

Room artworks by Richard Lee, except for the following by John Egan: 84–5, 106–7, 235, 237, 239.

Ergonomic diagrams by David Ashby.

KITCHEN

All kitchen plans by Johnny Grey, except 44–5, 52–3, 60–1.

Stylists: Michelle and Yvonne Roberts.

All photographs by Peter Anderson and Matthew Ward, except:
(Kitchen designers are named in brackets.)
Peter Aprahamian (Johnny Grey) 20, 46–47; Interior Archive/Tim Beddow (John Pawson) 50bl; Simon Brown (Johnny Grey) 51; Michael Focard (Johnny Grey) 59; Ray Main 18bl, 46tl, and 46bl, 54tl, 55, 58tr; Diana Miller 18t, 43tr; James Mortimer (Johnny Grey) 16b; David Parmiter (Claudia Bryant) 46br, 50tr and 50br; Colin Radcliffe Design 58bl; Trevor Richards (Johnny Grey) 16, 19, 58tl and 58br, 66br; Paul Ryan/International Interiors (Fell-Clark Design) 62bl; Paul Ryan/International Interiors (Gerry Nelisson) 62br; Deidi von Schaewen 62tl; Colin Walton 297tr.

The following companies kindly lent us their photographs:
Aga-Rayburn 23tl, 36t; Alternative Plans 43b; Chalon 50bl; Jenn-Air (CV4380PG) 34t, (WW27210PG) 37bl; John Lewis of Hungerford 68tr; Kohler 33b; Newcastle Furniture Company 50tl; Snaidero 46cb; Sub-zero 26bl.

We would like to thank the following companies for allowing us to photograph in their showrooms: Arc Linea; Bulthaup; Chalon; C.P. Hart; Newcastle Furniture Company; Nicholas Anthony, and to Fired Earth, for use of their floorings.

We are also grateful to those who kindly supplied items for photography: American Appliance Centre; Amtico; Christoph Caffyn; La Cuisinière; David Mellor; Formica Ltd; Geneviève Lethu; Graham & Green; Hogarth & Dwyer; Jerry's Home Store; Mediterranean Imports; Moore Park Delicatessen; Pallam Precast; P.G. Kitchens & Bathrooms; RJ's HomeShop; Sinclair Till, and Viaduct Furniture Ltd.

LIVING AREA

Living room plans by Walter Strebel, GPS Architects 82–3; Barbara Weiss 84–5.

Stylist: Fiona Craig-McFeely; Kay McGlone.

All photographs by Jake Fitzjones, except:
Peter Anderson (architect: Barbara Weiss) 72b, (architect: Barbara Weiss) 73b, 78–9, (designer: Anthony Collett) 80–1, (architect: Barbara Weiss) 81tr; Bo Appletoft/Camera Press 86tl; Andy Crawford 78bl, 79tr; Richard Glover 72t; Chris Grayson/Abode 71br; Ray Main/Mainstream 71bc, 75br, 77tr, 86b, 86–7; Marianne Majerus 80l, 81br; National Trust Picture Library/Andreas von Einsiedel 70b; Ian Parry/Abode 71bl; Willem Rethmeier/ Belle/Arcaid 71t.

The following companies kindly lent us their photographs:
Bartholomew Conservatories 86tc; Ducal 76bl; Habitat 23br; Ligne Roset 74t, 75c; The Pier 76tl; Pivotelli 23cr; John Wilman Fabrics 75t.

Thank you also to Highly Sprung and Purves and Purves, who allowed us to photograph in their showrooms, and to Habitat, The Holding Company, and Malabar for supplying items for photography.

BEDROOM

Bedroom plans by Walter Strebel, GPS Architects 104–5; Barbara Weiss 106–7, 110–11.

Stylists: Tiffany Davies; Fiona Craig-McFeely; Kay McGlone.

All photographs by Jake Fitzjones, except:
Peter Anderson 91tr, 97cl, 99tr, 100tr, 101bl, 101tr, (architect: Barbara Weiss) 103br; Dominic Blackmore/Homes & Ideas/Robert Harding Syndication 112t; Brigitte/Camera Press 112br; Richard Glover (architects: Circus Architects) 112–13; Chris Grayson/Abode 108br; Cecilia Innes/The Interior Archive 98–9; Nadia Mackenzie (Mark Brazier Jones) 108tl; Nadia Mackenzie 108bl; Ray Main/Mainstream 91tl, 91b, 92b, 97br; Marianne Majerus (architect: Barbara Weiss) 103tr; Andreas von Einsiedel/National Trust Picture Library 90b; Fritz von der Schulenberg/The Interior Archive 102cl; Matthew Ward 100b, 101tl, 102t, 102–3; Zuhause/Camera Press 112bl.

The following companies kindly lent us their photographs: Berkeley AG 95c; Coloroll 92tl, 97cr; Ducal 97tl; Habitat 99br; The Holding Company 101b; Simon Horn 93, 94bl, 94–5t; Hülsta 97bl, 108–9; Ikea 96bl; Iron Design Co. 95tr; Ligne Roset 94–5br, 97tr; Gavin Lindsay 90t; Charles Page 98b; Sleepeezee 94tl; Stompa Furniture 92tr; John Wilman Fabrics 108tr.

We are also grateful to those who kindly supplied items for photography: Cologne & Cotton; Habitat; The Holding Company.

BATHROOM

Bathroom plans by: Ken Rorrison, Bushcow Henley 146–7; Dale Loth Architects 166–7; Joyce Owens, Azman Owens Architect 170–1.

Stylist: Fiona Craig-McFeely.

All photographs by Jake Fitzjones except:
Andy Crawford 127t, 135br, 141br, 143tr, 144bl, 145tr, 145c; Earl Carter/Belle/Arcaid (designer: Christian Liagre) 148bl; David Churchill/Arcaid (architect: Elspeth Beard) 172b; Mike Crockett/Elizabeth Whiting & Associates (designer: Fiona Cowan) 173; Michael Dunne/Elizabeth Whiting & Associates 164b; Andreas von Einsiedel/National Trust Picture Library 116tl, Andreas von Einsiedel/Elizabeth Whiting & Associates 172tr; Chris Gascoigne/View (architect: Simon Conder) 131cl; Dennis Gilbert/ View (architect: Bernhard Blauel) 149, (architect: AHMM) 168cr; Rodney Hyett/Elizabeth Whiting & Associates 172tl; IMS/Camera Press 152tr, 164tr; Simon Kenny/

Belle/Arcaid (designer: Andrew Nimmo & Annabel Lahz) 172cr; John Edward Linden/Arcaid (architect: John Newton) 124–5, (architect: Julian Powell Tuck) 152tl; Living/Camera Press 156tl; Nadia Mackenzie (designer Francois Gilles/IPL Interiors) 148tl, (owner: Paula Pryke) 153, (The Water Monopoly) 164tl; Marianne Majerus (architect: Barbara Weiss) 168t; (owner: Merete Steinboch) 168–9; James Mortimer/National Trust Picture Library 116–17; Ian Parry/Abode 156tr, 157; David Parmiter 156br; Spike Powell/ Elizabeth Whiting & Associates 152bl; Jo Reid and John Peck (architect: Simon Conder) 133br; Elizabeth Whiting & Associates 168bl; Schöner Wohnen/Camera Press 160tl, 164–5; Friedholm Thomas/ Elizabeth Whiting & Associates 160bl; Petrina Tinslay/Arcaid (designer: Phil & Jackie Staub) 161; Henry Wilson/ Interior Archive (designer: Patrick Jefferson) 156bl.

The following companies kindly lent us their photographs: Jacuzzi UK 130bl; Armitage Shanks 118tc; Ideal-Standard 128tr; Dimplex 145tc; Jaga 145tl; Shires 129tr; Lefroy Brooks 129bl; Mira 135tc; Myson 145cl; Showerlux 128cr, 133bl; Twyfords 141bl; Vent-Axia 145bl, bc.

We would like to thank the following companies for allowing us to photograph in their showrooms and showhomes: Alternative Plans; C.P.

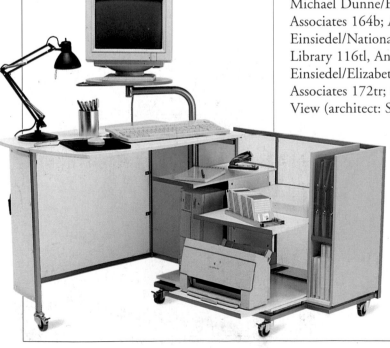

ACKNOWLEDGMENTS • 311

Hart; Leftley Bros Ltd; Original Bathrooms; Sitting Pretty; The Water Monopoly; West One.

We are also grateful to those who kindly supplied items for photography: Alternative Plans; Aston Matthews; Bisque Radiators; Bobo; Christy Towels; Cologne & Cotton; Descamps; Fiona Craig-McFeely; Habitat; The Holding Company; Innovations; Muji; Natural Products; Newman Tonks Architectural Hardware; The Pier; Pru Bury; Smith & Nephew; Mr Tomkinson Carpets; The Source; Yves Delorme; Ever Trading.

HOME OFFICE

Home office plans by: Allford Hall Monaghan Morris 224–5; Birds Portchmouth Russum 220–1; Cany Ash and Robert Sakula 216–17; Studio MG Architects 212–13; Mary Thum Associates 208–9.

Stylist: Emily Hedges.

All photographs by Peter Anderson and Andy Crawford, except: Abode/Ian Parry (Marjorie McDougall) 193tl; Otto Baitz/Esto 222br; Brigitte/Camera Press 200l, 203tl, 210tl, 210bc; Jeremy Cockayne/Arcaid 211; Mark Darley/Esto (architect: Brenda Levine) 218cr; Christopher Drake/Options/Robert Harding Syndication 177; Jake Fitzjones 214bl; Dennis Gilbert/Arcaid (architects: Allford Hall Monaghan Morris) 223; Jeff Goldberg/Esto (Nancy Levine and Rita Marks) 192cl; Living/Camera Press 222bl; Ray Main 214tl; Derry Moore courtesy of Architectural Digest 176tl, 176b; Michael Nicholson/Elizabeth Whiting and Associates 190br; Paul Ryan/ International Interiors (architect: Korinne Kalesso) 198l, (designer: Maeve Mougin) 206tl, (architect: Ian Hay) 206b, (designer: Sam Blount) 207, (designer: Sasha Waddell) 210bl, (Wolfgang Joop) 215; Schöner

Wohnen/Camera Press 197br, 214tr, 218b, 222tl; Solvi Dos Santos 183, 207tr, 226tl, 226b, 227; Fritz von der Schulenburg/The Interior Archive 226tr; Ian Skelton/ Homes & Ideas/Robert Harding Syndication 191br; Tim Street-Porter/ Elizabeth Whiting and Associates (designer: Lloyd Ziff) 218cl; Colin Walton 190tr.

The following companies kindly lent us their photographs: Ikea Ltd 210ct; Newcastle Furniture Company 197tr, 197tl; Neville Johnson Fitted Furniture/GGT Direct 218t; Nice House 203br; Silent Gliss 199br; Vitra 179tr, 193br, 188, 189tl.

We would like to thank the following companies for allowing us to photograph in their showrooms: Atrium; Co-existence; Haworth; Herman Miller; Just Desks; Marcatre.

We are also grateful to those who kindly supplied items for photography: Aero; The Back Shop; Sebastian Bergne; Bond Street Carpets; Nel Brett; Caz Systems; The Chelsea Gardener; The Holding Company; Clare Mosely Gilding; Nicholas; Primrose and Primrose; Retro Homestores; RJ's HomeShop; Gillian Roberts; Shiu-Kay Kan; Gerard Taylor; Vitra.

ANCILLARY SPACE

All plans designed by Barbara Weiss.

Stylists: Tiffany Davies; Shani Zion.

All photographs by Jake Fitzjones and Matthew Ward, except: Peter Anderson (designer Anthony Collett) 235tl, 235tr; Andreas von Einsiedel/Homes & Gardens/Robert Harding Syndication 230b; Andreas von Einsiedel/Elizabeth Whiting and Associates 232bc, 234tr; B. Femina/ Camera Press 240tl; Richard Glover (architect: Alastair Howe) 231; Rodney Hyett/Elizabeth Whiting and Associates 232br, 237tr, 240bl; Ray Main/Mainstream 240tr, 241; Marianne Majerus (designer: Léon Krier) 234b; Jonathan Pilkington/The Interior Archive 237c; Elizabeth Whiting and Associates 232bl; Zuhause Wohnen/Camera Press 236.

STUDIO LIVING

Studio living plans by: Andrew Hanson and Nazar al-Sayigh of Circus Architects 278–9; Jason Cooper Architect 270–1; Seth Stein Architects 282–3; Simon Colebrook of the Douglas Stephen Partnership 274–5; Voon Yee Wong of VX Designs 266–7.

Stylist: Shani Zion.

All photographs by Jake Fitzjones, Andy Crawford, and Matthew Ward, except:

Peter Anderson 260tr; Richard Bryant/Arcaid (architect: Pierre D'Avoine) 285; Jeremy Cockayne/Arcaid (architect: Yann Weymouth) 284tl; Peter Cook/View (designer: Hugo Tugman Partnership) 269; Friedheim-Thomas/Elizabeth Whiting & Associates 272tl; Chris Gascoigne/View (designer: Nick Hockley at Orms) 277, 284br; Graham Henderson/Elizabeth Whiting & Associates (designer: Sue Pitman) 272bl; Ray Main 272–3, 281; Nadia Mackenzie/Elizabeth Whiting & Associates 280bl; Ian Parry/Abode 280–1; Alberto Piovano/Arcaid (architect: Kris Mys) 284bl; Spike Powell/Elizabeth Whiting & Associates 251br; Roger Ressmeyer/© Corbis 244bl; Trevor Richards/Abode 272tc; Paul Ryan/International Interiors (designer: John Michael Ekeblad) 276tr; Paul Ryan/International Interiors (designer: Kristina Ratia) 268tl; Andreas von Einsiedel/Elizabeth Whiting & Associates 280tl; Schöner Wohnen/Camera Press 256tr, 264tr, 264cr; C Scott Frances/Esto (Thomas Leeser, Architect) 276bl; Elizabeth Whiting & Associates 265br, 268bl, 268c, 276tl.

We would also like to thank the following individuals and companies who lent us photographs and items for photography:

Abet Ltd; Aero; Helen Allen; Alouette Innovation Ltd; Antique Baths of Ivybridge; Arc Linea; Ariston; Alouette Innovation Ltd; Tomoko Azumi; Cheryl Bell; Belling Appliances Ltd; James Bermudez; Bisque; But Furniture; Campbell and Young; Cato; China & Co; Crabtree Kitchens; Crucial Trading Ltd; Dimplex; Divertimenti; Elizabethan Photographic/Abet Limited; Susan Fairminer; Jonathan Field; First Floor; Fitzroy's Flower Workshop Ltd; Robert Fleming Designs; Futon Company; Graham & Green; Habitat; Thomas Hall; Ian Hay; Heal's; The Holding Company; Simon Horn; Innovations; Key Industrial; The Kitchenware Company; John Knights; Manhattan Loft Corporation; Meyer; Muji; Paperchase; Pivotelli; Poggenpohl; Precious McBane; Primrose & Primrose; Radiant Distribution; Rainbow Carpets & Curtains Ltd; Rembrandt Arts & Crafts; The Rug Warehouse; Scotts of Stow; Winfried Scheuer-Authentics; Simply Bathrooms; John Strand; Strouds of London; N.V. Vasco; Tefal; Tenco; Viaduct; Vola UK Ltd; Whirlpool; Alison White; Zanussi Ltd.

We are also grateful to Guy Greenfield Architects (245, 254bl, 258–9tc) and Clifton Page Architect for help with other locations.

PLANNING DETAILS

Stylists: Fiona Craig-McFeely; Tiffany Davies; Emily Hedges; Kay McGlone; Michelle and Yvonne Roberts; Shani Zion.

All photography by Peter Anderson, Andy Crawford, Jake Fitzjones, and Matthew Ward, except:
Otto Baitz/Esto 288t; Rodney Hyett/Elizabeth Whiting & Associates 296br; Suomen Kuvapalvelu/Camera Press 296tl; Ray Main 292l; Simon McBride (designer: Kaffe Fasset) 294tl; Ianthe Ruthven 290l.

The following companies kindly lent us their photographs: Novatec 289tc; Charles Page 303tr.

Thanks also to Tim Head for permission to photograph his work of art "Levity", 291bc.

Every effort has been made to trace the copyright holders. We apologise for any unintentional omission and would be pleased to insert these in subsequent editions.